D0072336

DAILY LIFE IN COLONIAL NEW ENGLAND

The Greenwood Press "Daily Life Through History" Series

The Age of Sail
Dorothy Denneen Volo and James M. Volo

The Ancient Egyptians
Bob Brier and Hoyt Hobbs

The Ancient Greeks
Robert Garland

Ancient Mesopotamia
Karen Rhea Nemet-Nejat

The Ancient Romans
David Matz

The Aztecs: People of the Sun and Earth
Davíd Carrasco with Scott Sessions

Chaucer's England
Jeffrey L. Singman and Will McLean

Civil War America
Dorothy Denneen Volo and James M. Volo

Early Modern Japan
Louis G. Perez

18th-Century England
Kirstin Olsen

Elizabethan England
Jeffrey L. Singman

The Holocaust
Eve Nussbaum Soumerai and Carol D. Schulz

The Inca Empire
Michael A. Malpass

Maya Civilization
Robert J. Sharer

Medieval Europe
Jeffrey L. Singman

The Nineteenth Century American Frontier
Mary Ellen Jones

Renaissance Italy
Elizabeth S. Cohen and Thomas V. Cohen

The Spanish Inquisition
James M. Anderson

Traditional China: The Tang Dynasty
Charles Benn

The United States, 1920–1939: Decades of Promise and Pain
David E. Kyvig

The United States, 1940–1959: Shifting Worlds
Eugenia Kaledin

The United States, 1960–1990: Decades of Discord
Myron A. Marty

Victorian England
Sally Mitchell

DAILY LIFE IN COLONIAL NEW ENGLAND

CLAUDIA DURST JOHNSON

The Greenwood Press "Daily Life Through History" Series

GREENWOOD PRESS
Westport, Connecticut • London

Library of Congress Cataloging-in-Publication Data

Johnson, Claudia D.
Daily life in colonial New England / Claudia Durst Johnson.
p. cm.—(The Greenwood Press "Daily life through history" series, ISSN 1080–4749)
Includes bibliographical references and index.
ISBN 0–313–31458–6 (alk. paper)
1. New England—Social life and customs—To 1775. I. Title. II. Series.
F7.J59 2002
974'.02—dc21 00–061721

British Library Cataloguing in Publication Data is available.

Library of Congress Catalog Card Number: 00–061721
ISBN: 0–313–31458–6
ISSN: 1080–4749

First published in 2002

Greenwood Press, 88 Post Road West, Westport, CT 06881
An imprint of Greenwood Publishing Group, Inc.
www.greenwood.com

Printed in the United States of America

The paper used in this book complies with the Permanent Paper Standard issued by the National Information Standards Organization (Z39.48–1984).

10 9 8 7 6 5 4 3 2

For Caroline West Pearson,
Nathaniel Durst George,
and Genevieve West Pearson

Contents

Introduction

On June 12, 1630, the *Arbella*, one of seventeen vessels carrying close to 1,000 English men and women, landed on the bleak, wild shore of Cape Ann, Massachusetts, northeast of what would be the city of Boston, in territory that in 1614 John Smith had christened "New England." John Winthrop, a twenty-nine-year-old lawyer, had been elected by the members of the Massachusetts Bay Company to lead the group of religious dissenters, entrepreneurs, and indentured servants.

After they landed, Winthrop records that most of the new settlers were in no hurry to leave the *Arbella*, remaining on board for several days before disembarking at Cape Ann and proceeding to Salem. One can only imagine that the ship itself was their last tie with home and civilization and that they left it warily and with some regret, despite the troubles they had endured in the passage. Still, the settlers arrived in New England full of hope, secure in the belief that they would find a thriving two-year settlement of Englishmen in Salem, Massachusetts, people who, they had been led to believe, had prepared the way for them. The wilderness around the immediate settlement would have been cleared, shelters would be ready for occupation, crops would be established, and stores of food and other necessary supplies would have been put in for the winter. Instead, they were shocked with what they found, aghast at the situation that they had planned to be their hedge against a brutal winter in a wild country, peopled with a strange and frightening civilization. One-fourth of the Salem settlers had died the previous winter, and the survivors were sick and weak. According to one observer,

An English merchant vessel from the early seventeenth century. From George Francis Dow, *Every Day Life in the Massachusetts Bay Colony* (Boston: Society for the Preservation of New England Antiquities, 1935).

the Salemites, from bad government planning and general laziness, had not prepared for the newcomers at all. The structures the new settlers saw were few and shabby, entirely inadequate for the winter they would soon face. The corn and supplies that were to have carried them through a long winter would not last through the fall.

Within a week, John Winthrop sized up the situation, formulated a plan of attack, moved his people to Charlestown (hence, to Boston proper), which seemed a more favorable location than Salem, and set to work at hard labor with his hands, along with the lowliest indentured servant. In a few weeks, they had temporary shelters for the winter and at least some provisions. There can be little wonder that in the thriving community that sprang up across the Charles River in Boston, idleness became a cardinal sin and industry a shining virtue.

MOTIVATION FOR LEAVING ENGLAND

A primary impetus for this voyage to the New World was to avoid the religious persecution that had worsened in England in 1625 with the

The landing on Cape Cod. From Ralph Henry Gabriel, *Toilers of Land and Sea* (New Haven: Yale University Press, 1926).

accession of Charles I to the English throne. The new settlers were mainly Congregationalists (or Puritans), a sect that had risen to prominence in England at the end of the sixteenth century, its people suppressed and imprisoned in England because they were in substantial disagreement with the established Church of England. In this atmosphere of increasing hostility, even those who showed sympathy for the Puritans were harassed. To gather or to hold a service in a Congregationalist church or to read Scripture was to commit a crime against the state.

These Boston Puritans, unlike their Plymouth neighbors who had landed in 1620, were non-Separatists who believed that eventually they would be able to effect changes to their satisfaction within the Church of England. In 1628 the Massachusetts Bay Company was formed, a trading company designed to make money and to guide their settlement. Unlike Spanish and French corporations in the New World, which had their headquarters in the parent countries, the Massachusetts Bay Company was initially run from and by the colony itself.

English persecution led to the phenomenal growth of the Massachusetts Bay Colony, the 1630s becoming known as the years of the Great Migration from England to the Massachusetts Bay. By 1643, thirteen years after the Puritans arrived on Cape Ann, 20,000 people had joined the Massachusetts Bay Colony and were living in New England. Boston, its religious and political center, had become the largest town in the colonies.

Although religious persecution brought many of these emigrants to the New World, this was not the sole or even the main reason for settlement in New England. Some, unabashed financial entrepreneurs, came for fortune. Many others were people of humble social status, including indentured servants, with little interest in religion. They came to the New World primarily for a better life, especially what seemed the impossible dream of one day owning land—impossible because land ownership for these people had been inconceivable in England for generations. And Massachusetts was particularly attractive because it was the only settlement in the New World where land was deeded to settlers without charge or obligation.

PREDECESSORS IN THE NEW WORLD

The almost 1,000 English men and women who landed in New England that summer day in 1630 were not the first Europeans to settle in North America. The first were the Spanish, who had set up forts in Florida in 1565 and dominated the Far West and the Southwest. A group of speculators from England had made an abortive settlement in Roanoke, Virginia, in 1585 and a successful settlement in Jamestown in 1607. The Dutch had made incursions into New York beginning in 1609. Anglicans and dissenters from Europe settled the Carolinas. In addition to the Salem residents who had arrived in 1629 under the leadership of John Endicott, other English had already braved the harsh climate of New England, some in collectives and some alone. For instance, a group of English, who shared the Bostonians' religious views in most respects and are usually called the Pilgrims, had been living in Plymouth, forty miles south of Boston, for a decade by the time John Winthrop's group arrived on Cape Ann. One of the more eccentric individuals who preceeded Winthrop's group was the Reverend William Blackstone, an Anglican cleric who was said to amuse himself by riding cows on his farm in the middle of the Shawmut Peninsula (which came to be called Boston). He was there to welcome the Winthrop Puritans, but left disenchanted when they appropriated most of his land for a "common," where the whole community could graze its cows.

PARAMETERS OF TIME AND PLACE

The original charter for a settlement in New England was for a grant of land that extended from the Atlantic Ocean to the Pacific Ocean and

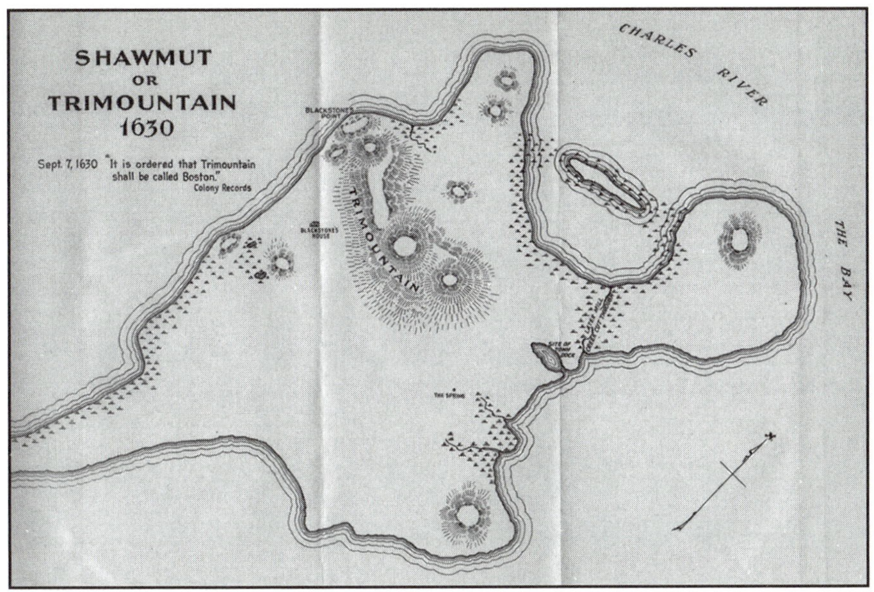

Map of Shawmut Peninsula, 1630. From Annie Haven Thwing, *The Crooked & Narrow Streets of the Town of Boston 1630–1822* (Boston: Marshall Jones Company, 1920).

Blackstone's House on the southeast side of Beacon Hill. The first house in Boston, it was built by William Blackstone ca. 1628, before Winthrop's party arrived. From Robert M. Palmer, *Palmer's Views of Boston* (New York, 1910).

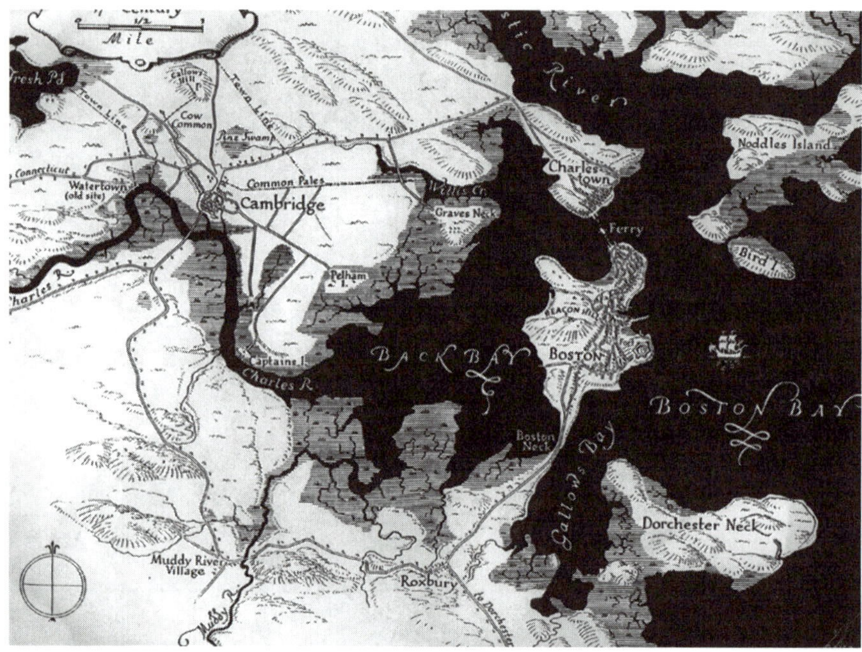

Map of Boston, Cambridge and Environs in the seventeenth century. Reprinted by permission of the publisher from THE FOUNDING OF HARVARD COLLEGE by Samuel Eliot Morison, Cambridge, Mass.: Harvard University Press, Copyright © 1935 by the President and Fellows of Harvard College.

from three miles north of the Merrimack River to three miles south of the Charles River. Eventually the Massachusetts Bay Colony appropriated most of the land in what are now Massachusetts, New Hampshire, and Maine. Two other strong colonies, at New Haven and Hartford, were also settled by Puritans. Rhode Island, part of New England, remained independent of the Boston-centered Massachusetts Bay.

The colonial age in New England encompasses two fairly distinct cultural periods. The first period covers the years of Puritan domination, roughly between 1630 and 1700. The second period, from about 1700 to 1776, covers the years of Puritan decline and the rise of the Age of Reason, and the most oppressive years of the English occupation, leading up to the American Revolution.

PARADOXES AND AMBIGUITIES

The Puritans, who dominated colonial New England for over 100 years were studies in paradox and ambiguity. As a group, they arose from revolution, in defiance of the authority of the Catholic and Anglican churches and a hierarchical clergy. They were among the most nonconformist of Protestants, whose radical cry was, "Each man his own priest." In rebelling against the established church, they also defied the king, opening themselves to charges of treason.

Yet despite their radicalism in England, by the time they reached the New World, they had become an authority-ridden people, having invested their own Congregational church and its clergy with immense and intrusive power over the private lives of citizens.

Their relationship to the state in England had been adversarial. They were dissidents, the victims of intolerance. In the New World, they changed from being the oppressed to being the oppressors, refusing to allow members of other Christian denominations to live in the confines of their community and refusing to tolerate doctrinal disagreements among members of their own faith. In this New World community ruled by old men, toleration became a term of disparagement.

Their balancing of godly and worldly concerns was also fraught with contradictions. They saw themselves as a pious people who maintained a godly society and emphasized the need for cultivation of spiritual matters above worldly ones. At the same time, they were the progenitors of capitalism. Their actions as businessmen often showed that what they valued most was not charity or piety but industry and profit. The mark of a man loved by God was material wealth.

They were Christians who seemed far more comfortable with the Old Testament God of vengeance and wrath than the New Testament messiah of love and forgiveness. They were a homogeneous group that gave rise to a nation of many nationalities, religions, cultures, and races. They were candid in admitting their intention to rule by tyranny, yet they gave rise to a country founded on freedom of speech and religion.

FALLACIES

Much of the traditional mythology that grew up regarding the lives and beliefs of colonial New Englanders was either patently false, a distortion of the truth, or oversimplified. For instance, it is often said that these English came to the New World to establish religious freedom; that they had no class system; that, unlike their southern neighbors, they refused to traffic in slaves; that they wore only black, white, and gray clothing; that they were sexually repressed; and that they refused to imbibe alcohol. These popular assumptions will be challenged throughout this book in the course of examining how they conducted their lives.

THE PURITANS' INFLUENCE AND IMPACT

One tradition that is continually demonstrated to have validity, however, is that this group that landed near Salem, Massachusetts, in June of 1630 and eventually settled the city of Boston gave colonial New England its identity. More than that, it placed its stamp on American character and culture for all time. Indeed, the intellectual and cultural impact of colonial New England on the rest of the country was for two centuries more significant than that of any other single group of settlers, and greatly disproportionate to their population or land mass.

Many of the traits of the Massachusetts Bay community have endured in the national character in a positive way. The country was shaped by New England's nonhierarchical religious sectarianism and the value it placed on the spiritual life. The New Englanders' "Protestant ethic" continued to live in the importance the nation accorded to hard work and independence. And the country was shaped by the value these New England settlers placed on education.

At the same time, much of the impact of colonial New England on the nation was negative. For instance, the nation inherited from the Puritans a suspicion of art, particularly the performing arts. And the occasional eruptions in the country of fanaticism and narrowness have been traced to our New England roots.

The nation and individuals have spent much time and energy in reacting against the narrowness and intolerance of its New England past. For example, the founding fathers of the new republic, many of whom embraced or were strongly influenced by Deism, a philosophical anathema antithetical to Puritanism, insisted on an emphatic separation between church and state and made freedom of expression a cornerstone of democracy.

THIS WORLD AND THE NEXT

The influence of colonial New England would endure, but even by the mid-seventeenth century, many of their number despaired that in the day-to-day struggle for survival, the lofty design was being lost. In April 1657, one of their clerical leaders, Richard Mather, looked back on their twenty-seven-year struggle in New England in a treatise intended as a summary and a caution. His statement in *A Farewell-Exhortation to the Church and People of Dorchester in New-England*, is a fervent hope that New Englanders would remember to imbue their worldly concerns with religious meaning. Yet despite New England's godly beginnings, the imperative and vivid reality of life and work in the world was insistent, especially a new world unshaped by Western civilization.

It is to the this-worldly business of everyday living, shaped in large measure by other-worldly concerns, which we now turn attention.

EVERYDAY LIFE

Life in New England was shaped by various political, military, and ideological conflicts as well as natural disasters. Despite the great distance and their initial autonomy, events in England continued to have profound effects on New England. Puritans and other dissidents who remained behind in England struggled with the British Crown after members of the Massachusetts Bay Colony left. In 1642, after a bloody civil war, the Puritans won their battle against the Crown, deposing King Charles (who was executed in 1649), and placing a Puritan leader, Oliver Cromwell, at the head of state. As long as Cromwell was in control in England, the Puritan communities in New England enjoyed prosperity and autonomy. The death of Cromwell, the execution and exile of friends of the Massachusetts Bay Colony in Cromwell's government, and the restoration of the Crown, with Charles II as king in 1660 had a profound influence on colonial New England.

One of the first insults suffered by Massachusetts Bay was the passage of the punishing Navigation Acts in 1662, taking away the colony's freedom to trade with Europe. After intense and futile negotiations, the colony's ability to govern itself was lost in 1662 with the revocation of their charter. With the ascension to the English throne of James I in 1685, the colony's loss of autonomy accelerated. A series of royal governors, beginning in 1686 with the tyrannical Edmund Andros, was visited on the once-independent Boston government. These governors, acting in the name of the English king, had veto power over colonial legislation. Andros also insisted on formalizing the toleration of the Church of England by authorizing the building of an Anglican church in Boston. Although citizens of Massachusetts Bay drove out one governor after another, they realized by 1691 that it was useless to continue hoping for restoration of their original charter.

The heavy ruling hand of the English king continued to be apparent in an increasingly unhappy New England. In 1764, in an attempt to create revenue, the English began levying a series of taxes on goods imported into the colonies. Rhetoric became heated in the call for more colonial representation and less of an English military presence, building inevitably toward revolution.

The conspicuous quartering of British troops in the streets of such cities as Boston and the posting of military broadsides were infuriating to the residents, who felt that their homes had been turned into occupied countries. On March 5, 1770, one of the most notorious pre-Revolutionary events occurred in Boston when an angry mob of citizens confronted the British soldiers in their streets. As tempers flared, the soldiers fired pointblank, instantly killing three people, mortally wounding two others, and injuring six more. As a result of what came to be called the Boston Massacre, British troops were temporarily removed from Boston to the harbor islands, and the captain of the militia and eight soldiers were arrested for murder.

Whether or not a direct response to the Boston Massacre and other colonial objections, the English tax was lifted in all commodities except tea, and the act enforcing the quartering of English soldiers in colonial towns was not renewed.

In contrast to the Boston Massacre, the second most notable pre-Revolutionary War incident, the Boston Tea Party, might be described as clever and comical. It was precipitated by the continuing tax on tea imported from England. When a ship carrying tea landed in Boston Harbor, the angry residents decide to send the ship back to England without paying the tax. The royal governor, Thomas Hutchinson, whose family was profiting from the tax, declared that the ship would not be allowed to leave the harbor until the tax was paid. On December 16, 1773, 8,000 citizens gathered in an angry protest meeting. Later, in the middle of the night, a group of men disguised as Indians boarded the ship and dumped 342 casks of tea overboard.

Natural Disasters

Natural disasters as well as political conflicts shaped colonial New England. Such occurrences, which plagued the colonists, convinced them that they were the particular targets of God's eternal wrath and that the devil was working to defeat their cause. From 1660 to 1689 they were beset by smallpox epidemics, the worst occurring in the years 1684 and 1689. On top of smallpox, the year 1688 brought a killing epidemic of measles.

Guilt and paranoia built toward hysteria with other natural disasters, notably the drought and plague of locusts and other insects that devastated crops in 1687. The colonists suffered through an equally killing drought in 1749, which left them with insufficient fodder and threatened their livestock. As a result, New England had to import hay from England and the other colonies.

Military Struggle with Indians

New England's principal military struggles before the American Revolution were with the Native Americans in the area. From 1633, the New Englanders were involved in constant conflict with the Pequot and Narraganset tribes. In 1637 the Massachusetts Bay militia succeeded in wiping out the Pequot. For over thirty years, as the settlers became hungry for more land, relations between the colonials and the Indians worsened. In 1675, after years of disputes, bloody warfare broke out between the colonists and Indians under the command of "King Philip," chief of the Wampanoag, who joined forces with the French. The war did not end in some parts of New England until 1677, and the devastation on both sides was enormous. The two most notorious massacres of European settlers by Indians in the colonial Northeast were west of Massachusetts at Schenectady, New York, in 1690 and Deerfield, Massachusetts, in 1704.

The French and Indian War, waged primarily in the Ohio Valley, began on May 28, 1754. In the following year, the French were turned away from the New England colonies, but war raged on in nearby New York State. Not until February 1763 did the French and Indian War end with English victories in Canada.

Internal and External Ideological Struggles

Internal and external tensions over religious dogma marked the New England settlement from the beginning. Over the matter of religious liberty, Roger Williams, a Congregational minister, was a thorn in the sides of New England's religious leaders from the moment of his arrival in Boston in 1631. He was one of several religious protesters (these included Baptists) who founded the colony of Rhode Island as a haven for supporters of religious freedom.

No other series of events was so divisive and damaging to the New England community as the arrest on grounds of heresy and treason of Anne Hutchinson, another of its own who commanded a large and sympathetic following in Boston and Cambridge. After being found guilty of treason in 1637 and of heresy in 1638, she was banished from the Massachusetts Bay Colony and escaped to Rhode Island.

With the arrival in Massachusetts of the Quakers in July 1656, the New Englanders found themselves in another heated debate over dogma, which culminated with the hanging of three Quaker men in 1659 and a Quaker woman, Mary Dyer, in 1660.

The last and most notorious internal disruption came in 1692 with the Salem witchcraft trials, resulting in the execution of twenty citizens of Massachusetts Bay and the arrest of hundreds.

Each of these events had an intense effect on the daily lives of the citizens of colonial New England, shaping education, the individual's relationship to church and state, the response to outsiders and eccentrics, and personal matters of shelter and health.

BIBLIOGRAPHY

Adams, James Truslow. *The Founding of New England*. Boston: Atlantic Monthly Press, 1921.

Bridenbaugh, Carl. *Cities in the Wilderness*. New York: Ronald Press, 1938.

Morgan, Edmund S. *The Puritan Dilemma*. Boston: Little, Brown, 1958.

Morrison, Samuel Eliot. *Builders of the Bay Colony*. Boston: Houghton Mifflin, 1930.

Palfrey, John Gorham. *History of New England*. 5 vols. Boston: Little, Brown, 1856–1890.

Shurtleff, N. B., ed. *Records of the Governor and Company of the Massachusetts Bay*. 6 vols. Boston: W. White, 1853–1854.

Wertenbaker, Thomas J. *The First Americans*. New York: Macmillan, 1927.
———. *The Puritan Oligarchy*. New York: Scribner's, 1947.
Young, Alexander. *Chronicles of the First Planters*. Boston: C.C. Little, and J. Brown, 1846.

Chronology

1565	Spanish settlement in St. Augustine, Florida
1588	John Winthrop born
1590	William Bradford born
1591	Organization of first Puritan church in England Anne Hutchinson born
1603	Roger Williams born
1607	English settlement at Jamestown, Virginia
1608	Puritan settlement in Holland
1614	John Smith names the territory he explores "New England"
1620	Puritan settlement in Plymouth, Massachusetts, under William Bradford
1624	Dutch settle New York
1625	The Reverend William Blackstone settles in Boston Charles I assumes the British throne, and persecution of religious dissenters intensifies
1626	Settlement at Salem, Massachusetts Thomas Morton settlement at Merry Mount, Massachusetts

1628	Plymouth settlers, led by Miles Standish, attack Thomas Morton's Merrymounters Arrival of John Endicott and settlers in Salem
1628	Organization of Massachusetts Bay Company in England
1629	John Winthrop elected governor 400 settlers arrive in Salem
1630	John Winthrop and 900 colonists arrive in Salem and move on to Charlestown, where the first legislature meets; Boston becomes the seat of government, and the first church is established there
1631	Roger Williams arrives in Bay Colony Adultery becomes a capital offense
1633	John Cotton and Thomas Hooker arrive in Boston The Boston Latin School is founded Law against idleness enacted
1634	Anne and William Hutchinson follow John Cotton to Boston
1635	Roger Williams ordered exiled
1636	Henry Vane elected governor John Cotton's *Judicals* (proposed laws) Thomas Hooker leads group from Cambridge, Massachusetts, to found Hartford, Connecticut Roger Williams founds colony in Rhode Island based on religious liberty Money appropriated for Harvard College
1637	Winthrop wins governorship over Vane Anne Hutchinson tried in civil court, sentenced to be banished, and placed under house arrest awaiting church trial Pequot camps at Stonington and New Haven, Connecticut are destroyed
1638	Anne Hutchinson excommunicated by church and leaves with family for Rhode Island First mention of slaves brought to New England from Africa
1640	Salem ship *Desire* goes to Africa for slaves

1641	Massachusetts Bay assumes an area of New Hampshire Nathaniel Ward's Body of Liberties Law legalizing slavery in Massachusetts
1642	Civil War begins in England, with Oliver Cromwell at head of the Puritans
1643	Colonies of Connecticut, Massachusetts, Plymouth, and New Hampshire join to establish the United Colonies of New England
1647	Massachusetts Bay passes legislation requiring establishment of schools
1648	*The Laws and Liberties of Massachusetts* Margaret Jones is hanged as a witch in Boston Code of Laws for Bay Colony finalized
1649	King Charles I is executed; Commonwealth under Cromwell established in England One of Maine's many attempts to gain independence from Massachusetts Bay and to establish religious liberty John Winthrop dies
1651	Three Baptists banished from Massachusetts Bay First Navigation Act, limiting colonial trade, passed by England 150 prisoners of war, primarily Scottish, sent to New England from England Law enacted in the Massachusetts Bay regulating dress according to social status
1652	Slavery declared illegal in Rhode Island Cromwell sends 270 Scottish prisoners to Massachusetts
1656	First Quakers arrive in New England
1658	Cromwell dies; the monarchy, publicly favoring the Anglican church, regains the throne Katherine Scott, Anne Hutchinson's sister, is publicly whipped in Boston for her religious beliefs
1659	Two Quakers hanged on Boston Common William Bradford dies

1660	Charles II returned to English throne Quaker Mary Dyer hanged on Boston Common Appeals made to the Crown to halt Puritan persecution of Quakers, Baptists, and others received sympathetically by King Charles II England's expanded Navigation Act angers New England
1660–1689	A series of shipwrecks result in great monetary losses Continual epidemics of smallpox plague the Boston community
1661	English Crown interferes to halt execution of Quakers John Eliot publishes a translation of the Bible into a Native American language
1662	Crown challenges the old charter, which allowed Massachusetts Bay freedom to govern itself Michael Wigglesworth publishes "Day of Doom"
1663	Cotton Mather born
1665	First non-Puritan church, a Baptist one, is allowed in Boston
1671	Hostilities began escalating between settlers and natives
1672	Publication of the General Laws and Liberties of the Massachusetts Colony
1674	First year of Samuel Sewall's diary
1675–1676	King Philip's War
1676	The North Church and forty adjacent houses in Boston catch fire and burn to the ground
1677	The Puritans again perceive an unchecked threat from a new wave of Quakers within their borders The Crown appoints a council to examine the laws of Massachusetts and issues objections to them
1679	A fire spreads through the business district of Boston, burning almost all of the city's businesses to the ground Anglicanism is introduced into the Puritan colony
1684	Charter of the Massachusetts Bay is revoked; Joseph Dudley appointed governor One of the most damaging outbreaks of smallpox occurs

1685 James I ascends throne
150 Huguenots arrive in New England

1686 Sir Edmund Andros is named governor-general of New England
Colonial legislatures abolished
Andros asks colonials to share Old South Meeting House with Anglicans

1687 Crops are destroyed by locusts and other insects, along with a drought

1688 Measles epidemic causes many deaths
Andros orders Old South turned over to Anglicans
James II is deposed; William and Mary assume British throne

1689 Andros is recalled but work he has begun on an Anglican church for Boston continues
New wave of hostilities with Indians
Colonists, especially those in Maine, fear an imminent invasion by the French from Canada
Another devastating smallpox epidemic

1690 Indians attack Schenectady, New York, completely burning it and damaging other outposts; several hundred are killed, and sixty are taken prisoner

1691 Despite hopes for reinstatement of the original charter, restoring self-government with a religious purpose, a new charter is issued, in which property ownership rather than church membership determines voting rights; royal governors continued
Cotton Mather publishes an alarming account of a witchcraft case in Boston

1692 January: Young girls in the Reverend Samuel Parris household in Salem begin acting strangely
February: First charges of witchcraft are made; aggressive interrogations begin
March: Three women are sent to prison, and others are charged; afflictions prompt day of prayer; Reverends Lawson and Parris deliver sermons that stir up the populace; Martha Corey, Rebecca Nurse, and Sarah Good's four-and-one-half-year-old daughter are examined and sent to prison

April: John and Elizabeth Proctor, Giles Corey, and George Burroughs are among the twenty-three more people jailed
May: Governor Phips appoints panel of judges to hear cases as arrests mount
June: Bridget Bishop is the first hanged; a group of ministers in Boston convey their alarm to the governor; five more sentenced to death
July: Rebecca Nurse among those hanged on Gallows Hill
August: John Proctor among those brought to trial and executed
September: Giles Corey is pressed to death; Martha, his wife, is among the last—a group of eight—people hanged
October: The governor forbids any more arrests and dissolves the witchcraft court, but another is appointed and some trials go on

1693 May: Governor orders the release of all accused witches upon payment of their fees

1697 January: A fast day is held in Massachusetts in penance for witch trials; Judge Samuel Sewall apologizes, and jurors apologize

1699 Captain Kidd the pirate is arrested in Boston and sent to England to stand trial

1700 Joseph Sewall publishes *The Selling of Joseph*

1701 Yale College founded in Connecticut

1702 Publication of Cotton Mather's *Magnalia Christi Americana*
Queen Anne's War (in colonies; settlers and English war with French, Indians, and Spanish)

1703 Disgrace officially removed from those accused of witchcraft and compensation ordered

1704 Indian attack on Deerfield, Massachusetts

1706 Benjamin Franklin born in Boston

1709 Quakers are allowed to build a meeting house in Boston

1712 First capture of sperm whale by Americans; whaling industry begins in New England

1719 120 Presbyterians from Northern Ireland come to New England

1728	Cotton Mather dies
1729	Last year of Samuel Sewall's diary
1741	Beginning of the Great Awakening, a religious revival under the leadership of Jonathan Edwards and George Whitefield
1747	Beginning of new religious outlook in a Boston church: denial of the trinity and belief in free will and toleration
1749	Deadly drought in New England
1754	Beginning of French and Indian War
1760	Devastating fire in Boston George III becomes king of England
1763	End of French and Indian War
1764	Beginning of new series of British taxes on colonies Founding of Rhode Island College (later Brown University)
1765	Quartering Act, requiring the housing of British troops Stamp Act
1767	Townshend Acts
1770	Boston Massacre
1773	Boston Tea Party
1774	First Continental Congress

1

The Doctrinal Foundation of Colonial Life

The Puritans who emigrated to the New World from England were the absolute rulers of the principal New England colonies—Massachusetts Bay, Plymouth, Hartford, and New Haven—and their religious beliefs shaped every aspect of daily life in colonial New England for over two hundred years. Their religion determined who was allowed to vote (only church members in most colonies), the laws that were enacted (to enforce church attendance by all citizens and to exclude other denominations and dissenting doctrines), the clothes that they chose to wear, the entertainments that they tolerated, their attitude toward work, and all other aspect of secular existence. Historian James Truslow Adams wrote in *The Founding of New England* that nothing in everyday life in New England could be seen as separate from politics and religion.

In approaching a study of the daily lives of the New England colonists, it is necessary to look first at the all-encompassing, predominant religious beliefs that decided all else in colonial New England life.

RELATIONSHIP TO THE CHURCH OF ENGLAND

Protestantism was established in England in the sixteenth century under the direction of Henry VIII, who expelled the Roman Catholic church and established the Anglican church, also known as the Church of England, in its place, with himself, rather than the pope, at its head. The king's motives, unlike those of Martin Luther, the leader of the Protestant Reformation, and other religious reformers, were political and personal rather than theological. Henry was interested in having the power and property that once belonged to the pope and priests, and he was infuriated at the pope's refusal to annul his marriage to Catherine of Aragon so that he could marry Anne Boleyn. Probably for this reason, the changes in the established English church were not as substantive as those proposed by many reformers, especially those rebellious Anglicans who came to be known as Puritans. Despite the reformers' dissatisfaction with the Anglican church, many remained as Anglican priests for as long as they could, trying to work and compromise within the system.

When the king divorced his wife, the English church divorced the pope in Rome as well. The king was also responsible for the destruction of the corrupt monastic orders in England. But the Anglican service remained virtually the same. The prayer book was altered very little, and an ecclesiastical hierarchy remained in place under the direction of the archbishop of Canterbury, appointed by the King.

THE RISE OF PURITANISM

Although the English church was no longer officially under Roman Catholic control, reformers saw that old abuses and corruption died hard. Not only did the old Catholic service and hierarchy remain intact, but poorly educated clergy remained in place, and financial corruption within the church persisted. Reformers within the Anglican church pressured the king and bishops to purge the churches of images, issue new prayer books, and replace church altars with communion tables. These reforms were largely amenable to the king. However, he found unacceptable some changes that reformers insisted on to "purify" the church, particularly the elimination of clerical robes or vestments and the substitution of sermons for scriptural readings. The ensuing controversies during Henry VIII's reign forced many reformers into exile, where they were influenced by theologians like John Knox, a Scot who had been exiled first to Frankfurt and then Geneva, and John Calvin of Geneva. The Puritan assumption of Calvin's religious ideas caused them to be described as "Calvinistic."

Leading dissenters remained in exile throughout the reign of Henry's daughter, Mary Tudor (1553–1558), a staunch Catholic who tried to restore Catholicism to England. But most of the Protestants returned from exile when Elizabeth I came to the throne in 1558 as a Protestant monarch. Some of these returning exiles were now willing to compromise with the Anglican establishment. By the time of Elizabeth, the monasteries were gone (having been destroyed in the reign of Henry VIII), and the Anglican hierarchy had lost interest in closely supervising some of the smaller churches, leaving some radicals free to conduct their churches as they pleased. But many reformers were not content to work in any way within what they perceived to be a corrupt Anglican system, and they set themselves up as itinerant preachers and household chaplains completely outside the official church. Puritans were prominent members of this renegade group.

The radical changes that the Puritans and other dissidents insisted on in England, and which came to identify Puritanism in New England, included purging the church of what they saw as the following "popish" practices:

The use of vestments and other clerical robes

Making the sign of the cross

Baptism by midwives

Confirmation rites

Kneeling at communion

The use of the ring in marriage ceremonies

The ceremony of the purification of women after childbirth

The use of the terms *priest* and *absolution*

Celebration of saints' days

Bowing at the name of Jesus

Organ music

Singing in parts

Responsive readings

The ecclesiastical hierarchy

Strangely enough, the reform that the established Church of England and English monarchs found most unacceptable was the prohibition of clerical garb. In 1565 this controversy came to a head when Elizabeth defied reformers by ordering the clergy to wear proper clerical clothing. Many clergymen refused and were dismissed. In the 1570s, as Puritans felt increasingly alienated, they substituted Bible study in regional religious conferences for participation in lawful Anglican church services. In 1576 Elizabeth declared these meetings illegal, driving Puritans further underground.

The Puritans had reason to hope that James I, who followed Elizabeth in 1603 and hailed from Presbyterian Scotland, would be more sympathetic to them than his predecessor was. But except for James's sponsorship of the English-language Bible, the dissidents were even more alienated than before. James vowed to chase all of them out of England.

James's son, Charles, who came to the throne at James's death in 1625, enraged the Puritans and drove them further underground by reintroducing high church rites into the Anglican service. John Eliot, a Puritan leader who objected to what he called papist practices, died in the Tower of London in 1632. Eight other dissidents were also arrested with him.

Despite Charles's open hatred of the Puritans, he was in a sense the father of colonial New England, for it was he, in his eagerness to be rid of the Puritans, who granted a charter in 1629 to the governor and Company of Massachusetts Bay in New England for the express purpose of Puritan settlement there.

After Elizabeth's death, the Anglican church not only returned to services that the Puritans despised; it also retreated theologically. The Calvinistic doctrine of predestination, one of the cornerstones of their faith, was eroded in the reign of James and then was openly forbidden by Charles I.

The Separatists, a group of dissenters within the ranks of the Puritans, were Puritan in all but one respect: they discontinued any attempt to reform the Anglican church and abandoned any hope of ever operating within it. Most Puritans, on the other hand, hoped for reforms and remained Anglican. Three of the Separatist leaders were executed in England in 1593 for urging English to leave the Anglican church and for preaching that ministers and sacraments were unnecessary in religious life. A large group of separatists secretly left England for the Netherlands in great numbers in 1608. But they became increasingly dissatisfied as their children were lost to Dutch culture, leading some of them to migrate to America under a charter for an English joint stock company. Thirty-five Separatists were among the 102 passengers aboard the *Mayflower*, which sailed for the New World and landed in Plymouth, Massachusetts, in 1620. They became the working partners and neighbors of the Winthrop party that settled Boston in 1630. But in 1620, the large majority of Puritans remained in England.

By 1629, with Bishop Laud presiding over the church as the archbishop of Canterbury, with a continuing history of royal alliances with Catholic countries, and with the Massachusetts Bay Company charter in hand, the time was ripe for the migration of Puritans from England.

COVENANT THEOLOGY: THE NATURE OF GOD

The Puritans who dominated colonial New England were committed to the establishment of a "godly" state in the New World, a theocracy in which church and state were virtually the same. It would be a "City on the Hill," as John Winthrop biblically described it, an Olivet where heaven and earth came together. Although three-quarters of the new settlers of 1630 were not members of the Puritan church, the settlement's godliness, to which the leaders aspired, was predicated on governmental adherence to a belief system known as *covenant theology*, which derived from an unusual view of biblical history based on a series of covenants or contracts. From this biblical history arose their concept of God, especially his power and his attitude toward humanity; their view of human nature, human obligation, and human destiny; their belief about nature and society; and their vision of the past and the afterlife. The Puritans' covenant story informed every aspect of public and private life in the New England they founded and dominated for so long.

The story that shaped Puritanism and life in seventeenth- and-eighteenth-century New England begins at the very beginning with the creation of the world. The Creator, who set the world in motion, was very like the Supreme Being of the Old Testament. The Puritans would never describe God chiefly as a God of love and benevolence. Rather he contained all things: hate and love, mercy and justice, light and dark, pride and humility. His power was shown in his ability to determine all events before the beginning of time. The Calvinistic doctrine of predestination, over which the Anglicans and Puritans had fought, meant that God not only knew from the first all events that would ever happen, he determined all events from the beginning of time.

THE FIRST COVENANT

Puritan theology is laden with the language of business. Each turning point in God's relationship with humans is expressed as a "covenant" or "contract." Because the concept of the contract is so basic to the Puritans' complex view of history, it is helpful to glance at its reciprocal nature: a contract is an agreement wherein specific actions by one party are demanded in exchange for specific actions by a second party. A mundane example of a contract occurs when one person hires another person to paint a house. In signing the contract, the painter agrees to paint the house, and the owner agrees to pay a specified sum for the painter's services. Thus, both are placed under an obligation. Having signed the contract, the owner is under an obligation to pay the painter who paints the house, whether he wants to pay him or not, whether he likes him or not. So the contract places limitations on the owner that he may not like. The covenant between humans and God was similar in construction, placing limits on the behavior of both. In covenant theology, this critical concept meant that God, in entering into a covenant of works with humans, agreed to place limits on his own actions or works. He had to honor his part of the agreement, whether he wanted to or not.

What was God's contract or covenant with Adam, the representative of humans? In the beginning of the world, God's part of the bargain was to allow humans to live protected in the Garden of Eden, a place untouched by change and adversity. Adam's part of the bargain was to praise God and obey him, specifically by avoiding the fruits of the Tree of Life and the Tree of the Knowledge of good and evil. As long as Adam obeyed God, God was obligated to keep Adam in paradise.

THE FALL

Imagine on the mundane level that the house owner, who has a contract with the painter, pays the painter several thousand dollars and that the painter breaks the contract by taking the money and failing to paint the house. This is what happened on a cosmic level between the creator of the universe and Adam. God kept his part of the bargain by providing Adam and Eve with a paradise, but Adam and Eve broke the contract. Satan, in the form of a snake, approached Eve, convincing her that if she and Adam ate of the forbidden fruit of the Tree of Knowledge, they would be greater than human; they would take on the power of God. Adam and Eve, as representatives of all humanity, broke their part of the bargain by disobeying God and eating the fruit of the Tree of Knowledge.

If a house owner is righteously angry at being cheated out of several thousand dollars when a painter breaks a contract, imagine the all-consuming wrath of power incarnate when Adam and Eve break their part of the bargain, thinking they can double-cross God. Adam and Eve's sin was worse than deception. In Calvinist theology, they committed the worst sin of all, pride, out of a desire to be like God, as Satan had falsely promised.

THE CONSEQUENCES

With humanity's breaking of the covenant of works, God's attitude toward humanity underwent a cataclysmic transformation, for God now became enraged beyond human imagination. His wrath was all-consuming, smoldering, furious, inescapable. Wrath became the Almighty's fundamental quality. He would no longer tolerate humans in his presence.

And as a result of divine wrath, the entire physical world, human nature, human destiny, and God's relationship with humankind changed utterly. In the first place, nature—the physical world—changed. Before, in the Garden of Eden, nature was a perfect mirror of the divine. Humans had only to look at nature to see the face of God reflected in it. But after the Fall, it was if a massive fist had come down to smash the mirror to smithereens. Thereafter, nature gave back to human beings only a fragmented, distorted, and partial image of God.

Nature changed in other frightening ways. Instead of existing in harmony with humankind, nature was now cruel, discordant, destructive.

Before, in Eden's "Peaceable Kingdom," the lion and lamb lay peacefully down with one another. After the fall, the lion sprang for the lamb's (and humans') throat. Diseases and natural disasters plagued the human race. Nature, which had once been a human paradise and playground, now became hostile ground.

As bad as was the change in nature, however, the worst change was yet to come. This was the alteration in human nature itself. Every faculty of the human being "fell," that is, was ineffably weakened and corrupted. In the first place, the human mind fell: people were never again able to understand, to grasp full knowledge of, God or things divine. More than that, their will, their ability to make choices, was paralyzed. Worst of all, their hearts became defiled and corrupted. They became capable of, even desired, to commit every possible horrible sin. They wanted to commit every horrible sin. In the Puritans' view, this condition, known as natural depravity, was true of every person for all time, including even the tiny unborn infant and the most pious, charitable saint. According to Puritan doctrine, a person was evil not because he committed a sinful act, but because he had in his heart the capacity to commit a sinful act. Since the Fall, everyone without exception had in his heart the capacity to sin.

Because of human disobedience and depravity, God prepared a dreadful destiny for them as punishment. Adam and Eve were thrown out of paradise into a world of time and change and mortality. They and all other people who came after them would now suffer, grow old, and die. They would always be at war with nature and removed from and hated in the sight of God. After they died, they and all other men and women, whom they represented, would inevitably go to hell.

In the Puritan view, human beings faced a guilty, shameful past; lived a hard life of toil, sickness, and danger; and faced a horrible future of eternal damnation. And because of their sins and worthless hearts, they deserved whatever befell them.

The Almighty, for his part, decided that because of human disobedience, he would never again enter into a covenant of works (which would place him under obligations and limitations) and he would never again enter into any kind of covenant at all with humankind.

THE COVENANT OF GRACE

In the Puritans' interpretation of Scripture, however, something happened that gave *some* human beings something of a respite in this bleaker than bleak existence in which they were constantly punished by a wrathful God. Jesus Christ, the son of God, appeared in human form. Since God would never again enter into a contract with humankind, Jesus himself, in his great compassion for the human race, made his own contract with God on behalf of all people. And since God would never again bind himself with a covenant of works that required of him contractual actions, the new covenant would be a covenant of grace, which placed no obligations on him. By virtue of this new covenant, God was free to do whatever he wanted to do—to give benefits as he wished, never to be contractually bound to provide benefits.

This, in essence, is what the covenant of grace provided. In exchange for Jesus's self-sacrifice, God agreed to "elect" (or choose) a very few human beings for salvation; that is, he would save them from going to hell. Such fortunate people were known as members of God's elect. In the strictest interpretation of Puritan doctrine, there was absolutely nothing one could do to become a member of the elect if one was not chosen by God before the beginning of time, and absolutely no way one could ever positively know if someone was a member of the elect. And according to the dictates of predestination, all that transpired—including the breaking of the covenant of works, the coming of Jesus, his death, the covenant of grace, and the knowledge of which people were chosen to be saved or damned—was in the mind of God before the beginning of time.

JUSTIFICATION

In all this process, human beings were largely helpless, being possessed of weak wills, weak understanding, and corrupt hearts. They were under the control of a wrathful God whom they had cheated and who had determined their fates before the beginning of time. In such a deterministic world, however, the covenant of grace provided an opportunity and obligation for human beings to improve their situations. This stage in the spiritual journey was called *justification*, an experience that justified a person, somewhat, in the eyes of God.

The journey of justification was, in essence, a trip to hell in this life. Classical and religious literature is replete with such journeys to hell. Ulysses went to the underworld in Homer's epic. Aeneas went to the underworld in Virgil's epic. Dante went to hell in his Christian epic. In each of these and many other cases, the trip to hell is a journey provided especially to the heroic, larger-than-life character, often at his request or instigation. In hell, these heroes receive knowledge from the dead to which the living are rarely privy. Unlike most other people who go to hell, the hero is able to get back out, and his life thereafter takes on direction and purpose.

In the Puritans' story of the trip to hell, every person, not just the hero, was under obligation to take a trip to hell in this life. Furthermore, it was an internal journey—a "dark night of the soul," as St. John of the Cross had written. One version of hell, the Puritans believed, existed in the interior of the human heart, and it was to this nightmarish land that one had to go to be justified. The Puritan version was formulaic. There was a set way to undertake the journey, and there were particular things one needed to learn on the journey. The results of the journey for different individuals were also the same.

Justification was asked of every Puritan, elect and nonelect alike. Both profited by such a journey. For the elect, justification was necessary to secure their election or salvation. But the nonelect could also benefit from such a journey. Although it would not change the fact of their eternal damnation, it made life easier for them in the here and now. God's eternal wrath was somewhat softened toward elect and nonelect who went through a valid justification, and, as a result, the lives of both the elect and the nonelect were less horrible in this temporal world than they would have been otherwise. There might, as a result, be fewer deaths in the family, less illness and pain, fewer community catastrophes, and, above all, less spiritual pain. Obviously it was in the best interest of everyone to try to undergo the experience.

PREPARATION FOR JUSTIFICATION

The making of the journey was not easy. One could not just sit down under a tree one day and decide to be justified. It was often a long, complicated process, requiring intense and frightening meditation. To complete the full and true justification, a Puritan actually had to experience two trips to hell, the first a minor trip to hell undergone in preparation for the major journey. Such a preparation was deemed necessary because the human heart, into which one had to journey, was encased in a thick crust that could be penetrated only after it had been softened by meditation and then opened by God. And the heart could be softened only by meditating on hellish subjects: sin, death, the last judgment, and hell—meditating until the horror of each became a painful and terrifying reality.

The Puritan clergyman, as we shall see, saw his chief function as assisting in this preparation for justification, often by preaching unsettling hellfire sermons. There was little theological incentive for a hellfire sermon to inspire the congregation to change their lives to avoid going to hell, for their salvation had already been determined before the world began. Except for the elect who needed to secure their salvation in justification, there was nothing they could do to change election. But the clergyman's hellfire sermon *could* prepare them for the journey into their hearts by making the subjects of sin, death, the last judgment, and hell intensely real.

THE INNER JOURNEY

After the Puritans had sincerely meditated on sin, death, the last judgment, and hell, it was assumed that God would open their hearts and allow them to enter the inner sanctum. It is not surprising to learn that this inner territory, according to Puritans, was a repugnant, loathsome, hellish landscape. Puritans knew this because doctrine and the clergy so often enlarged on it. But justification, if correctly done, brought one to feel, to experience what before was only known intellectually. One minister said that it was difference between just looking at a country on a map and actually traveling there.

Every abomination lay within the human heart—every sin, every perversity, every cruelty. One minister wrote that the human heart has many rooms, and every room is smeared with every sin. To emerge justified from this frightening inwardness, one had to feel and accept the full force of one's own horror.

All people had to come to know that they were capable of committing every despicable sin and that they were completely helpless in the matter of their own spiritual renewal. The man being hanged for mass murder was in his heart no worse than any other person, including oneself. To think otherwise, the Puritan believed, was self-delusion of the worst kind. After this wretched self-knowledge had left one lying helpless on the ground, metaphorically speaking, God lifted one out of hell to a higher plane, was less angry, and determined that the justified person would be less troubled in this life than he or she would have been otherwise.

Yet many people who thought they had been justified had actually gone through a false justification. The elect among these deluded people were in danger of going to hell, and the nonelect were in danger of continuing to incur God's punishment. Consequently it was important to test whether their journeys to an inner hell were in fact valid. The clergy applied tests of true justification in sermons and essays, putting them in the form of questions: Do you think there is any sin of which you are incapable? Do you think you have even a bit of strength to affect your own spiritual renewal or salvation? Anyone who answered yes had not had a true journey of justification.

QUESTIONS ABOUT DOCTRINE

There was no exact agreement on all matters of doctrine, even among Puritans. Controversies among clerical leaders arose about many matters, including the extent to which people had free will or awareness of God's intent, whether justification could be instant or protracted, or just how much of a difference faith made in the life of the nonelect.

The whole doctrine taught by Puritan clergy to the people of colonial New England also raised many questions in the minds of the laity, just as it does for us. The way the clergy dealt with these questions instructed the congregation in the mysteries of Puritan doctrine:

If all people went to hell after the breaking of the first covenant and before the appearance of Jesus, does that mean that the grand old biblical figures like Moses and Joseph went to hell? Yes. They remained in hell until Jesus brought them out after his crucifixion.

If everything on earth is determined before the beginning of time, then are human beings lacking in free will? Essentially, yes. What is at issue, however, is that human beings have no free will with regard to their salvation or to alter the nature of their hearts.

If we have no free will, then how can we be blamed for anything we do? God knows the nature of your evil heart and how you would have chosen or acted in any given situation. Some Puritans believed that people did have very limited free will within very narrow limits.

It was Adam and Eve (not me) who disobeyed God in the Garden of Eden. Why should I suffer for what they did? God knows that if you had been there, you would have done the same thing. Besides, the blame for what Adam did is like an inheritance. You either accept the whole inheritance, or you turn it all down. If you had been given a choice, you would not have refused to inherit the good things you got from Adam, so you are obligated to take the bad things as well. Therefore, you are implicated in the Fall and must accept the blame for it along with Adam.

We are taught that God saved Adam retroactively at the time of Jesus's resurrection from the dead. Adam was the one who caused the fall yet we who have not anything directly to do with the Fall and have lived good lives are likely damned. Why? God is under no obligation to save anyone. He is free to save whomever he wants. He wanted to save Adam, his first human, and he does not want to save you.

According to the doctrine of election made possible by the second covenant, God has chosen certain people to be saved and others to be damned. Are the elect pure in heart and the nonelect depraved? No. All people, including those elected for salvation, have depraved hearts. God saves them despite their evil hearts.

Isn't a good person one who does good deeds? No. Deeds are just external actions. The condition of the heart determines whether a person is good or bad. And all people since the Fall have bad hearts. While they might not actually hurt anyone or do anything immoral outwardly, they want to hurt others, and they want to commit immoral acts. In the eyes of God, the person who actually commits adultery and the person who only has lust in his heart (as everyone has) are essentially no different.

Isn't it possible for a person who is not chosen for election to save himself by acting holy and doing good deeds? No. There is absolutely nothing a nonelect person can do to change his damnation. People who do good deeds in an effort to avoid going to hell are just hypocrites trying to buy their way into heaven.

Then does good behavior not matter? Why should a Puritan do good deeds and act morally when it might just be more fun to seek pleasure? Good behavior does not reverse God's decision made before the creation of the earth to eternally save or damn someone. However, there are many pressing reasons that good behavior matters in other ways. First, God is pleased by good behavior. If you are good, he will be less likely to punish you in this life; if you are bad, he will be more likely to give you pain in this life. Second, the community requires good behavior to hold it together and to diminish God's wrath. There are community laws and customs demanding good behavior. If you break those laws, you will be severely punished by the community.

So good deeds do not get one to heaven. But what about faith? Isn't this one thing that a person can do to help save himself? Here there was genuine disagreement among the clergy. Some declared that even true faith was a gift from God to his elect and that no one could take control of his salvation, even by having faith in Holy Scripture. More accommodating Puritans would argue later that the least amount of God's grace was enough to get into heaven and that God would give the least amount of grace to anyone who had the least amount of faith.

What about innocent infants and little children who die? Do they also go to hell? Are some of them members of the elect and able to escape going to hell? This was a matter much contested among the congregation and has often been one of those issues blamed for tearing down Puritanism. However, the official answer from the Puritan clergy was this: in the first place, infants and little children are not innocent. They are depraved from the moment of conception, and they do go to hell. They *all* go to hell. Although some might have been elected by God for salvation, all members of the elect must secure their salvation by going through justification, and children who die young never have an opportunity to do that. Therefore, they go to hell. The Puritans offered some concessions at this point, however: they taught that children who die young are consigned to an easier room of hell.

Why would anyone believe such a wretched, hopeless doctrine as that taught by the New England Puritans? They believed it was true. A person who breaks his leg does not say, "This is so awful I won't believe it."

PERTINENCE OF DOCTRINE TO DAILY LIFE

The force of Puritan doctrine on private and public daily life was unceasing, invasive, and authoritative. The notion that nature had fallen reinforced their view that the land they had come to settle was little more than the devil's domain and the native peoples were the devil's fiends. As a consequence, their treatment of the wilderness and the natives was fortified by doctrine. Every catastrophe that occurred was irrefutable evidence of God's anger against them for the Fall and for their own wicked natures. Every law and every episode of community intolerance flowed from the notion that they must purge themselves of behavior and beliefs unsuitable in the sight of God, toleration of which might bring on the next plague or massacre. Thomas Dudley, first lieutenant governor of the Massachusetts Bay, eventually governor, and father of the poet Anne Bradstreet, wrote the following poem (found in his pocket at his death) illustrating the New World Puritans' peculiar view of tolerance as an evil and dangerous practice (a cockatrice is a crocodile):

> Let men of God in courts and churches watch
> O'er such as do a toleration hatch
> Lest that ill egg bring forth a cockatrice
> To poison all with heresy and vice. (from Jones, 227)

Their belief in their own depravity burdened them with guilt for the most ordinary desires and frailties, and it led them to discipline themselves and their children with psychologically crippling severity. Their conviction that individuals and nature were corrupt made the saving grace of a church and a godly society of utmost importance in redeeming both the elect and nonelect in this life. The conviction that human beings were floundering for spiritual truths with imperfect understanding in a fragmented universe led them to develop a comprehensive system of education and to rely heavily on a highly educated clergy.

DECLINE AND ENFORCED TOLERATION

By the end of seventeenth century, Puritanism, which was still powerful enough in 1692 to fuel the Salem witchcraft trials, was in decline. During the presence of the royal governors, the Anglican church was introduced to New England, and the Puritans were forced by the British to tolerate other religious denominations. The Baptists, Quakers, and Huguenots found places in New England society from which they had previously been expelled. There were internal pressures on the Puritan leaders to change their policies with regard to religious toleration. The people of Rhode Island had founded their colony on religious freedom, and the people of Maine, long unhappily under the thumb of the Massachusetts Bay Colony, expressed their desire for religious liberty for themselves.

Furthermore, Puritan clergymen and congregations themselves were moving in different directions in the eighteenth century. Puritan clergy had always felt that their foundation lay on a crucial balance in religious experience between head and heart. When this balance was lost, Puritanism splintered. One group, which placed more emphasis on the heart and emotions, became part of what was known as the *Great Awakening*. It was their intent to energize Congregationalism with revivals. Unlike the older Puritans, the followers of these ministers tended to let their emotions get away with them at highly charged meetings.

Another group placed more emphasis on the head—the intellect—than the old Puritans tolerated. These Congregationalists evolved into the strong Unitarian church of New England. As the name implies, they did away with the idea of the Trinity. They also greatly modified or entirely dropped Calvinistic ideas of salvation by election and grace alone.

To this mix of different Christian sects and new versions of Congregationalism was added a radical new philosophy called Deism, which flowered in the Age of Reason and influenced the fathers of the American Revolution, including Thomas Paine, Thomas Jefferson, and Boston's own Benjamin Franklin. Deism was never popular with most citizens of New England. Indeed, Thomas Paine, who had once been lauded as a national hero, was seen as the devil incarnate after he made his deistic views known in *The Age of Reason*. New Englanders were not prepared to accept his views that the Bible was not the revealed word of God and that miracles were untrue concoctions of the church to cement its own power. Still, the philosophy of the Age of Reason had an impact on modifying and reshaping much of New England religion in the eighteenth century.

BIBLIOGRAPHY

Adams, James Truslow. *The Founding of New England*. Boston: Atlantic Monthly Press, 1926.

Bartlett, Robert Merrill. *The Faith of the Pilgrims*. New York: United Church Press, 1978.

Bercovitch, Sacvan. *The Puritan Origins of the American Self*. New Haven, Conn.: Yale University Press, 1975.

Bremer, Francis J. *The Puritan Experiment: New England Society from Bradford to Edwards*. Rev. ed. Hanover, N.H.: University Press of New England, 1995.

Byington, Ezra Hoyt. *The Puritans in England and New England*. New York: B. Franklin, 1972.

Foster, Stephen. *The Long Argument: English Puritanism and the Shaping of New England Culture*. Chapel Hill: University of North Carolina Press, 1991.

Hall, David D. *Puritanism in Seventeenth-Century Massachusetts*. New York: Holt, Rinehart and Winston, 1968.
Heimert, Alan, and Andrew Delbanco, eds. *The Puritans in America: A Narrative Anthology*. Cambridge, Mass.: Harvard University Press, 1985.
Hill, Douglas Arthur. *The English to New England*. London: Gentry Books, 1975.
Jones, Augustus. *The Life and Work of Thomas Dudley*. Boston: Houghton-Mifflin, 1900.
Miller, Perry. *The New England Mind*. 2 vols. Boston: Beacon Press, 1939.
———. *The Puritans*. New York: American Book Co., 1938.
Reintz, Richard. *Tensions in American Puritanism*. New York: Wiley, 1970.
Rutman, Darrett Bruce. *American Puritanism: Faith and Practice*. Philadelphia: Lippincott, 1970.
Smith, Chard Powers. *Yankees and God*. New York: Hermitage House, 1954.
Stavely, Keith. *Puritan Legacies: Paradise Lost and the New England Tradition, 1630–1890*. Ithaca, N.Y.: Cornell University Press, 1987.
Ziff, Larzer. *Puritanism in America*. New York: Viking Press, 1973.

2

Clergy and the Church

CHURCH ORGANIZATION

Among the first business conducted by the Plymouth, Salem, and Boston settlers was the establishment of churches, using as their model the church order of the English Independents or Congregational churches. The process began when a group of men presented themselves as candidates for "pillars of the church." After being investigated and confirmed by their peers, these men, after having determined that there were enough people to conduct church business, formed themselves into a new congregation. If there were too many people to meet in one modest structure, a second church was formed.

Each church had at least one pastor; large congregations like the one in Boston had two. By 1634, five years after the arrival of the Winthrop party, there were about thirteen clergymen in New England, most of whom had been educated at Cambridge or Oxford and some of whom had held positions as clergymen in the Church of England. In sharp contrast to the papal system of hierarchy, churches were independent entities, directed by the officers of the individual church, and Puritan clergymen were not ordained by other clergy but by church officers. In New England, ministers were usually maintained through public taxes collected from every resident, church members or not, a practice that second- and third-generation New Englanders began to find objectionable.

The second minister of each New England church was called a teaching elder. His duties were to reinforce doctrine. About half the teaching elders in New England had also been educated at Cambridge or Oxford. Teaching elders were often men of property with impressive connections to powerful aristocrats and businessmen.

Other church officers included ruling elders who were responsible for the discipline of individuals in the congregation. Often with the pastor, they would visit and warn congregation members who were behaving unacceptably—those who were not working hard enough, were drinking too much, were lax in their church participation, were in altercations with their neighbors, or were spending too much money on clothes and household treasures, for example.

Another category, the church deacon, was the business officer of the church. He received church offerings and distributed church funding to the minister and church members who were in need. Ministering to the sick was done in the church's name by elderly women who were called ancient widows. Tithing men, another class of church officer, were chiefly responsible for keeping order in the meeting house itself.

Tithing men were the meetinghouse policemen. A large congregation had several tithingmen, each responsible for about ten families. Their responsibilities in the meetinghouse consisted primarily of keeping the members of their families awake with a long rod, with a feather on one end and a ball on the other. Women were usually wakened from sleeping in the pews by being tickled in the face with a feather. Men were smacked on the head with the rod or ball. Thomas Scott, a worshipper in Lynn, Massachusetts, was so abruptly awakened from his loud snoring that he leaped up and knocked the tithingman to the floor. The tithingman assigned to the pews where young boys were seated had such a hard task that he was often paid up to 20 shillings a year for the job of keeping the boys still, quiet, attentive, and suitably solemn. It was his responsibility to correct them when they smiled or laughed and to report their misbehavior to the authorities.

CHURCH ATTENDANCE

The union of church and state is found in legal documents that required church attendance of all citizens of the Massachusetts Bay, even though most of the ordinary people who emigrated were likely not Puritans. In 1634, the legislators, prodded by the clergy, became sufficiently alarmed at the laxity of the community with regard to church attendance to reenforce community expectations:

> Whereas complaint hath been made to this Court that divers persons within this jurisdiction do usually absent themselves from church meetings upon the Lord's day, power is therefore given to any Assistants to hear and censure, either by

fine or imprisonment (at their discretion) all misdemeaners of that kind committed by any inhabitant within this jurisdiction, provided they exceed not the fine . . . for one offence. (Shurtleff, vol. 1: 140)

CHURCH MEMBERSHIP

Although all citizens of the Massachusetts Bay were required by law to attend church, only a small percentage were actually members of the church. Church membership was a privileged position in that only members were allowed to vote or hold office.

Securing church membership was usually an arduous process. First, the candidates let the officers of the church know of their desire to become members. The elders and the minister would examine the candidate to determine if his or her knowledge or religious experience merited a recommendation of membership. The candidate would then be presented to the congregation, who were asked to report any moral failings on the part of the candidate or to testify to the candidate's good character. Male candidates would describe their conversions to the church in public, and females would convey their stories in private to the minister, who would then report to the congregation. After the testimony, the candidate might be publicly questioned by the congregation. The examination concluded with the candidate's profession of faith, followed by a vote of the congregation.

Samuel Sewall, a prominent judge in colonial Boston, describes his own election to church membership in his diary:

March 30, 1677. I, together with Gilbert Cole, was admitted into Mr. Thacher's Church, making a Solemn covenant to take the L. Jehovah for our God, and to walk in Brotherly Love and watchfulness to Edification. Goodm. Cole first spake, then I, then the Relations of the Women were read: as we spake so were we admitted; then altogether covenanted. Prayed before, and after. (Sewall, vol. 1: 41, 42)

The faith and behavior of all members were closely scrutinized by the rest of the congregation and the elders. Church members needed the permission of the congregation to move from the area and needed recommendations from the congregation to join churches in other locations. A story is told of a couple, Colonel James and Elizabeth Davis, who applied for membership in a New Hampshire church, only to have their former minister send a list of reasons why he encouraged the congregation to decline them, including that Colonel Davis had spoken against the minister's receiving a raise.

A church member who was excommunicated and not restored to the

Boston's first meeting house, 1632. From Robert M. Palmer, *Palmer's Views of Boston* (New York, 1910).

church within six months could be fined, imprisoned, banished, or "other"—meaning put to death.

THE MEETINGHOUSE

Worship took place in the meetinghouse, usually a square structure about fifty feet long and forty-five feet wide, built in the center of every village. In keeping with Puritan belief that churches should refrain from the extravagance and corruptions they saw in the Catholic church, the meetinghouse was extremely simple and plain to the point of homeliness or severity—no ornamentation, no vaulted ceilings, no statues whatsoever, no decorative carvings, no religious candles, and no stained-glass windows. Some were described as roughly put together, crowded, dark, drafty, and unheated. The Second Church in Boston was so cold that in the middle of winter the communion wafers froze hard as stone.

The usual meetinghouse had folding doors on three sides with semicircular molding over each door. The windows were small, diamond-shaped panes set in lead. Pews were owned by individual church

Interior view of the reconstructed Old South Meeting House, Boston, showing family pews. In this church, Samuel Sewall apologized for his part in the Salem witch trials. Photo courtesy of the author.

members or were owned by the congregation and assigned to church members. Although the rule of simplicity always applied, there were many different pew sizes and designs within a given church as various families and individuals had their own pews built to their specifications. Some were small and some large; some were in the shape of a U with seating on three sides and some with seating on one side only; some were round and some oblong with seating all around; some were made of oak and others of pine. In the middle of a square- or round-shaped family pew, there was a chair for the head of the family.

Social stratification was very much apparent in the meetinghouse. The pews of the wealthy were usually large and decorated with columns. Others, rented for most of the worshippers and the poor, were often no more than rough plank benches. There was a very high, elevated pew in one corner for black worshipppers. (The segregation of black worshippers continued in Boston churches well into the nineteenth century.) And there was a special range of pews assigned to the white community's poor.

In most congregations, every person was seated by votes of village selectmen according to a social ranking based on a combination of wealth, position in the community, or sometimes age. At times rankings caused division and havoc among the congregation, some of whom, dissatisfied with their assignments, would take the seats of others and would be hauled out and fined. In Hadley, Massachusetts, the meeting house contained 128 seats; each seat rented for about 3 shillings per year. Women generally sat on one side of the church and men on the other. A section of the church was also devoted to young boys.

In the larger churches, there were as many as fifteen ranks determining church seating. The first seats around a table were for the trustees of the church and the judges and for those who contributed 40 shillings to the church. The first six pews were reserved for males who contributed substantial amounts for their seats, the first one costing 30 shillings and the sixth 9 shillings. The seventh pew was for young men. The eighth was for boys. The ninth was for ministers' wives and widows and for women whose husbands were 40-shilling contributors. The next three pews were for women whose husbands were lesser contributors. The fourteenth rank and pew was for girls. And the fifteenth was for anyone.

THE CHURCH SERVICE

Two services were held on Sunday, both during daylight hours. All the Sunday services followed a prescribed pattern. Thomas Lechford, an early settler, reported back to old England on the prevailing practice in New England in 1640. The service began with an extemporaneous prayer of about fifteen minutes, delivered by the minister. This was followed by either the minister's or teacher's scriptural reading and an explanation of it. Next was the singing of psalms, the only hymns allowed at first.

A large committee of Puritan clergy translated the Psalms from the Hebrew into everyday English in *The Bay Psalm Book* (1640), principally for use in the service. Their aim was not only to have an accurate translation; their view of the beauty of paintings and music as devilishly or popishly seductive led them to create singsong verses with none of the lyrical poetry of the Hebrew sources or the English King James Bible. A comparison of four lines of the Twenty-Third Psalm of the King James Bible with *The Bay Psalm Book* illustrates just where the minister's suspicion of poetry (and need to create Psalms that were easy to memorize) led them:

The Lord is my Shepherd
I shall not want.
He maketh me to lie down in green pastures.
He restoreth my soul.
(from the King James Bible)

The Lord to me a Shepherd is.
Want therefore shall not I.
He in the folds of tender grass
Doth cause me down to lie.
(from *The Bay Psalm Book*)

No organ or piano or other instrumental accompaniment was permitted.

The center of the service was a one-hour sermon, timed by an hourglass kept at the pulpit. Some report, however, that if the minister were not finished when the sands had completely run down in the hourglass, he would turn it over and keep on going. The teaching elder concluded the service with a prayer and a blessing.

There were no responsive readings and no readings of Scripture without explication. Such readings, the centerpieces of the Anglican service, were contemptuously labeled "dumb readings." Neither the sign of the cross nor kneeling was part of the ceremony.

OTHER MEETINGHOUSE ACTIVITIES

The New England community in colonial times was entirely church centered. Besides the two services on the Sabbath, at least one other instructive church meeting was held each week. Often there were church meetings of some kind every day of the week. Community members could expect that on one day of the week (in Boston it was Thursday) important lectures and other critical activities would be held. On Thursdays in Boston, for example, engagements to be married were announced. Other announcements were made at Thursday lectures. Moreover, those who had misbehaved were scolded at Thursday meetings. More serious offenders were placed in the stocks or publicly whipped on Thursdays, on either side of the meetinghouse, where their punishments served as a major entertainment for all and an opportunity for the minister to draw a moral for them. Many chose the time of this meeting to confess their sins.

SABBATH LAWS AND CUSTOMS

The Sabbath began at sundown on Saturday and lasted until sundown on Sunday. During this time, the only holy day recognized by the Puritans, no one was supposed to participate in recreation or work. The original *Judicals*, a book of Mosaic laws proposed by the Reverend John Cotton of Boston, called for the death penalty for persons found prophaning the Sabbath. Among the activities that were forbidden in New Haven, Connecticut, which had some of the most stringent Sabbath laws, were walking in the garden or in the fields, cooking, making beds, sweeping, cutting hair, and shaving. The Reverend Michael Wigglesworth, a Harvard professor, became dejected that one of the Harvard students was going to hell because Wigglesworth found him laughing on the Sabbath. According to one student of colonial New England, Alice Morse Earle, in 1656, a Captain Kemble of Boston was apparently placed in the stocks for two hours for kissing his wife in public on the Sabbath after returning from a three-year voyage.

Some clergymen were under the conviction that lovemaking on the Sabbath, even between husband and wife, was the gravest of sins. And they also believed that they could determine when many of such misbehaviors occurred, for it was thought that a child was born on the same day of the week when it was conceived. So some clergymen were certain that a child born on Sunday was conceived on Sunday. The Reverend Israel Loring of Sudbury, Massachusetts, was especially well known for punishing couples whom he thought had made love on the Sabbath. He steadfastly refused to baptize children who were born on Sunday, convinced that they had been conceived on the Sabbath. His policy changed when his own wife gave birth to twins on the Sabbath.

HOLY DAYS

Other days deemed holy by most Christians—Christmas, Good Friday, and Easter—were not celebrated at all. Stiff fines were even levied on any member of the colony who was caught celebrating Christmas. Note the following law from *The General Laws And Liberties of the Massachusetts Bay Colony*:

> For preventing disorders arising in several places within this jurisdiction, by reason of some still observing such Festivals, as were Superstitiously kept in other Countries, to the great dishonour of God and offence of others;
>
> It is therefore Ordered by his Court and the Authority thereof, that whosoever shall be found observing any such day as Christmas or the like, either by forbearing labour, feasting, or any other way upon any such account as aforesaid, every such person so offending, shall pay for every such offence *five shillings* as a fine to the County. (57, 58)

FAST DAYS AND DAYS OF THANKSGIVING

Although the Puritans refused to recognize the usual religious holidays, they regularly designated days of prayer for fasting and praise as they thought they were needed. These were called fast days, days of humiliation, or days of thanksgiving. In some cases, as around the time of colony-wide elections, fast days were mandated by the legislature. Usually upon the instigation of the clergy, official fast days were also appointed and announced by the legislature in times of serious community crises—for example, during battles with Indians, epidemics of disease, and internal strife or disintegration. The colony records indicate that the legislature declared a fast day for October 19, 1652, as a response to natural, social, and spiritual emergencies—torrential rains and flooding, wars in England, and worldliness and hard-heartedness among the people. Such days were appointed with some frequency throughout the year, sometimes as many as one every month. Later in the century, after the Restoration and the appointment of a royal governor to the colonies, disputes arose over the power of the legislature to dictate public fast days. The royal governor would on occasion refuse to add his authorization for fast days called by the legislature upon clerical urging, especially fasts prompted by the colony's unhappiness with England.

On public fast days, citizens led by public figures and church members were expected to be in church. Church members who failed to appear received solemn visits and reprimands from church elders. Church services on these days continued for eight or nine hours of preaching and scriptural explication, during which the ministers elaborated on the sins that had caused the calamity at hand and predicted further troubles if the community and its members refused to repent and change their behavior. These fast day sermons, or jeremiads, were the rhetorical culmination of Puritan culture.

Besides public, authorized fast days, there were private meetings of fasting and prayer in residences, where friends gathered during family trouble like an illness.

Only two sacraments were recognized by the Puritan church: holy communion and infant baptism. Puritans did not, as did Roman Catholics, believe in transubstantiation—that the wine of communion became the blood of Christ and the wafer became the body of Christ. Nor did they approach an altar to be given communion by the pastor. Instead they sat in their seats and placed the wine and wafer in their own mouths. Marriage was not considered a sacrament and was performed by a magistrate, not a clergyman. There were no last rites and no religious burials for the dead.

The church was unquestionably the center of the life of any New England community. Only church members could vote, and only church members could sit on the general court of magistrates or the court of deputies or elect other members of legislative bodies, despite the fact that church members were in a decided minority.

THE POWER OF THE CLERGY

The Puritans, who despised the power of the Catholic hierarchy, believed that "each man is his own priest" and that the Roman Catholic system of intermediaries between God and humans was corrupt. But in few other societies did the appointed men of God have as much power in public and private life as they did in colonial New England. Although the clergy were not allowed to hold office, they held unquestionable power in the public and private spheres. No person could be elected without the open support of the clergy, and no legislation was successful without the endorsement of the clergy.

We need look no further than the first pastor of the First Church of Boston, the Reverend John Wilson, who worked openly and successfully in seeing that the renegade Anne Hutchinson was exiled for treason as well as heresy and in ensuring that Quakers were driven out of the colony, jailed, mutilated, or even hanged. We see clergymen like Increase Mather attempting to negotiate politically with the English king and Parliament in the best interests of the colony to keep from losing its charter. We find Cotton Mather proposing legislation and working the crowds and the legislature to reinforce the witchcraft trials while his father, Increase, worked with the new governor of the colony to halt the trials.

The clergy could not hold office themselves, but they were the chief advisers of the legislators and judges, and they used their pulpits and weekday meetings and their election day addresses to instruct their congregations how to lobby the legislature on a variety of social measures and how to vote in elections.

The clergy were so powerful that any criticism of them or challenge of their authority was considered close to treason and heresy, as Anne Hutchinson discovered, to her sorrow. Stories abound of citizens who were punished for speaking ill of clergymen. One Nathaniel Haddock was "severely" whipped for saying that he got no profit from listening to his preacher's sermons. Another man, Thomas Maule, was sentenced to receive ten stripes (lashes of the whip) because he said that his pastor was a liar and a man of the devil.

Preaching

Not only did the Puritan clergy have political clout; they assumed power in the church community as preachers. Their congregations realized that the clergy was indispensable in many ways. Most important, congregations needed an educated clergy to explain doctrine to them, for they knew that every person's intellect had become hopelessly weakened after Adam's disobedience and that they needed help to know Scripture intimately and to figure out what God required them to do to secure any call to election or to please God in order to make life on this earth less painful. For this reason, among others, the Puritans needed a highly educated clergy who could interpret Scripture for them.

Harvard University was established in 1636 not only to educate the youth who could afford it but to provide subsequent generations with well-trained ministers. Covenant theology was not a simple message to explain. There were many complicated legalistic conundrums to unravel. (For example, how could humans have no freedom of will yet shoulder such guilt?) Furthermore, there were many beliefs that went against the grain of human understanding and sympathy. (How could God damn all deceased infants to hell, even to an easier room of hell?)

The sermon was not only a necessary interpretation of Scripture; it was also a conveyer and interpreter of current happenings in the world and the community. The Puritans believed that God and Satan were in a constant battle in the present life; everything that happened in daily life, whether an outbreak of disease or the death of an important or beloved person, was directly caused or allowed by God. Sometimes such events were God's way of metaphorically conveying truths to humans. The role of the clergy was to interpret these things. So if an earthquake, for instance, shook the earth in some remote place, the congregation got news of the catastrophe from the pulpit. The community learned of an earthquake from Increase Mather in 1706 and had the event interpreted for them as God's warning of the hell that lay at the pit of the world and at the pit of man's soul—a hell that could unsettle the very foundation of existence in ruinous fury at any time as a result of God's anger. Sermons were sometimes the only means of continuing education for the congregation. They were also the chief ways in which the clergy provided moral instruction on specific behaviors. Increase Mather is again an example, preaching on drunkards in 1673, against dancing in 1648, and on the more serious crime of murder in 1682.

Preparing for Justification

One of the most important roles of the clergy, which gave them power in the lives of everyday citizens, was their responsibility (they believed it was their chief responsibility) in preparing church members to experience justification and to determine whether they had been through a true justification or a false one. In this critical journey, which secured salvation for the elect and softened God's wrath against elect and nonelect alike, clergymen were trained to help the unjustified feel the full horror of sin, death, the last judgment, and hell. Much of this was done through sermons like the famous one, "Sinners in the Hands of an Angry God," delivered by Jonathan Edwards in 1741 in Enfield, Connecticut. On this occasion, he painted a picture of a vengeful God holding man over the pit of hell as he would a spider and longing to drop man in. As a means of stimulating his hearers to prepare for justification by intensely feeling the horrors of hell, Edwards's sermon has few equals. Eyewitnesses claim that there was such groaning and loud weeping in the audience, that Edwards had to ask them to quiet down so he could finish:

> O Sinner! Consider the fearful danger you are in: it is a great furnace of wrath, a wide and bottomless pit, full of the fire of wrath, that you are held over in the hand of God, whose wrath is provoked and incensed as much against you, as against many of the damned in hell. (From Lauter, 561–562)

Michael Wigglesworth's 1662 poem, "Day of Doom" was another famous instance of clerical assistance in preparation for justification by meditating on sin, the last judgment, and hell. His poem is a vivid picture of iniquity before the end of the world—people "wallowing in all kind of sin," then Judgment Day when people go amok and even tear their own flesh in an attempt to escape, and hell, where monsters drag off the nonelect and unjustified in chains to burn miserably forever.

Sometimes this gruesome preparation for justification would last for months; sometimes it would last for only a few days. But during this time, the church member who was preparing for justification or going through the process of justification might visit the minister's study daily. And the clergyman was the one who in private counseling guided members through the process, leading many to describe pastors as physicians of the soul. Indeed, preparation was not unlike modern psychoanalysis, and the clergy's role was not unlike that of a psychiatrist.

Standers in the Gap

Through their multiple private functions as explainers of Scripture, moral teachers and disciplinarians, comforters and guides, and their public roles in affecting community legislation and politics, many prominent clergy took on a mythic stature as protectors of the community: "standers in the gap." Ministers were not the only people who functioned as standers in the gap, but most of the people who were so regarded came from the clerical ranks. This label usually surfaced in funeral rhetoric when beloved leaders died.

The idea was that in the Garden of Eden, the human race lived within a protective circle. But the disobedience created a gap in the circle. Through this chasm or gap, God rained down his constant anger on human beings, causing disease, physical pain, hunger, spiritual confusion, psychological torment, untimely death, and war. But sometimes a community was fortunate to have a very special, good person to serve as a stopper in the gap. He or she stood in the gap through which God ordinarily visited his anger and displeasure, and because God loved the person, he held back his anger. In short, the whole community was protected from God's anger by the beloved leader. When such a person died, the community's grief was great—not only because it had lost a loved one, but because it feared that it would again be subject to God's wrath raining down on the community through the breach no longer occupied by the stander in the gap.

CHANGES IN THE POSITION OF CLERGYMEN

The first clergymen, by the force of their characters, held absolute power over their congregations and their communities—if not in law, certainly in practice. It was a power that the congregations seem to yield to their charismatic ministers without much question. With the second generation, however, the authority of the ministers began to be questioned by a changing, broadening population. When the force of character was insufficient to command control, the clerical response was to dig in their heels and to legislate and insist on their authority, arguing that it came not from their congregations but from Christ himself—a position very akin to the papal view to which the Puritan church had originally objected. By the eighteenth century, as Puritanism was declining sharply, many prominent ministers were absolute despots ruling over congregations, which often resented the control.

As ideas from the Age of Reason came to the colonies from Britain and Europe in the eighteenth century, more citizens were suspicious of all organized religion. Influential individuals like Thomas Paine and Benjamin Franklin were classed among the unchurched.

Even the Puritan or Congregational churches were themselves changing rapidly. The rigid and, to many parishioners, harsh doctrine, especially concerning the insignificance of good works in salvation and the damnation of infants, would be reconsidered. But the Protestant church, chiefly shaped by Puritanism, would remain the strongest single institutional influence in the United States throughout the eighteenth and nineteenth centuries.

BIBLIOGRAPHY

Andrews, Charles M. *Colonial Folkways*. New Haven, Conn.: Yale University Press, 1919.

Bealle, Otho T., and Richard H. Shryock. *Cotton Mather*. Baltimore: Johns Hopkins University Press, 1954.

Child, Frank Samuel. *The Colonial Parson of New England*. New York: Baber and Taylor, 1896.

Dow, George F. *Everyday Life in the Massachusetts Bay Colony*. Boston: Society for the Preservation of New England Antiquities, 1935.

Earle, Alice Morse. *The Sabbath*. New York: Macmillan, 1891.

The General Laws And Liberties of the Massachusetts Colony: Revised & Reprinted. Cambridge, Mass.: Samuel Green, 1672.

Lauter, Paul, ed. *The Heath Anthology of American Literature*. Lexington, Mass.: D.C. Heath, 1990.

Miller, Perry. *The New England Mind.* 2 vols. Boston: Beacon Press, 1953.
———. *Orthodoxy in Massachusetts.* Cambridge, Mass.: Harvard University Press, 1933.
Morgan, Edmund S. *The Diary of Michael Wigglesworth.* New York: Harper and Row, 1946.
Sewell, Samuel. *The Diary of Samuel Sewall.* 2 vols. New York: Farrar, Straus and Giroux, 1973.
Shurtleff, N.B., ed. *Records of the Governor and Company of the Massachusetts Bay.* 6 vols. Boston: W. White, 1853–1854.
Solberg, Winton U. *Redeem the Time.* Cambridge, Mass.: Harvard University Press, 1977.
Walzer, Michael. *Revolution of the Saints.* Cambridge, Mass.: Harvard University Press, 1965.
Wendell, Barrett. *Cotton Mather.* 1891. New York: Chelsea House, 1980.
Wertenbaker, Thomas J. *The Puritan Oligarchy.* New York: Scribner's Sons, 1947.
Winslow, Ola E. *Meetinghouse Hill.* New York: Macmillan, 1952.

3

Government and Law

Mary Wilson, Sara Lynch, and Martha Coleman, three young girls of sixteen, decided after a hard week of kitchen work to take a walk on a beautiful spring Sunday afternoon in the countryside around Plymouth, Massachusetts. A neighbor who saw them leaving the house reported their transgression to the town constable, who arrested them for violating a law that forbade dishonoring God and the Sabbath day by walking in the fields on Sundays. It was the third time that Mary Wilson had been admonished for taking a stroll on the Sabbath. Her master decided not to pay her fine, so she was publicly admonished at the Thursday lecture and given five stripes with a whip.

John and Anne Hansen had nine-year-old twin sons who spent most of the week at their school desks or in church meetings with their parents. The boys loved the out-of-doors and repeatedly managed to escape to the back yard on Sunday afternoons, where they engaged in games that got noisier and noisier. The Hansens' neighbors complained that the noise of the children was desecrating the Sabbath and disturbing their meditations. As a result, Hansen was brought before the court, fined ten shillings, and made to stand on the public gallows to be admonished before the community.

Esther and Thomas Bryan had suffered through a troubled twenty-five-year marriage. His faults were laziness, irresponsibility, and a fondness for the bottle. Her fault was nagging. One day, after a particularly acrimonious argument, Thomas called the constable to arrest Esther for the crime of "Exorbitancy of the Tongue, in Railing and Scolding." A magistrate found her guilty and sent her home with a gag in her mouth, which she had to wear for a week. On subsequent occasions, she was given the appropriate sentence for repeat offenders: she was set on a stool on a public platform and her head dunked three times into a trough or bucket of water.

William Brown, an orthodox member of the Anglican Church while still in England, came to the New World as part of the Massachusetts Bay Company although he did not share the Puritan beliefs of their leaders, for the opportunity to own land and become economically independent. Though he acquiesced to the law that he and his family attend the first Church of Boston, his past as a traditional Anglican coupled with his humble social position made it impossible for him to join the church. As a consequence, he could not vote in any elections. Yet as he began to enjoy success as a farmer, he was required to pay taxes to support a church of which he was not a member and a government in which he could neither vote nor participate. When Brown repeatedly objected, voicing his opinions to friends, he was arrested, charged, and found guilty of vilifying the authorities. His ears were cut off, and he was fined, publicly whipped, and banished from the Massachusetts Bay Colony.

John Meredith, a blacksmith in Salem, was notorious for his colorful language. Several men who did business with him and were offended by his cursing called the constable to his shop on several occasions, after which he was arrested and sentenced to wear a cleft stick on his tongue (a cleft stick was a stick split three-quarters of the way down lengthwise).

Peter Johnson, a sixteen-year-old servant who was arrested for stealing two chickens from his master's barn, was beaten for the offense and branded with the letter *T* on his arm. When he was again found guilty of stealing apples from the orchard and having no money to reimburse the orchard owner three-fold, as decided by the judge, he was sold as a slave to work six years to pay for the stolen apples. This was justified by the Bible in Exodus 22:3: "If he have nothing, then he shall be sold for his theft."

The people listed above are fictional, but the rules, laws, and punishments cited as prevailing in the Bay Colony, Plymouth, and New Haven were all too real. For people who had escaped tyranny in old England, there was tyranny in New England. Some escaped religious persecution only to set up a government founded on religious intolerance in the New World. Legislation was enacted outlawing cruel punishments, but in the New World society, beatings through several towns, branding, the cutting off of ears, and driving stakes through the tongues of miscreants were not regarded as cruel corrections. And every government decree, tyranny, intolerance, and cruelty was carried out in the name of the Lord.

RELIGIOUS DOCTRINE AND GOVERNMENTAL MISSION

The view of the world inherent in the reformed theology that brought most of the English Puritans to New England shaped the grand vision of a godly government and had a direct bearing on the laws the Puritans chose to pass and the severity of their punishments. Their mission was shaped by their interpretation of biblical history in that they viewed themselves as biblical Israelites, chosen by God to establish his kingdom on earth. The king of England was, to them, the Egyptian pharaoh of the Bible, virtually enslaving them by denying them the right to worship freely as they pleased. The perilous Atlantic Ocean was like the desert of the Bible over which the Israelites fled. And New England was the holy land, or the Canaan of the Bible, where they would set up a godly government.

They used another biblical metaphor, this one from the New Testament, in calling New England an "Olivet," or the Mount of Olives, where Jesus prayed before he was arrested and crucified. The Mount of Olives, made holy by Jesus' presence there, was a raised plot of earth where earth and heaven symbolically came closest together. Boston, that city where Beacon Hill stood so prominently raised above sea level, became Olivet in their minds. John Winthrop, Massachusetts Bay's first governor, borrowed a phrase from Scripture to describe the Olivet of the New World in his essay "A Model of Christian Charity"; he called it a "City on a Hill." Boston, this center of New England, would be a government in which the affairs of state would be guided by God and by Puritan principles, through the agency of godly leaders, including the clergy. It would therefore be a religious government, with no pretense at separating church and state. The union of church and state was felt in the daily lives of most New Englanders in the governmental dictate that restricted the vote and office-holding to church members only and forbade any expression of belief other than that sanctioned by the Puritan church. There were a few exceptions, but for the vast majority, the franchise and speech were limited by the state.

THE SOURCE OF LEGISLATIVE POWER

Ultimately European and English settlers in the New World received their authority to establish government from the kings and queens of their home countries, who had paid for the exploratory expeditions and then decreed that specific New World territories belonged to them. Trading companies were given charters, or contracts, by European monarchs to mine the New World for natural resources, particularly fish and furs. To assist in the process, the companies often established settlements.

The preeminent authority for the colonies of New England was the king of England, who invested his authority in the trading companies that had received his permission to create settlements. The trading companies, in turn, sent members of their company or their delegates to the New World settlements to run them.

SYSTEM OF GOVERNMENT IN MASSACHUSETTS BAY

The main New England settlements were at Plymouth, Salem, and Boston, Massachusetts; Hartford and New Haven (only the latter known as Connecticut); Providence, Rhode Island; and smaller scattered communities throughout New Hampshire and Maine. The people in each of these settlements developed governments unique to their situations.

The most formidable, far-reaching, and influential government in colonial New England was the Massachusetts Bay Colony, with its capital in Boston. In Cambridge, England, on March 19, 1629, King Charles I granted a charter to the Massachusetts Bay Company to establish a settlement in New England. The charter, with specific requirements dictated by the king, became, of necessity, the constitution for everyone living in the Massachusetts Bay Colony, eventually including all of what is now Massachusetts, most of Connecticut, and most of Maine and New Hampshire. The charter gave the company authority

> to make, ordeine, and establishe all manner of wholesome and reasonable orders, lawes, statutes, and ordinances, directions, and instructions, not contrarie to the lawes of this our realm of England, as well for setling of the forms and ceremonies of government and magistracy fitt and necessary for the said plantation, and the inhabitants there, and for nameing and stiling of all sortes of officers, both superior and inferior, which they shall finde needeful for that government and plantation, and the distinguishing and setting forth of the severall duties, powers, and lymytts of every such office and place. (Quoted in Morgan, 84–85)

Even before the group left England, it was decreed that the business of the colony would be conducted at four meetings a year of the "Great and General Court," consisting of the twelve members of the company plus the governor. However, a loophole in the charter and some clever political moves made the governing of this colony different from previous ones: no meeting *place* was specified. A meeting could occur anywhere with the governor and only six members present, and the governor and ten members were planning to emigrate. Therefore, there would always be a legal quorum in the colony, so the seat of government could be moved to the colony itself rather than remaining in England to be ruled from England. When this prospect became clear, the members

John Winthrop, first governor of the Massachusetts Bay Colony. Courtesy of the Massachusetts Historical Society.

of the company who did not plan to emigrate resigned, and the charter was placed in the hands of the company members who did emigrate.

The charter specified that the colony was to be managed by a governor, a deputy governor, and a council of eighteen assistants to be elected annually by the company. John Winthrop, one of twelve members of the company, was elected governor and Thomas Dudley was elected deputy governor before the journey to New England even began. These men would constitute the first legislature. At the time of settlement, the eleven or so other members of the company were the only settlers designated as *freemen*—those who could vote.

The charter decreed that once every year the General Court would meet to elect or reelect the governor and no more than eighteen assistants, who would meet every month on their own and also be present at meetings of the General Court. The power to make laws and elect the governor was to be in the hands of the General Court.

But once in New England, the Massachusetts Bay Company, rather than developing a government in which a portion of the population had a voice, filled all the places on the General Court and all the places on the Court of Assistants with the same the ten or so members of the company. Although the charter had called for from eighteen to twenty assistants, only about ten were actually chosen at first so that places could be saved for other important men who would emigrate later. After four years, there were only two new assistants named beyond the original ten, and one of those was the son of Governor Winthrop. For fifty years, the number of assistants remained about half the number specified in the charter. Yet in 1630 alone, over 1,000 people arrived in territory controlled by the Massachusetts Bay Company. A year later there were 2,000. In ten years the colony had grown to 26,000 members. The same eleven or twelve men, including the governor and deputy governor, continued to rule over a population of thousands.

The General Court was intended by the charter to be the legislating body, made up of those who were franchised. But at the time the settlers arrived in Boston, only the company members (about twelve men) had the franchise, and the Court of Assistants was very slow to grant the vote to the many who applied. Then it was determined that only those who were church members could vote. But securing church membership was an arduous process, which only only a small minority of the settlers were able to complete successfully, though the law required church attendance of all settlers. None of the women or indentured servants could vote.

In further undermining the voice that the people could exercise through the General Court, the governor and Court of Assistants decreed, in sharp contradiction to the terms of the charter, that virtually all powers to legislate and the power to select the governor would reside with them, and not with the voting men on the General Court. This plan failed when some of the settlers demanded to see the charter for themselves, and the General Court emphatically rejected it. In spite this successful check, the political leaders of the colony, strongly supported by the powerful clergy and buttressed by the policy of allowing only church members to vote, successfully squelched continual attempts to bring significant representation to the government and exiled or ran off anyone who spoke for more representation. New England was literally an oligarchy (absolute rule by a few) and a theocracy (rule by the church).

A practical effect of government by the few on the lives of many was illustrated when the General Court met for the first time in August 1630. Their primary business was to place a ceiling on wages that could be earned by building trade workers, whose services were urgently needed to construct shelters. It is interesting to speculate on the fate of this legislation had the vote not been restricted to some ten or twelve men who composed the company at the time.

SMALL STEPS TOWARD GREATER REPRESENTATION

In 1631, a situation developed in the colony that inadvertently forced the government to open up to more participation on the part of its citizens. The original plan in 1630 was to make Newtown (what is now Cambridge), not Boston, the seat of government for the Massachusetts Bay. Anticipating this, the deputy governor, Thomas Dudley, had built his house there. But Governor Winthrop and the assistants changed their minds and declared that Boston instead would house the General Court and Court of Assistants. Dudley was furious and mollified only when Winthrop promised to pour extra money into fortifying Newtown where Dudley had already invested in a house. To pay for the fortifications, Winthrop and the Court of Assistants levied a general tax on all Massachusetts settlements. The village of Watertown, however, refused to pay the tax, which had been levied without consultation. As a consequence, the government allowed two deputies to be elected from each township to advise the Court of Assistants on matters of taxation.

This was the beginning of a slightly more representative government. The number of freemen was growing, and more people were needed to conduct the everyday business of the colony. Moreover, representatives chosen among the freemen by the towns began to voice their suspicions that the charter was being violated by the governor, his deputy governor, and the elite Court of Assistants in denying them representation. These situations led to the organization of a second legislative body in May of 1634. The Court of Assistants would constitute an upper house, and deputies or representatives from each township were elected to serve as members of a lower house. Until 1644, when the two bodies had a bad-tempered fracas over the ownership of a dead pig, they met at the same time in the same hall. After 1644, they met separately, with each body having veto powers over the decisions of the other.

TOWN MEETING

Frustration had been growing in the first three years over the inability of most settlers to have a meaningful voice in government, and they soon realized that the level at which they could most substantially have a voice was in the town or village. The formal beginnings of town meetings were in 1633 when the towns of Watertown, Dorchester, and Newtown took the initiative in spontaneously forming governments at the town level, where decisions were made that touched the daily lives of settlers.

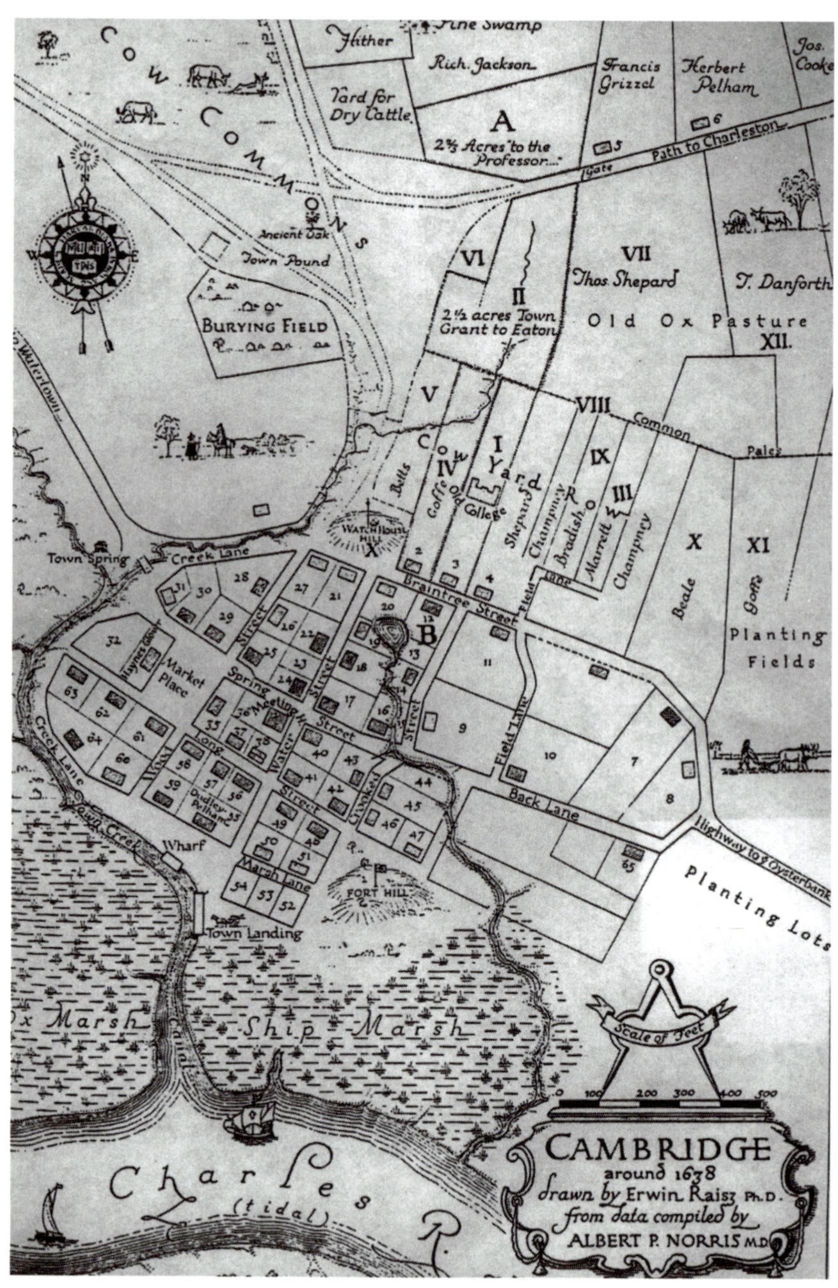

Map of Cambridge, 1638. Reprinted by permission of the publisher from THE FOUNDING OF HARVARD COLLEGE by Samuel Eliot Morison, Cambridge, Mass.: Harvard University Press, Copyright © 1935 by the President and Fellows of Harvard College.

Selectmen or representatives were often chosen by the entire free male population, not always just those who had votes at the colony level. Here all the settlers, not just the freemen, were given an opportunity to voice their opinions, and even nonfreemen served on local committees. At town meetings, citizens would make known their wishes and suggestions regarding local matters, such as taxes, roads, schools, public nuisances, and charities. It was then the responsibility of the chosen selectmen to see that the wishes of the community were carried out. The New England town meeting has often been called the true beginning of grassroots democracy in America.

Town government was formalized in Massachusetts in 1636 with the establishment of the Town Act, giving freemen power to allocate lands and take care of local business, including the levying of fines. Following English tradition, town officials included a recorder, a pound keeper, a herdman, a fence keeper, and sometimes a bellman and a drummer.

The most important town officers were the constables, charged with law keeping and seeing that punishments levied by the General Court were carried out. At first, they were chosen by the General Court from men of property and influence. The Town Act of 1636 allowed the town itself to choose its constables.

Just as the Court of Assistants had to approve anyone who wished to settle in the colony, so town leaders had to approve anyone who wished to settle in their communities.

IMPULSE FOR DEMOCRACY: RHODE ISLAND AND HARTFORD

Despite the addition of a lower legislative body of representatives from villages and the ability to participate in town meetings, the vote at colony level was still restricted to the comparatively few men who had been admitted to church membership. On this matter, the leaders of Massachusetts Bay were not willing to change, though there were two strong voices against the policy within the community. The more radical was Roger Williams, a Puritan clergyman who was a thorn in the side of the leadership on this and a number of other issues. In January 1635, Williams was ordered by the Massachusetts General Court to leave the colony and return to England. But he escaped and found his way to what is now known as Rhode Island. There he founded a colony where church and state were entirely separate, the franchise had nothing to do with church membership, and all settlers were free to worship, or not worship, as they pleased. Massachusetts Bay's animosity toward Rhode Island was such that when, in 1643, the Bay Colony formed a confederacy of other colonies for self-protection, Rhode Island was excluded from membership.

In the same year, the Reverend Thomas Hooker, another Puritan minister, though not so radically abrasive as Williams, also broke with the Massachusetts Bay Colony, largely on the issue of representative government. Hooker had openly expressed his opposition to a franchise limited to church members, and his congregation at Newtown enthusiastically supported him in his opinion. It was not, however, an enthusiasm shared by the power structure in Boston or by Newtown's powerful resident, Deputy Governor Thomas Dudley. John Cotton, the charismatic assistant pastor of Boston's First Church, countered Hooker's opinion (as he had Williams') with a lengthy tract arguing against democratic government. Cotton was of the opinion that "if the people be governors who shall be governed?" (Hutchinson, vol. 1: 437). Most of his fellow ministers, whose sympathies were invariably with the upper house and the aristocracy, concurred with Cotton. And Governor Winthrop, a fairly mild-mannered man, tried to change Hooker's mind in a letter, arguing the aristocratic position that the mass of common people are not wise enough to govern themselves: "The best part is always the least, and of that best part the wiser part is always the lesser." There was, Winthrop wrote elsewhere, no such government as a democracy "in Israel." (Winthrop, 2:430). But Hooker was firm in his democratic convictions and argued that representative government was fairest and safest.

In June 1636, the same year that saw the departure of Roger Williams, the Reverend Hooker, with over one hundred members of his congregation, left the Boston area for the Connecticut Valley, finally choosing to settle in what is now Hartford. After one year, the settlement was governed by a General Court at Hartford to which all freemen, not just church members, chose representatives. Hooker expressed satisfaction with the form of representative government adopted in Hartford, speaking to the General Court on May 31, 1638. He declared that the foundation of government lies in the consent of the people, who have the right to choose their representatives and to set limits on the power of their leaders. In January 1639 all the freemen of the towns around Hartford met to draft a constitution based on Hooker's philosophy.

In New Haven, Connecticut, however, the story was different. Their guiding light, the Reverend John Davenport, established policies that limited the freedoms and rights of his community even more severely than those of Massachusetts Bay by making it more difficult to secure the church membership required for voting and office-holding and by dispensing with trial by jury (because the Bible makes no reference to juries).

RELIGIOUS RATIONALE FOR THE LACK OF REPRESENTATION

The Massachusetts Bay's refusal to allow a representative form of government was consistent not only with the monarchy but also with Calvinist views of human nature and society. Because of their evil nature (since the Fall), humans were wild beasts who, it was remarked on more than one occasion, needed to be fenced in by a strong government run by the few wise and godly men among them. This sentiment was expressed on August 23, 1630, just two months after John Winthrop's party arrived, when he called the first General Court. Despite the radical Protestant notion that each person was his or her own priest, it also incorporated the very conservative idea of secular calling, which insisted that one should remain in the station to which one is called, that is, to which one is born. Some are called to lead and legislate, and others—the commoners—are called to follow. This view authorized the idea that the colony's leaders should be only the highest born and best educated. The lower classes were not called to choose their leaders and would be going outside the calling to which God intended for them if they were allowed to vote or hold office.

ENGLISH RULE, 1684 TO THE AMERICAN REVOLUTION

Losing the Charter

For fifty years, New England was governed without serious interference from England, without the slightest regard for the various kings of England, and without regard for the directives written into the charter that made their settlement in the New World possible. The toppling of James I and then Charles I just before either could impose restrictions on New England, followed by years of Puritan rule in England under Oliver Cromwell who gave them free rein to do as they pleased, allowed the colonies to go their own way and ignore any and all legalities.

As early as the mid-1670s, England's displeasure with the New England colonies was beginning to take on an ominous tone that the settlers could not ignore. Charles II was becoming weary of New England's refusal to obey the Navigation Acts, which imposed tariffs on the colonies, and to pay allegiance to him as their legal sovereign and their flaunting of the law by coining their own money. Moreover, despite repeated warnings from England, the Massachusetts Bay persisted with religious persecution and refusal to accord any but church members the right to vote. Finally on July 21, 1684, Charles II revoked the charter of the Massachusetts Bay Colony and simultaneously negated the practice of requiring church membership of voters.

Changes for Landowners

One large change for landowners occurred with the intrusion of England into the affairs of the colonies: the authority for their whole system of government ultimately and legally rested in the British Crown, not the Massachusetts Bay Company, not the governor or the Court of Assistants, and not Boston or the various other towns. Legally, the Massachusetts Bay Company had never had the right to grant land to either the towns or to individuals. As a result, titles to farms and plots on which houses were built were extralegal, and the British questioned titles to all property. The challenge to all land titles created panic among those who had left England and, for the opportunity of owning land, had crossed an ocean at great peril. Fortunately the English generally decided not to threaten property holders who paid the government a fee of one-third of a penny per acre. The government did take possession of the hundreds of acres of unassigned land and the public land, like the Common in Boston and elsewhere used as pastures or woodlands common to all.

Changes in Representative Goverment

In the 1680s the English moved in to take control over their colonies, especially the large and powerful Massachusetts Bay, which had steadfastly refused or ignored all requests for changes in government made by the Crown. The executive and judicial branches of the government were now placed in the hands of a royal governor and council appointed by the Crown. Property ownership rather than church membership became the standard for the franchise, and local self-government was restored to the villages. Nevertheless, the Congregational or Puritan church continued to control the government of Massachusetts Bay until 1812. As Cotton Mather noted in a letter to a friend, his father Richard Mather, a Puritan minister of note, had managed to get prominent Puritans appointed to the council, the governorship, and all political offices in the 1680s. The strongest evidence of continuing church control is the Salem witch trials of 1692.

BIBLIOGRAPHY

Adams, James Truslow. *The Founding of New England*. Boston: Atlantic Monthly Press, 1921.

Bridenbaugh, Carl. *Cities in the Wilderness*. New York: Ronald Press, 1938.

Cushing, John D. *The Earliest Laws of New Haven*. Wilmington, Del.: M. Glazier, 1917

———. *The Laws and Liberties of Massachusetts*. Wilmington, Del.: Scholarly Resources, 1976.

———. *The Laws of the Pilgrims*. Wilmington, Del.: M. Glazier, 1977.

Haskins, George Lee. *Law and Authority in Early Massachusetts*. New York: Macmillan, 1960.

Hutchinson, Thomas S. *The History of Massachusett's Bay By Mr. Hutchinson*. 3 vols. London: M. Richardson, 1766–1828.

Kawashima, Yasuhide. *Puritan Justice*. Middletown, Conn.: Wesleyan University Press, 1986.

Konig, David Thomas. *Law and Society in Puritan Massachusetts*. Chapel Hill: University of North Carolina Press, 1979.

Miller, Perry. *Orthodoxy in Massachusetts*. Cambridge, Mass.: Harvard University Press, 1933.

Morgan, Edmund S. *The Puritan Dilemma*. Boston: Little, Brown, 1958.

Morris, Richard. *Government and Labor in Early America.* New York: Columbia University Press, 1946.

———. *Studies in the History of American Law.* New York: Columbia University Press, 1930.

Morrison, Samuel Eliot. *Builders of the Bay Colony.* Boston: Houghton Mifflin, 1930.

Palfrey, John Gorham. *History of New England.* 5 vols. Boston: Little Brown, 1856–1890.

Shurtleff, N.B. ed. *Records of the Governor and Company of the Massachusetts Bay.* 6 vols. Boston: W. White, 1853–1854.

Smith, Joseph H. *Colonial Justice in Western Massachusetts.* Cambridge, Mass.: Harvard University Press, 1961.

Wertenbaker, Thomas. J. *The First Americans.* New York: Macmillan, 1927.

———. *The Puritan Oligarchy.* New York: Scribner's Sons, 1947.

Winthrop, R.C. *Life and Letters of John Winthrop.* 2 vols. Boston: Little Brown, 1869.

Young, Alexander. *Chronicles of the First Planters.* Boston: C.C. Little and J. Brown, 1846.

4

Crime and Punishment

The processes by which citizens were tried in Massachusetts and elsewhere were attended to from the early days of settlement. The Court of Assistants established several lower courts including town courts for minor local matters and various "inferior courts" of five judges each in several circuits throughout the colony. These tried civil cases involving judgments of under £10, divorces, probate of wills, and minor criminal cases, which were not serious enough to call for the death penalty, mutilation, or banishment. Appeals could be made from the town court to the inferior court, then to the Court of Assistants, and on to the General Court. Unlike British citizens in other colonies and in England, there was no final appeal to the king.

Each of the main New England colonies had separate legal systems and codes, but their laws, with the exception of Rhode Island, were similar to one another and distinctive in Western world societies in being so decidedly shaped by mosaic, that is, biblical, dictates. When substantial communities of settlers arrived in New England, their written legal codes were virtually nonexistent. In Plymouth Colony, this system consisted of the Mayflower Compact, which was not a list of procedures, rights, and laws but rather an agreement of general social attitudes. Very few specific laws were designated there. These included a list, based on the Ten Commandments, of eight crimes for which one paid with one's life, laws regarding marriage and widows' dues, laws about the transfer of real estate, the making and sale of liquor, and the trespass of animals.

The first legal document in the Massachusetts Bay Colony was the corporation's charter, which had only the specific stipulation that no laws be created in contradiction of English law, a detail that the Massachusetts Colony promptly and knowingly ignored. As well, there was no due process to which citizens could refer. Nor were there constructed systems of laws, systematic statements of citizens' rights and duties, clear statements of what evidence the state needed to convict a person of a crime or what punishment went with what crimes. It was possible, for example, to be tried twice and receive two punishments for the same crime—once by the Court of Assistants and once by the church.

Instead of a written code, all law was in the hands of the ten or twelve colony legislators. These few powerful men who composed the Court of Assistants preferred this impromptu, individualized method of handling the legal business of the colony. Laws were drafted one at a time by these men to suit particular occasions (as, for example, in regulating the wages of carpenters when the Assistants first met in Massachusetts.) They were in no hurry to compose a body of written law because the absence of such a document consolidated power in their hands, leaving them free to rule on individual matters as they liked, without being limited by a code. They refused for another reason: if nothing were written down, there were fewer opportunities for the king to be able to prove just how far they had gone in violating the charter, which forbade them from countering English law.

As the volume of legal business quickly reached a level that one small group of men could no longer handle, minor local matters were turned over to town officials to settle.

To carry out trials in the English tradition, the legislators in Massachusetts and most of the other colonies eventually established jury systems. However, leaders in New Haven, in what was known as Connecticut, refused to allow juries to sit in judgment on any matter whatsoever.

Soon after settling, citizens in Massachusetts Bay, frustrated with their arbitrary and unstable situations with respect to law, began entreating the magistrates to provide them with a comprehensive written code of laws, outlining their rights and obligations. Despite constant pressure from the citizenry, the Court of Assistants made no significant response, though committees were appointed of equal numbers of powerful clergy and legislators to look into the matter.

With the ever-present exception of Rhode Island, the most important generalization that can be made about law in colonial New England as it affected the daily lives of its citizens is that it was created and administered under the influence of Puritan clergy on the basis of Puritan religious principles. Although the magistrates eventually acknowledged the need to incorporate the English legal code, it was always clearly of secondary importance—almost an afterthought to placate the English.

The law that they turned to first and the one that was most important to them was biblical law, specifically, the Ten Commandments. And their constant advisers were not legal scholars but clergyman with little or no legal training.

It comes as no surprise that in 1636, as pressure for a code increased, it was the Reverend John Cotton, a formidable pastor at Boston's First Church and one of the most influential powers behind the legislature, who wrote his own biblical version of the laws of Massachusetts, ironically entitling it, "An Abstract of the Laws of New England, as they are now established"—ironical because there were no established laws of New England. Cotton's code is important even though it was never adopted in Massachusetts Bay as he wrote it, because parts of it were later incorporated into a final version and because it was adopted almost verbatim in New Haven. It is also important as an illustration of the Puritan mind—this peculiar view of law rendered from Scripture as a guide for virtually every aspect of secular human endeavor.

Cotton, who had no legal knowledge, modeled his code on the Old Testament. Governor Winthrop, who, by contrast, was a lawyer, approvingly called Cotton's code "Moses his judicals." It mandated an array of behavior, much of it based on religious belief and authorized by specific Bible verses, which justified the death penalty. In addition to murder and kidnapping, the following were capital crimes: blasphemy, idolatry, witchcraft, false worship, Sabbath breaking, lying, cursing, hitting parents, and criticizing magistrates. The first five of these clearly rested on a unique Puritan view of the universe. Technically any citizen with a religious conscience in sympathy with non-Christians, and also with Baptists, Presbyterians, Catholics, or Lutherans, should, according to Cotton, be hanged. Anyone caught laughing on Saturday night was technically a Sabbath breaker, who deserved to be hanged. In short, most of these capital crimes were generated from a particular religious ideology buttressed by a church-state relationship and would, had they been adopted, be even more blatantly in violation of the charter than ever.

By this time, the legislators in Boston were convinced that they had to act, and multiple committees began working in earnest on an acceptable legal code. In 1641 a second minister, Nathaniel Ward, came up with a body of laws entitled *The Body of Liberties*. Ward had been serving on one of these committees with Cotton, though, unlike Cotton, he had had some legal experience. The first provision in Ward's document expressly addresses the fears of citizens who felt threatened with arrest and losses made arbitrary by the absence of any written laws:

> No man's life shall be taken away; no man's honor or good name shall be stained; no man's person shall be arrested, restrained, banished, dismembered, nor any

ways punished; no man shall be deprived of his wife or children; no man's goods or estates shall be taken away, nor any way endangered, under color of law, or countenance of authority, unless it be by virtue or equity of some express law of the country warranting the same, established by the General Court and sufficiently published, or, in case of the defect of the law in any particular case, by the word of God, and in capital cases, or in cases concerning dismemberment or banishment, according to that word to be judged by the General Court. (Quoted in Palfrey, 280)

Ward's treatise established a code for judicial proceedings; the rights and responsibilities of freemen; the proper treatment of women and children, servants, and foreigners; and the humane treatment of domestic animals. He outlined ten offenses that called for the death penalty, which he buttressed with biblical authority, omitting, however, the death penalty for older children who strike their parents or for anyone who fails to keep the Sabbath. Offspring of slaves, according to the code, were not held in servitude. This document provided the magistrates with far too much latitude and, like Cotton's, was not adopted as written, though much of it was incorporated into a later version.

As a variety of legislative committees continued to meet to draft a code of law, they examined whatever they wrote in the light of English statutory law, though there is little evidence that differences in the two worked as impediments, for in November 1646 a large number of laws were added to the existing miscellany, including one group that designated as criminal various actions totally religious in nature: blasphemy, heresy, contempt of the Bible, contempt of ministers, absence from church, disturbing church services, and Indian pow-wows.

Finally, in 1648, eighteen years after the settlers arrived in Boston, the Bay Colony got a formalized legal code. Called *The Laws and Liberties of Massachusetts*, it incorporated Ward's *Body of Liberties*, the body of laws that had already been enacted, and new laws. The first extant version of this code is a revision printed in 1660. A compilation of supplements, included in a third 1672 version, is the most widely available version today.

LAWS OF MASSACHUSETTS BAY

The body of law with which most of the citizens of New England were presented can be roughly analyzed (in no particular order) into the following subjects, though there is obviously some overlap:

Government and due process

Trades, commerce, and the economy

Capital crimes

Nuisance and serious (but not usually capital) crimes detrimental to the work of the community (such as nuisance suits, breach of peace, theft)

Paganism and heresy, in which native Americans and Quakers are addressed

Actions, aside from heresy, criminalized by the church (such as dancing, desecration of the Sabbath, the drinking of toasts)

Family and household matters (such as marriage and children)

Here we look at capital crimes and nuisance and lesser crimes. Any discussion must be informed by recognizing that the source of the laws was a relatively small minority of men—legislators and clergy—who formed the committees.

Crime in New England

The category of capital crimes illustrates clearly that the leaders had forced a mosaic code on the lives of the settlers, leavened somewhat by the laws of England as well as the independent needs of their frontier community as they had come to experience it for the previous eighteen years. Seventeen crimes could result in the death penalty. All but the crimes of rape and nonappearance in a capital trial invoked specific scriptural authority from five Old Testament books: Exodus, Deuteronomy, Leviticus, Numbers, and Samuel. In the order in which the legislators listed them, they are:

idolatry
witchcraft
blasphemy
murder
poisoning
bestiality
sodomy
adultery
man stealing (kidnapping)
false witness
rebellion and conspiracy
hitting or cursing of parents
rebelliousness in sons
rape
rape of a child
nonappearance in a capital crime

Six of the seventeen crimes, for which the sentence was execution, involved acts of violence against another human being. Three of the seventeen were religious crimes. Two crimes with the death penalty were speech acts alone: blasphemy and cursing a parent. Three were sexual crimes, usually of a nonviolent nature. And three were for crimes of rebellion: against parents, church, or state. In most cases of so-called capital crimes (adultery and cursing a parent, for example), the ultimate penalty of death was rarely carried out, although the language in most cases reads that the miscreants "shall surely be put to death." And the threat of execution for nonviolent crimes like adultery continued to hang over the heads of the citizenry.

The most notorious cases of the death penalty being carried out for crimes other than violence against citizens were the executions of "witches" in Salem and other places and the executions of four Quakers because they were Quakers and kept turning up in the colony when they had been ordered not to return.

Crimes that did not carry the death penalty but were nevertheless considered sufficiently serious to warrant grave consequences were lying, burglary and theft, fornication, assault and battery, Sabbath violations, lewd behavior, swearing, and vilifying authorities. Nuisance crimes of lesser importance included galloping through the streets, gambling, dancing, drinking toasts, smoking near buildings that could catch fire, disturbing the peace with loud noises, and celebrating Christmas.

In studying the court records throughout the Massachusetts Bay Colony and Plymouth, Edwin Powers presents a good idea of what the most frequent crimes were in various areas of New England and what the punishments were for the crimes. Across the board, the most frequent crime brought into colonial New England courts was fornication—sex between men and women not married to each other, including betrothed couples who married shortly thereafter. (Charges were sometimes brought by the state long after the event occurred and the couple was married.) The chief punishments for this crime were whippings along with fines. Arrests for fornication in almost every year and in every colony exceeded arrests for petty thefts, which included stealing apples from orchards.

A surprising number of the other fifteen to twenty most frequently punished crimes seem unjustifiable to the contemporary mind, though vestiges of them may still exist. In Suffolk County Court, for example, the fourth most frequently tried crime was "Lord's Day violations." Number six was "vilifying authorities." Number seven was "lewd, lascivious, wanton behavior." Number nine was drunkenness, which occasionally included being in the company of drunks. Number ten was going to a Quaker meeting. Number fourteen was swearing, and number seventeen was idleness. Other lesser-heard cases that are rare or nonexistent today were crimes of card playing, living alone, scoffing at religion, calling a man a rogue or a woman a whore, traveling on Sunday, disturbing church services, living apart from one's husband for four years, and lying.

Punishment

The 1648 code contained an article forbidding cruel punishments, yet the protection would not have been very comforting to citizens for two reasons. First, practical applications of punishments show that the definition of *cruel* was so narrow as to be nonexistent and, second, the many qualifications in the law seem to cancel out the intent to outlaw cruelty:

> *And for Bodily Punishments;* We allow amongst us none that are Inhumane, Barbarous or Cruel.
>
> And no Man shall be beaten with above *forty stripes* for one Fact at one time, nor shall any Man be punished with Whipping, except he hath not otherwise to answer the Law, unless his Crime be very shameful, and his course of life vicious and profligate.
>
> And no man shall be forced by Torture to confess any Crime against himself or any other, unless it be in some Capital case, where he is first fully convicted by clear and sufficient evidence to be guilty, after which if the case be of that nature, that is very apparent there be other Conspirators or Confederates with him, then he may be Tortured, yet not with such Tortures as are Barbarous and Inhumane. (*General Laws And Liberties*, 129)

The modern reader finds the last sentence confounding because, unlike the magistrates of Massachusetts Bay and others of their day, our culture cannot conceive of a form of punishment classifiable as torture that is not "cruel, barbarous and inhumane." Looking at the punishments that were actually carried out with some regularity in New England, it is hard to imagine just what they might have avoided as cruel.

Whippings, for example, were not always just whippings. In Salem a woman who preached unsanctioned religious doctrine near the church was stripped to the waist, dragged through the streets by a cart, and beaten with a whip. The law specifies that no man will be given more than forty stripes at one time, but sometimes the community leaders found that it was not enough to just give a miscreant forty stripes at the whipping post, conveniently situated at the center of town; he or she would be sentenced to be whipped through several towns—forty stripes through the street of Salem, forty more through Boston, then forty more through Cambridge.

By far the most frequently used punishment was public whipping. John Legge in 1631 was whipped through the streets of Boston and then Salem for hitting a man. For theft and fornication, Nicholas Frost was, in 1632, "severely" whipped, branded in the hand with a hot iron, fined, and banished.

Branding people on the forehead, like cattle, was another popular form of punishment not considered barbarous or cruel. The brand identified the miscreant for life: *B* for burglary, *T* for theft, *F* for forgery, *AD* for adultery, *V* for lewdness, *D* for drunkenness, or *I* for incest (which usually meant marrying the widow of a brother).

Mutilation was evidently not considered excessively cruel by the Puritans. Phillip Ratliffe of Salem, who in 1631 had both his ears cut off for criticizing the government, probably never realized that his punishment was not cruel, barbarous, or inhumane. Indeed, the chopping off of ears was a mutilation often chosen as punishment by the authorities for a variety of crimes, including being a Quaker. The piercing of the tongue with a red-hot iron was another form of punishment for those who used their tongues to malign authorities or to express heretical opinions. In 1631, for example, Joseph Gatchell for his blasphemy was sentenced by the court to "have his tongue drawn forth out of his mouth and pierced through with a red hot iron." We know also that torture was used to elicit confessions from accused witches and that in 1692 one Giles Corey was slowly pressed to death with heavy stones placed on his chest.

RELIGIOUS JUSTIFICATION OF CRUELTY

The wide range of actions criminalized by the Puritans and the severity of the punishments they inflicted for these crimes were explained and justified by their interpretation of Scripture and biblical history. Their intent was to establish a godly community on this earth, and to those ends, they believed that they had to exclude what they found to be ungodly behavior—desecration of the Sabbath, failure to attend church services, and toleration of beliefs other than their own Puritan one, for example.

Finding themselves on a cruel, uncharted frontier, they found it even more urgent than usual to enforce laws that would organize and buttress the community. To be lenient with disobedient children and community rebels was to undermine the fabric of a community that needed to be united and well disciplined to survive.

Moreover, the frontier that they were encroaching on was seen by them as sinister, the devil's territory, and as such it was incumbent on them to do everything they could to avoid being engulfed in evil and to avert the eternal and unmitigated wrath of God. They saw their oppressiveness as a practical necessity. They believed that God's anger would damage the community (with floods, disease, droughts, Indian raids) if they allowed behavior to persist that displeased him, like drunkenness, swearing, and fornication. So they were unsparing in their laws and, to discourage behavior that might anger God, cruel in their punishments.

BIBLIOGRAPHY

Cushing, John D. *The Laws of the Pilgrims.* Wilmington, Del.: M. Glazier, 1977.

Faber, Eli. "Puritan Criminals." *New England Quarterly* 15 (1942): 591–607.

The General Laws And Liberties of the Massachusetts Colony: Revised & Reprinted. Cambridge, Mass.: Samuel Green, 1672.

Haskins, George Lee. *Law and Authority in Early Massachusetts.* New York: Macmillan, 1960.

Kawashima, Yasuhide. *Puritan Justice.* Middletown, Conn.: Wesleyan University Press, 1986.

Konig, David Thomas. *Law and Society in Puritan Massachusetts*. Chapel Hill: University of North Carolina Press.

Miller, Perry. *Orthodoxy in Massachusetts*. Cambridge, Mass.: Harvard University Press, 1933.

Morgan, Edmund S. *The Puritan Dilemma*. Boston: Little, Brown, 1958.

Palfrey, John G. *History of New England*. 5 vols. New York: Huld & Houghton, 1856–1890.

Powers, Edwin. *Crime and Punishment in Early Massachusetts*. Boston: Beacon Press, 1966.

Shurtleff, N. B., ed. *Records of the Governor and Company of the Massachusetts Bay*. 6 vols. Boston: W. White, 1853–1854.

Smith, Joseph H. *Colonial Justice in Western Massachusetts*. Cambridge, Mass.: Harvard University Press, 1961.

Young, Alexander. *Chronicles of the First Planters*. Boston: C. C. Little and J. Brown, 1846.

5

Labor

RELIGIOUS DOCTRINE AND WORK

Economic life and work, like other aspects of colonial New England life, was influenced by religious dogma. The religious doctrine that had reference to social and economic life, including work, was the conservative doctrine of secular calling. The idea, expounded by Martin Luther and adopted with fervor by the Puritans, was that God called men and women to perform particular tasks or work in this life: women were invariably called to be housewives and mothers, and men were called to specific work as farmers, carpenters, ministers, and so on. People were responsible for identifying the work God intended for them and then for faithfully following their true callings.

To identify God-intended work, a believer considered his own talents and inclinations. If he was powerfully built, had an artistic bent, and was good at working with his hands, he might suspect that he had been called to be a blacksmith. If he liked to work outdoors and had a way with animals, he might suspect that he had been called to be a farmer. However, inclination and talent were not the only matters to be considered in identifying true secular calling, and here is where the conservatism of the doctrine came into play. Puritan clergy made it clear that the social status into which one was born helped one identify the calling God aimed for a person to follow, for certain work belonged to certain social levels. For example, ministers, legislators, and merchants did not come from the lower classes. And it was blasphemy to assume a calling or work outside the social level to which one was born. A person born into a peasant family was not to try to follow work unsuitable for someone of this humble social station. Thus, John Bunyan, an Englishman, was imprisoned for preaching because such work was considered unsuitable for a man like him of lowly social status.

Conflicts arose from the dictate to work and remain in the station in which God placed you. What if your talents and inclinations were clearly for work outside your social station? We have already seen that the calling of leaders and legislators belonged to only a handful of well-born men in the Massachusetts Bay Colony—men who believed that it was unwise to allow any citizens but themselves and their clerical friends to have any voice in central government, much less to function as leaders.

In actuality, the doctrine did not allow most people much choice of work. Peasants born on the bottom of the social ladder rarely had a choice about their life's work. Poor men and women were confined to hard physical labor.

Although women performed many kinds of work, they were largely precluded from any labor outside the house and adjacent land. A woman's ability to perform work as a professional or artisan was, with few exceptions, defined by her husband's vocation. For example, if he were a lawyer, she was able to assist him in his profession and even to carry on the family profession if he died. But the choice always lay with him, not her.

SECULAR CALLING AND COLONIAL ECONOMICS

The identification of one's God-given vocation did not seem so urgent in the early days of the New England settlements. Survival meant that everyone immediately turned their hand to whatever needed to be done rather than meditating on what specific work God intended. But in these early days, the doctrine of secular calling, as well as the hard environment to be conquered in America, did have an immense impact on economic life. Both doctrine and circumstance led New Englanders to take work very seriously. No other virtue was greater than working hard and diligently. No other vice was more despised than idleness. Survival itself was dependent on such an attitude. In the October 1, 1633, meeting of the Massachussetts Bay Colony Court of Assistants, it was decreed that

> no person, house holder or other shall spend his time idly or unprofitably, under pain of punishment as the Court shall think meet to inflict; and for this end it is ordered, that the constable of every place shall use special care and diligence to take knowledge of offenders in this kind. (Shurtleff, vol. 1: 109)

The value placed on economic success was also reinforced by the doctrine of secular calling, which led New Englanders to begin to look for signs of success in their work. It was believed that someone who worked sufficiently hard and well at his God-intended calling was bound to accumulate capital and land. Almost unconsciously, wealth came to be thought of as the mark of a good, hard-working person, and poverty was thought to be the result of shiftlessness. Moreover, success in one's work was regarded as a mark of God's approval. Partly as a consequence of this attitude, few limitations were placed on money making. Sociologist Max Weber argued that the Puritan doctrine of secular calling prepared the way for the rampant, unregulated capitalism in post–Civil War America.

The leaders in the Massachusetts Bay Colony were Englishmen with enough wealth to secure a charter. Reasoning from the doctrine of secular calling that successful businessmen were chosen by God, they felt entirely justified in keeping political power exclusively for themselves and in passing legislation that served to benefit themselves. With the legislative tools at its disposal to manage the colony's commerce, the court set about forming monopolies and restrictions on labor to harvest the rich natural resources of the new world.

The idea in the calling that reinforced social station and justified the perogatives of a privileged class was very much alive in New England, especially in matters of leadership, dress, and education. But the station to which one was born did not seem to limit one as much in choosing suitable work. And through success in work, one could more easily move up the economic and social ladder. Sir William Phipps serves as an illustration. He came to Boston at the age of eighteen as an illiterate ship's carpenter and managed, by various shady business dealings, to secure a fortune for himself and a knighthood from the British, marry the daughter of John Hull (one of the wealthiest merchants in Boston), and become royal governor of Massachusetts Bay.

In approaching the subject of work in the lives of colonial New Englanders, it is useful to imagine what jobs needed to be done immediately on their arrival in the wilderness. What provisions might they have been able to bring with them? What would they have to make or improvise after they got there? Having survived the first winter, what work would have to be done to establish their homes and farms? What would they have to import? What goods or services could they produce to pay for supplies?

After making a list of jobs that needed to be done, compare it to the following partial list of work that was actually done in the first decades of life in colonial New England:

barbing (or hair cutting)
blacksmithing
boating
brickmaking
brick and stone masonry
candlemaking
canoeing
carpentry
cider making
clock making
cooperage or barrel making
locksmith
plastering
fence builder
ferrying
field work
fishing
glassmaking
grooming of animals
innkeeping
leather work
logging
sawmill and grain mill work
metalworking
mining
mowing and reaping
nail making
nursing
message delivering
plowing and planting
rope making
sack making
sawing of boards
schoolteaching
shepherding
sheep shearing
shingling
shoemaking
slaughtering and butchering
soap making
spinning
stabling
surveying
tailoring and sewing
tanning
thatching
trapping
threshing and winnowing grains
weaving
well making
wheel making
printing
pottery making
paper making
dyeing
pencil making
doctoring
midwifery
making of guns and ammunition
basket weaving
hatmaking
apothecary work
shopkeeping
shipmaking
collection of tar and turpentine
lawyering
all manner of housekeeping

MAJOR ECONOMIC PERIODS

Work in the New England colonies can be divided into three periods. The first period, from 1630 to 1640, was a time when labor was scarce, and most settlers had to be jacks of all trades themselves or be wealthy enough to hire laborers with varied, though usually not highly specialized skills. The second period, from 1640 to about 1660, was a time of home industry, when much that was exported was produced in individual households. From the end of the seventeenth century to the Revolution, artisans and more specialized labor flourished in New England.

VOCATIONS

Businessmen

Merchants and artisans, who congregated in towns, made up from 15 to 20 percent of the total New England population. At the top of the work hierarchy in colonial New England in 1630 were the nine wealthy merchant-landowners who held the Massachusetts Bay Charter and formed the first Court of Assistants to govern the new colony. Each of them had lucrative holdings of land. Governor Winthrop and his family, for example, were powerful international exporters who controlled over 3,000 acres of land in the colony, where they raised cattle for sale. His family also had huge interests in shipbuilding and iron ore production. The Dudleys, the family of the deputy governor, and the Stoughtons, the family of another man who later became a member of the Court of Assistants, also immediately amassed immense acreage, not only in Massachusetts but in Rhode Island, Maine, and New Hampshire, and they acquired interests in mineral resources, furs, timber, and agricultural products.

The members of the Court of Assistants were continually awarding themselves land and monopolies. One example can be found in 1643, when the colony gave 3,000 acres to Governor Winthrop's son (himself a member of the Court of Assistants) and his partners to develop an ironworks. With the Winthrops, another member of the original Court of Assistants, William Pyncheon, controlled most of the fur trading in the first five years of the Massachusetts Bay settlement and later owned not only the town of Springfield, Massachusetts, but all of the laborers who entered the town, some of whom he used himself and some of whom he sold to other inhabitants.

The economy of the colony was tightly controlled, usually to the benefit of the nine wealthy men who sat on the Court of Assistants. They controlled all the land and could assign it as they saw fit. They made the laws and could assign monopolies in various areas and put ceilings on the wages of the workmen they had to hire. One of their first orders of business in 1630 was to place a ceiling on the wages of much-needed carpenters, joiners, bricklayers, sawers, and thatchers. These limits were repeatedly revised and restated. Limits were placed on the amount that innkeepers could charge for food and drink. Servants were not allowed to sell any commodity without the permission of their masters. No one could buy land from the natives without permission of the court. In 1631, the court ruled that no one could buy commodities directly from an incoming ship; all had to go through licensed merchants.

Not all merchants were wealthy international traders. Some were keepers of small stores that stocked a variety of goods. There were also roving peddlers who serviced remote rural areas.

Clergymen

The calling of the clergy was equal in importance to that of the wealthy landowner or merchant legislator. As the most highly educated people in the community, clergymen were the powers behind the legislators. From the beginning, their influence was tremendous. Clergymen were provided with good incomes, farms, and often slaves to work their farms.

The first order of business of the legislators on August 23, 1630, only weeks after their arrival in the New World, was to see to the "maintenance" of the ministers, making it a matter of official business that houses "be built for them with convenient speed, at the public charge" (Shurtleff, vol. 1: 10).

The pastors of the Boston and Cambridge churches (men like the Reverend John Wilson and, later, the Reverend Samuel Mather) spent as much of their time guiding the politics and legislation of the community and acting as negotiators with England as they did in their usual pastoral duties of preaching and ministering to their congregations. Other ministers, like the Reverend Michael Wigglesworth, paired their work as ministers with education, serving as professors at Harvard College. Clergymen in small communities, like Edward Taylor, the poet, who lived in Westfield, Massachusetts, doubled as physicians.

Lawyers and Teachers

Although Governor Winthrop himself was trained as a lawyer, the merchants and clergymen in the early days of the colony were suspicious of lawyers. Most legal functions were performed as part-time work by merchants who had minimal legal training. Lawyering as a specialized profession did not flourish until the eighteenth century.

Teachers and tutors were males on the lowest rung of the professional ladder. At best these functions were often performed part time by young men newly graduated from Harvard. The salary of a teacher was one-half to two-thirds of the usual clergyman's salary.

Farmers

The chief work to which nine-tenths of New England's first settlers believed they were called was farming. During the first several years in what for them was uncharted country, these farmers did the work belonging to many callings. In the first days of the settlement, every male had to be a carpenter to build even the simplest shelter. In the 1630s and 1640s, as farms were established in a land where labor was scarce, every farmer had to be his own carpenter (to build houses and outbuildings), mason (to build fireplaces and foundations), trapper (to secure food and hides for the family), and blacksmith (to forge farm implements and kitchen utensils). Farmers in rural areas built their own furniture, tanned leather, made shoes, and even ran stores. They fished, lumbered, and raised livestock.

The primary aim of most of these early farmers, in the ten years after the establishment of the Massachusetts Bay, was to put food on the table and barter for goods they did not produce, like cloth. After 1640, goods grown or made on the farm were also exported to Europe and other colonies.

Communal Farming. In many New England communities, land was set aside for the communal grazing of livestock. These commons are still in evidence throughout the area today. Certain chores would also be done communally; a community shepherd would watch the livestock, for example, and community milkers would milk the cows. In many instances, gardening was done in common areas as well.

Impressed Farm Labor. At critical periods of work on large farms, laborers, including shop owners and artisans, were rounded up by constables, forced to put down their own work, and escorted to work on farms where, for example, a large crop had to be harvested before it ruined. In some communities (for example, Salem, Massachusetts), workers were also required in the 1630s to devote their time and labor on one day in every month to public projects like road repair.

Routine of a Farmworker. In *Labor in a New Land* (1983), Stephen Innes describes the typical day of the owner of a small farm or a farmworker in central Massachusetts in the seventeenth century:

4:30 to 5:00 A.M.—rise and tend to livestock

5:00 to 6:30 A.M.—work in the fields

6:30 to 7:00 A.M.—eat breakfast

7:00 to 11:00 A.M.—work in the fields

11:00 to 11:30 A.M.—take a cider break

11:30 to 2:00 P.M.—work in the fields

2:00 to 3:00 P.M.—eat dinner

3:00 to 6:00 P.M.—work in the fields, tend livestock, repair tools

6:00 to 7:00 P.M.—eat supper

8:30 P.M.—go to bed.

EARLY INDUSTRIES

Two of the first industries, conducted on a small scale to meet local needs, were grain mills and sawmills. Fairly small sawmills were evidently established in New England as early as 1628. Larger ones, intended to assist in the business of lumber exportation, were built in New Hampshire around 1633.

It was imperative that settlers eventually have access to a miller who could grind their grain by a water-powered mill. Rough cereal could be made by grinding corn or rye by hand, but the refined bread, to which English settlers were accustomed, could be produced only by a mechanical mill run by a miller. The first water mill for grinding grain was likely established in Dorchester, Massachusetts, in the late 1620s, after Salem was settled. In any community, the miller was a pivotal political figure, likely because of the importance of his function.

The first large-scale exports from the colonies were the furs and skins brought in by trappers and traders. In high demand were beaver furs, out of which hats were made. Most of the trapping in the beginning was done by Indians, and traders bartered for hides to be sent to England and Europe. William Pyncheon, one of the original charter holders and one of the nine-member Court of Assistants, immediately went into partnership with Governor Winthrop and his family to export furs. In 1636 Pyncheon obtained permission to establish a fur trading post in Springfield, Massachusetts, the largest such enterprise in the colonies, a virtual monopoly in Massachusetts, run like a company town, which Pyncheon owned. The fur trade required workmen with numerous kinds of skills who Pyncheon imported: canoeists, teamsters, coopers, blacksmiths, and common laborers.

The collecting of skins and establishment of tanneries, especially for shoe leather, was a thriving industry by the mid-seventeenth century. Along with shoe manufacturing came the large-scale manufacturing of wooden shoe heels.

An equally important industry that arose in the first ten years of settlement was shipbuilding. Shipbuilders worked out of every port city in New England. By 1700 New England had 2,000 vessels on the seas. As in the fur trade, shipbuilding required many kinds of workers: sailors to man the ship, carpenters to build wharves, rope makers, sail makers, blacksmiths, coopers to make barrels, and wheelwrights to make carts and wagons.

One of the most important industries was the collection and refinement of bog iron, a valuable metal found at the bottom of swamps, bogs, and ponds. The smelting, forging, and refinement of iron was an important industry in Lynn, Massachusetts, from 1643 to 1683. Most house-

Saugus Iron Works, Saugus, Massachusetts. Photo courtesy of the author.

Forge and bellows at the Saugus Iron Works. Photo courtesy of the author.

hold utensils were pewter, which was produced in the New England colonies.

Other growing industries included the manufacture of gunpowder (so essential in hunting and in arming men for the Indian wars) and brick making demanded by the building industry.

Although the British passed laws to prohibit the importation into the colonies of machinery and manufacturing expertise, settlers from Yorkshire, England, were able to bring machinery and their knowledge of cloth manufacturing to Rowley, Massachusetts, in 1643. Here they set up the first textile mill for the manufacture of cloth and rugs.

Another industry crucial to building was established with the discovery of limestone in Newbury, Massachusetts, in the mid-seventeenth century. A wire factory was built in 1667, and Plymouth was known for its brick making. Numerous factories, called fulling mills, also existed for the processing of cloth to make it thicker.

The whaling industry, which in the nineteenth century would become the cornerstone of the New England economy, began to flourish in 1713. Whales provided New England households, businesses, and its exporters with oil for light, ivory, and perfume.

Other early exports included tar and turpentine, which was collected by laborers who might also work on farms or in industries that produced ships or furs.

THE ERA OF HOME INDUSTRIES, 1640–1662

Before 1640, settlers imported cloth, hats, gloves, and shoes, but England's Navigation Acts, with their tariffs and prohibition of trade in other than English ships, began to make trade more difficult. As a result, the Massachusetts Bay legislative bodies foresaw the need for the colonies to produce for themselves much of what they had imported.

Beginning in 1640, bills were passed to encourage production at home of cloth, shoes, and hats for both home use and export. For a brief period, bounties would be paid on all cloth made in the colonies; incentives were provided to teach servants and children to spin and weave; and spinning wheels were furnished by the government to numerous households. Wool production was encouraged by setting up common grazing areas for sheep and by placing a bounty on wolves, considered to be predators of sheep.

In addition to textiles, over 160 different articles were produced in the home to supply colonial needs and in some cases to export. These items ranged from guns to pewter plates, brushes to dishes, and knives to pencils.

An old loom like those used in home industry in colonial New England. From George Francis Dow, *Every Day Life in the Massachusetts Bay Colony* (Boston: Society for the Preservation of New England Antiquities, 1935).

ARTISANS AND SPECIALIZATION

In the early and mid-seventeenth century, only in centers of population like Boston did one find a significant degree of specialization. Here there were fishermen, shipbuilders, sail makers, innkeepers, and shopkeepers. At the close of the seventeenth century, more and more artisans had begun to flourish in New England cities, despite England's attempt to suppress them. Much of the nonfarm work done by the farmer and his household was now also done by specialists in urban areas, some of whom had been trained on farms, some of whom had emigrated from other countries, and many of whom had had training as apprentices. These craftsman set up shops along the main thoroughfares of colonial towns.

A typical street would have taverns, rope makers, a barber, ship masters, merchants, joiners, stave dealers, shoemakers, blacksmiths, silversmiths, tanners, hatters, and apothecaries. In addition, there were makers of leather goods (called saddlemakers) and of barrels (called coopers), dyers, brick makers, glass makers, paper makers, printers, and makers of alcoholic drinks (called distillers and brewers).

Despite New England's trouble with alcohol abuse and the frequent and brutal measures taken to curb drunkenness, early in their settlement New Englanders began the business of distilling rum from molasses imported from the West Indies. Brewers and distillers quickly became key elements in the economy because they required large amounts of capital and many workers, supported other industries like barrel makers, and saw an endless demand for their products. The attempt by England in 1733 to slow New England production by interfering with its importation of molasses for breweries and distilleries contributed to the growing unhappiness with the mother country. By some accounts, the distillation of rum was New England's greatest manufacturing industry at mid-eighteenth century. There were thirty distilleries in Rhode Island and sixty-three in Massachusetts, which produced 2.7 million gallons of rum in 1774.

As artisans rose in importance in the eighteenth century, and before they came to be displaced by factories, they began to join wealthy merchants in running colonial government. One of the famous Boston artisans prominent in American Revolutionary history is Paul Revere, a silversmith and brass smith. Not only does his legend as a famous Revolutionary survive, but his work as an artisan survives as well, for it was he who cast the dome for the Massachusetts State House.

Most of the arts and trades involved unique physical characteristics, specific and unusual tools and skills, peculiar terms and phrases, and decided mystiques. For example, the leather worker did his work straddling a special wooden contraption known as a horse, where his materials were clamped into a vise. Different arts and trades also involved unique risks. The dyer, for example, worked in a building filled with nauseating odors and blinding steam rising from vats sunk in the floor. The dye and steam made the floor so slippery that workers risked falling into the boiling vats.

WOMEN'S WORK

The work that women did depended on the situations in which they found themselves. A fair number of young, single women came to New England as indentured servants to work in households doing domestic and light farm work to help the wives of men who could afford to buy their labor for between four and seven years—shorter terms than those of male servants. A life in New England enabled European and English women to have at least a good chance of escaping the poverty that was inevitably their lot in their native lands. Single women from lower- and middle-class families already living in the colonies also worked in the houses of their families or in other people's houses doing domestic work. Most such young women married at the end of their contracts. In some cases, young women who worked for widowers married their employers.

Whether they were wives or employees, women's work was, with few exceptions, domestic, involving the rearing and education of young children; house cleaning; the growing, gathering, preserving, preparing, and serving of food; and most aspects of providing cloth and clothing—spinning, carding, weaving, and sewing.

It was also her job to support the work of the family, aside and apart from domestic chores. For most women, this involved farmwork, even that of the heaviest kind, including directing servants. Women plowed, planted, tended livestock, slaughtered animals, and knew basic carpentry.

Although most women lived on farms, many supported the work of the family as tradesmen or artisans, for they were expected to be their husband's helpmate in whatever calling he pursued. So women in colonial New England were found working as blacksmiths, silversmiths, tinworkers, shoemakers, shipwrights, tanners, gunsmiths, barbers, printers, butchers, and shopkeepers.

Whether on the farm or in trade, the woman's job was usually to keep informal accounts in her head, to be the guardian of the property, and to act as the center of communications with regard to servants and many customers and merchants.

Although a woman's work and business were always subordinate to her husband's work and her position was always determined by her husband's position, many women were expected to have complete control in running the family businesses when their husbands were away. Wives also assumed the running of the family businesses when their husbands died.

A number of women of modest means had their own small but thriving businesses—growing, drying, and selling herbs, for instance, or raising and selling fowl or dairy products or doing fine handwork for sale. In at least one instance, when a wife's small business became more lucrative than her husband's larger enterprise, he borrowed money from her. Another income available to women was piecework done at home—the same kind of spinning, weaving, and sewing she did for her own family, except on a larger scale.

In many ways, colonial New England women had more choices than their nineteenth-century descendants had, in that they could, and many did, inherit their husband's profession or business when their husband died. Nor was a woman hampered by false notions of work that was feminine and masculine. She was allowed to do almost any work her husband did. Although most of the work allowed a woman was domestic and done in the home, the nineteenth-century prohibition against a woman's working outside the home had not yet become entrenched, so wives and widows of artisans and tradesmen were free to continue nondomestic labor. Records tend to reveal that although a woman could not initiate a business without the sponsorship of a male, she was allowed, even expected, to protect and enlarge any business of her husband or father while either was alive or after their deaths. For example, an amazing 10 percent of the Port of Boston's mercantile firms were run by women in the early 1770s.

Nevertheless, the work situation was still far from ideal. It was not expected that women could be formally educated. It was expected that all men should be taught to read and write and figure, but families were only obligated to teach women to read. Of course, some families did teach women to write and figure, and some women educated themselves, but on the whole, their ignorance of math hindered them from keeping the formal account books needed in running large-scale, complex businesses.

APPRENTICES

It is important in any consideration of work to remember that the ranks of merchants, professionals, and artisans, whose work was so essential to colonial life, were trained and replenished by apprentices. These were young people of twelve or thirteen who were contracted out by their parents to learn a trade. The duty of their employer-trainers was to feed and lodge them, teach them to read and write if necessary, and, most important, teach them a trade. By tradition, at the end of their apprenticeship, when they supposedly had mastered the trade, their employers were to provide them with two suits of clothing. The duty of the apprentice was to do work for his master. Boys were usually apprenticed to artisans, merchants, and professionals like lawyers and physicians, and girls were apprenticed to households to learn spinning and weaving. The most famous apprentice of colonial New England, who left an account of his days as an apprentice, was Benjamin Franklin, whose father apprenticed him to his brother James, a Boston printer and journalist.

From Franklin and other sources, we know that setting up an apprenticeship required a formal, legal contract. Under usual circumstances, the apprentice who decided to leave his master before the allotted time was up broke the law and could be pursued like a runaway slave. Franklin was able to run away from his brother without consequences only because his contract had been legally suspended after his brother's arrest by the British authorities.

We also learn an unhappy fact about apprentice life from Franklin: it was the rare apprentice who was not ill treated by his master. Apprentices were often housed abominably, were not fed adequately, were worked far too hard, and often were beaten.

From the earliest days of settlement to the end of the colonial period in New England, most of the general physical labor in every area of life was performed by indentured servants and slaves. Their situation will be addressed in separate chapters.

DOGMA AND INDIVIDUAL WORK

By the end of the seventeenth century, with the growth of specialization—multiple industries and businesses and varied artisans and professions—young people whose families were not poverty stricken shouldered the burden of choosing the work they should adopt or, in the case of Puritan believers, of identifying the callings that God meant them to follow.

The magnitude of identifying one's proper work in the world continued to be a solemn business for those who had choices. Nowhere is this more graphic than in the case of diarist Judge Samuel Sewall and his troubled son. In the bitterly cold New England winter of 1696, a matter pressing on Sewall's mind was a painful crisis in his son's life. Young Samuel's depression and spiritual distress reached an acute stage in early mid-February. His physical symptoms understandably alarmed his father: the young boy complained of being unable to sleep, and his father reported that he suffered from fainting spells, chronic weakness, and uncontrollable weeping. The cause was not especially mysterious or insidious. It was not the dark threat of witchcraft in New England, with which his father had been associated only four years earlier in Salem, nor was it the fear of hell as it was for his sister in that same February of 1696. What assumed such great urgency in young Sam's life was whether his work as a merchant's apprentice was the calling for which God intended him. The elder Sewall's diary entries during the month of February disclose how keenly the father felt his son's distress:

> Last night Sam could not sleep because of my Brother's speaking to him of removing to some other place, mentioning Mr. Usher's. I put him to get up a little wood, and he even fainted, at which Brother was much startled, and advis'd to remove him forthwith and place him somewhere else, or send him to Salem and he would doe the best he could for him. Since, I have express'd doubtfullness to Sam. as to his staying there.
>
> He mention'd to me Mr. Wadsworth's Sermon against Idleness, which was an Affliction to him. He said his was an idle Calling, and that he did more at home than there, take one day with another. And he mention'd Mr. Stoddard's words to me, that should place him with a good Master, and where had fullness of Imployment. It seems Sam. overheard him, and now alleged these words against his being where he was because of his idleness. Mention'd also the difficulty of

Portrait of Samuel Sewall by John Smibert. Sewall, a judge during the witchcraft trials, later apologized for his involvement. COURTESY PEABODY ESSEX MUSEUM.

the imployment by reason of the numerousness of Goods and hard to distinguish them, many not being marked; whereas Books, the price of them was set down, and so could sell them readily. I spoke to Capt. Checkly again and again, and he gave me no encouragement that his being there would be to Sam.'s profit; and Mrs. Checkly always discouraging.

Mr. Willard's Sermon from these Words, What doest thou here Elijah? was an Occasion to hasten the Removal. (421)

On February 10, the elder Sewall prayed, "Give Rest unto my dear Son, and put him into some Calling wherein He will accept of him to Serve Him" (347–348). On Sunday, February 16, Sam's troubles are still on his father's mind: "I was very sorrowfull by reason of the unsettledness of my Samuel." Still troubled by his son's failure, he records on February 26 that he "prayed with Sam. alone that God would direct our way as to a Calling for him" (452).

It is not difficult to imagine why the elder Sewall would so empathize with his son in this crisis, for Samuel Sewall himself had reached a difficult vocational crossroads when he was about the same age. A religious and studious young man who believed himself called to the ministry, Sewall completed his studies at Harvard Divinity School before abandoning a calling in the church for the life of a businessman.

Long after the youthful crisis that affected his health, Samuel Sewall, Jr., continued to contend with the idea of secular calling on a very personal level when his calling as husband and father became greatly complicated by a profligate wife and an illegitimate child. His intellectual interest in the concept is also in evidence. After having become settled in his own vocation as manager of a book business in 1701, he arranged for Bartholomew Green and John Allen to print the most significant treatise on the calling to appear in America, *A Christian at His Personal Calling*, written by Cotton Mather.

In 1718 and 1719, the unreligious young Benjamin Franklin, approaching his teens, was just as unsettled about his choice of a profession, pondering which of the many avenues open to him would be the best. No matter what career his father proposed—religion, mathematics, candle making—Franklin rejected it as unsuited to his temperament or talents. Finally, he and his very frustrated father were able to settle on printing. Ironically, Franklin would soon be a master of many callings. He was always a printer but also, among many things, a journalist, an essayist, a humorist, a politician, a diplomat, a Revolutionary, a renowned inventor, a scientist, and an educator.

For the Puritans, work in the world, important as it was as a reflection of spiritual calling, was always, at least theoretically, subordinate to the work of the spirit. With the rise in the eighteenth century of the more secular intellectual like Benjamin Franklin, nothing exceeded the importance of one's work in the world, especially if one understands that work also embraced good deeds. While the secularization of the doctrine of work led to good, humanitarian deeds in the world, it also led to the opposite: the unbridled pursuit of personal economic success.

BIBLIOGRAPHY

Bailyn, Bernard. *New England Merchants in the Seventeenth Century*. 1955. New York: Torchbooks, 1964.

Dexter, Elizabeth A. *Colonial Women of Affairs*. Boston: Houghton Mifflin, 1924.

Innes, Stephen. *Creating the Commonwealth*. New York: Norton, 1995.

———. *Labor in a New Land*. Princeton, N.J.: Princeton University Press, 1983.

Koehler, Lyle. *A Search for Power*. Urbana: University of Illinois Press, 1980.

Matthaei, Julie A. *An Economic History of Women in America*. New York: Schocken Books, 1982.

McCracken, Elizabeth. *Women of America*. New York: Macmillan, 1904.

Morris, Richard B. *Government and Labor in Early America*. New York: Octagon Books, 1965.

Perkins, E. J. *The Economy of Colonial America*. New York: Columbia University Press, 1980.

Sewall, Samuel, *The Diary of Samuel Sewall*. 2 vols. New York: Farrar, Straus and Giroux, 1973.

Shurtleff, N. B., ed. *Records of the Governor and Company of the Massachusetts Bay*. 6 vols. Boston: W. White, 1853–1854.

Tryon, R. M. *Household Manufactures*. New York: Johnson Reprint Corp., 1966.

Ulrich, Laurel Thatcher. *Good Wives*. New York: Vintage Books, 1991.

Weber, Max. *The Protestant Ethic and the Spirit of Capitalism*. New York: Charles Scribner's Sons., 1958.

Weeden, W. B. *Economic and Social History of New England*. Boston: Houghton Mifflin, 1890.

6

Shelter and Attire

SHELTER

It is interesting to envision exactly how one would survive upon disembarking a ship thousands of miles from home, onto a land untouched by the kind of civilization to which one had become accustomed, especially in a climate that would prove brutally cold in winter.

Let us follow the hypothetical ordinary family of James and Annie Haselden as they face the challenge of providing shelter for themselves over the first fifty years of settlement in the Massachusetts Bay Colony.

James Haselden has been working as a carpenter, mason, and general laborer on a gentleman's estate in the English Midlands, and has been lured to the New World by the prospect of owning his own land. He has been able to save enough money for passage to the New World for himself, his wife, Annie, and their two young boys. They have few belongings of their own and are not able to carry many articles with them.

Temporary Quarters

When the ship lands in New England, James and the boys explore the area around Salem in the daylight hours and sleep on board ship at night for as long as they can, until the day the captain plans to return to England. The Haseldens have made friends with a family like themselves already settled in Salem, who allow them to spend a few nights near their hut after the ship leaves. They use the straw they scavenge to make beds on the ground cleared outside the crude Salem shack.

Governor Winthrop and most of the other colony leaders sleep in one

English teepees in the style of some of the first houses. From George Francis Dow, *Every Day Life in the Massachusetts Bay Colony* (Boston: Society for the Preservation of New England Antiquities, 1935).

or two of the few houses already built by Puritan leaders who had previously settled in the Salem area.

After a few days, Governor Winthrop leads the men to a new location, well south of Salem, in Charlestown, across the Charles River from what is now Boston. (Most of the women and small children stay behind in Salem while the men go on to the Boston area to size up the situation.) Boston, rather than Charlestown, however, will soon be their headquarters. Here the Haselden family and their friends must improvise temporary shelter. Although James is good with his hands and trees for building are plentiful, he cannot build a proper house for months because he and his friends lack the tools. Even if James owned a saw, readying enough wood for even a simple log structure is a long and arduous task, as trees must be sawed and fitted by hand.

Caves, Tents, and Teepees

James and most of the other settlers decide that the quickest way they can make shelters against the late summer rain is by digging caves into the sides of Boston's hills. This all four of the Haseldens begin to do, using the crude hoes and spades they are able to fashion from the tin cups they have brought with them. The small opening of their cave is covered with a dried animal skin that they find, abandoned by a native. A few other settlers find teepees made of skins that have been discarded by the natives. These have holes in the top that allow them to build internal fires. Some will modify the teepee style for a semipermanent structure, which will be called the New England teepee.

Frame for an English teepee. From George Francis Dow, *Every Day Life in the Massachusetts Bay Colony* (Boston: Society for the Preservation of New England Antiquities, 1935).

Interior of an English teepee. From George Francis Dow, *Every Day Life in the Massachusetts Bay Colony* (Boston: Society for the Preservation of New England Antiquities, 1935).

Some of the Haseldens' friends and all the wealthy gentry, who comprise the colony's leaders, have been able to bring tents over with them on the ship for use as shelter. Some of the more important members of the colony are lucky enough to continue fairly comfortably at night in the houses built by earlier settlers. One such frame house has been abandoned in Charlestown and is ready for use by the governor.

The First Houses of the Elite

Like William Bradford of the earlier Plymouth Plantation to the south of them, most of the gentry of the Massachusetts Bay Colony are able to begin construction of spacious, comfortable houses immediately. They plan for an entryway and staircase, three or four great rooms on the ground floor with a kitchen in the back, and three or four bedrooms upstairs. Two or three fireplaces and chimneys will provide heat for the kitchen and both downstairs and upstairs rooms.

The seat of government, where the Court of Assistants will initially meet, will be in Governor Winthrop's house for a time—first in the house in Charlestown and soon after in another house he has built in Boston. In addition, by act of the first meeting of the Court of Assistants on August 23, 1630, houses are planned for the two chief clergymen, the Reverend Wilson and the Reverend Phillips, built at public expense, though Wilson's house will not actually be completed for a couple of years.

These few fine houses can be begun with all due haste because their owners had the money to bring the necessary tools and materials with them and are able to hire laborers to begin construction. The raw materials they already know to be present in the New World, like oak and maple, can be put to use, using the hand tools they have brought. Other materials, like fired brick and iron beaten into nails, have been brought over as part of the ballast in the ship. Hewn stones to be used for their front steps, marble, glazed glass for windows, metal locks, painted wallpaper, and other finery can easily be imported from England on the next ship.

Those who arrive in the colony with money can also put to work at once not only the common laborers they have brought with them as indentured servants and slaves, but men like James Haselden who have building skills and a desperate need of money.

Obstacles

While James and Annie Haselden and their boys sleep in the cave they have excavated, they make plans to build a somewhat more stable structure to weather the coming New England winter. Any work they do on such a structure, however flimsy, will have to be slow, for James also has to make money doing as much general carpentry as he can in building the houses needed by the Bay Colony leaders so that he can purchase his own land for farming. In one sense, he is lucky, because there is no end to the demand for his skilled work. But he is disappointed that the very men who require and must hire him have, on August 23, their first day of business, placed a ceiling on all wages of skilled laborers. Not only must James work all day build-

Wattle and daub construction. From George Francis Dow, *Every Day Life in the Massachusetts Bay Colony* (Boston: Society for the Preservation of New England Antiquities, 1935).

ing other people's houses, he must participate in the governor's concentrated community effort to provide the colony with food for the coming year. A few of James's fellow settlers, unable to make much progress in their struggle to survive, continue to live in cave and tent shelters throughout the year.

The First-Stage House

Slowly, with the help of friends, James and Annie Haselden are able to begin building a more substantial, though still temporary structure, to get them through the winter. Like the settlers of Plymouth and Salem before him, James makes use of whatever materials are available to construct what was called a daub (clay) and wattle (woven sticks) structure. Lacking the tools to process logs, the workable materials include tree branches, mud, and clay. With these, James builds a simple one-room structure. He cuts and strips enough good-sized sticks to outline a low-ceilinged room about ten by twelve feet. These he plants upright as firmly in the ground as he can. This done, he collects leafy branches and interweaves them with the stakes. To this, he liberally applies mud and clay. Makeshift as the structure is, James realizes that it has to have a fireplace for heat to cook and keep them from freezing, but he has no means of firing bricks or of cutting stone, and no access to cement. For the meantime, he makes the fireplace of logs covered with clay. Like

Thatch-roofed one-room cottages at the 1630 Colonial Village in Salem. From George Francis Dow, *Every Day Life in the Massachusetts Bay Colony* (Boston: Society for the Preservation of New England Antiquities, 1935).

similar buildings of his neighbors, Haselden's shelter has no windows. This crude, cramped, windowless one-room dwelling—which we might call a shed or a hut or a shack—is the first house the Haselden family has ever owned. In fact, James cannot remember that anyone among his ancestors has ever owned a house. In this he is not unlike most of his neighbors, so it is not surprising that they refer to their hovels proudly as "cottages."

This structure has to serve the family during the first winter as a refuge from the cold, a place to sleep at night, as a place for Annie to cook food, however crudely, and a warm place to eat one or two meals a day. Very little reading, playing, or working can be done inside, though; not only is it cramped, but, being windowless, it is always pitch black except when a fire is burning in the fireplace. James has learned that he can provide the family with light as the natives do—by splitting a pine log in half, lighting it, and using it as a torch. But the inevitable heavy black smoke it creates in such close quarters is almost suffocating. The Haseldens have no way to make candles and no money to import them as wealthier people do.

The Second-Stage House

In the spring, after nine months in New England and having had constant work in building the houses of the gentry, James Haselden has saved enough money to secure his land and purchase some imported tools. The family is ready to build more livable quarters.

James begins by digging a six- by seven-foot-deep excavation about twenty by twenty feet wide. From the plenitude of trees, he cuts enough logs to line the excavation. Different families are covering their log walls with different materials. Some are using hides; some are using cloth; some are using sod, that is, dirt to which grass and other hardy vegetation is still attached (and what frontiersmen on the nineteenth-century plains would use); some are using tree bark. The Haseldens are lucky: they have managed to trade James' services as a carpenter for fifteen deer skins from a friend who makes his living trading with the natives. These skins and some large pieces of bark cover all but the fireplace wall. They make a roof of logs covered with bark, heavily daubed with clay to keep water out. Although the clay-daubed fireplace proves to be an obvious fire hazard and the Haseldens had almost lost their shack to fire three times when sparks ignited the wood, James again has no choice but to make the fireplace of wood and clay.

The floor is dirt and straw at first, but with the easy availability of trees, James is determined to lay a plank floor. This is the hardest chore in the building process and takes weeks to finish, because the logs have to be split and planed by hand.

Even so, it is a flimsy structure that soon begins to rot from the New England rain and snow. James spends some part of every day shoring it up with repairs. Once it is caved in by a storm and has to be reconstructed. He observes that it is the rare structure that does not burn down and have to be rebuilt entirely. Although one of these makeshift shelters can last for four years at the most, some continue to be in use well into the eighteenth century.

The First Permanent Structures

By the end of their second year on their own land, James and Annie are able to think about building a more stable house—one that will not blow down or rot. Moreover, James assures Annie that although it will still be a one-room house at first, it will be stable enough to expand eventually into a multiroomed house.

James begins with the excavation of a cellar about twenty by twenty feet. Above that he plans on one huge room with the addition of a loft, a true luxury. James drives heavy logs into the ground every few feet to form a solid skeletal structure. By this time there is a sawmill in the area, which can saw planks from the logs he cuts and brings to the mill. Some he uses for the floor of the main room above the cellar and to floor part of the loft. Others he himself prepares by painstakingly planing one edge of each plank so that the boards he secures to the log structure, inside and out, can overlap. This process, which he knows from his area of England, is called *clapboarding*. He must secure the clapboards onto the framing posts with home-crafted pegs; nails are still a rare commodity. He keeps the ceiling low; the six-foot James must stoop over to walk around inside. Some of his neighbors make their roofs of sod. Others use thatch, which is straw tied down in batches. But James considers thatch a fire hazard, so he makes wood and bark shingles instead, though they are more expensive and harder to install.

James and Annie are determined that this house will have windows, though they are little more than two slits. These he covers with oiled paper. He knows from experience that windows will need wooden shutters for protection, whether they be of leaded glass like that imported for the governor's mansion or of oiled paper or cloth in houses like his own.

He plans his doorway not with the aim of admitting light and sun, but rather to keep out bad weather and dangerous animals. He reasons that a small, low doorway will mean he will have at least some momentary warning if unfriendly people try to enter his house. The doorway ends up being so low and small that even a short woman like Annie is forced almost to bend double to enter.

James is still unable to afford the heavy metal hinges that the wealthier people import or have fashioned for them by local blacksmiths from imported metal, so his doors and shutters are tied on with leather thongs.

Despite the addition of windows, the interior is still dark and gloomy. Viewing such a house today, we might wonder why James had not made more and larger windows and more and larger doors to bring in the beauty of this pristine landscape for a light, cheerful, handsome interior. But James and Annie's perspective, typical of the time and place, is framed by their peculiar needs and their view of nature, altogether different from a twenty-first-century view. To James and his fellow settlers, nature is not synonymous with beauty and grace; it is instead a hostile enemy. Nature to them means chilling cold, ice, snow, brutal winds, predatory animals, and the baffling natives. They do not want to bring nature into their houses; they want to keep it out.

By the time Annie and James build their log house, the old chimneys, which had caused so many devastating fires that easily spread from house to house, had been outlawed by the community. James had no choice but to build his chimney of brick, which he himself formed of local clay and had fired in a local brick maker's oven.

James and Annie and their neighbors grow angry when visiting English gentry ridicule the houses scattered over the countryside, calling them ramshackle lean-tos. But they have to admit to each other that the wind blows through the walls and fireplaces of the houses of some of their less skillful neighbors, making their houses as cold on the inside as on the outside.

The single great room or hall of James and Annie's house serves as a kitchen, a dining room, a living room, a bedroom, and a workroom. The children sleep in the loft, which also serves as storage space.

Before another year has passed, the Haseldens follow their neighbors in improving on their log house. First they add a kitchen at the back of the house and a lean-to for storage. They also make a second small, enclosed room inside the great room. Here they can have privacy. It functions primarily as a master bedroom for Annie and James. In this inner room, their third child is born. The inner room is also used for more public occasions, like a parlor for entertaining guests once in a while. As they do more farming on their land, they build a barn, a shed, and a larger storage building.

Early Furnishings

The Haseldens' only furniture is still makeshift. The boys sleep in the loft on a bedroll brought from England. James and Annie have a straw bed covered with cloth brought from England. At first, their only chairs are blocks of wood that James has axed from the forest. But he wastes no time in fashioning benches for their new house. He chooses and planes a fine oak plank, which he rests on simple trestles he has made. This serves as a work and eating table. They keep some clothes and linens in the trunk they brought from England and hang their most often used clothes on wooden pegs.

Expanding the Basic Log House

As they anticipated, the Haseldens are able to expand their log house indefinitely. James prospers handsomely as a master carpenter, then as a master builder in charge of the construction of houses and shops, warehouses, and wharves. By 1650, he adds a second large downstairs room, a staircase that replaces a crude ladder, and two upstairs bedrooms. By 1660, this four-room house has doubled in size.

Native Building Materials

A number of situations affected the building of houses. Trees were obviously in abundance for use in building, though initially the process of planing logs into planks, shingles, and clapboards was a painstaking, arduous task, as it was then done by hand, before water-powered sawmills were established. Clay was available, but cement and plaster were rarely used at first because limestone was not discovered in significant amounts in New England until 1697. Stone quarrying and stone cutting were extremely difficult. Often the only parts of a permanent house that were stone were the steps and, though less frequently, the first story. Stone continued to be an expensive import until the American Revolution. The stones for King's Chapel, the first Anglican church in Boston, were imported between 1749 and 1754. The great fondness for hewn stone and its lack of availability created a curious scene in Salem, Massachusetts, where wood houses were painted to look like stone. Bricks, which had to be fired, were also hard to make and of unreliable quality. While some bricks of varying quality were fired in New England kilns, others continued to be imported. Wooden pegs held the humbler houses together, for nails and hinges had to be imported and were ex-

Reconstructed house of Rebecca Nurse, Danvers, Massachusetts. The original was built c. 1680 and is an example of a typical colonial house. Photo courtesy of the author.

pensive until bog iron was discovered and could be processed. The houses in different settlements had somewhat distinct characters, based partly on the materials available.

Expanding and Improving Furnishings

The Haseldens, like their neighbors, have only the scantiest floor coverings, so proud are they of their wood floors, which would have been unthinkable luxuries to their social equals in England. Small pieces of matting are placed here and there, and their only rugs are small ones placed beside their beds. Their house comes to be furnished with chairs, bureaus, tables, bedsteads, buffets, and cupboards, most of which James made at home and some of which they bought from local artisans who used the many available woods—primarily oak, pine, hickory, and maple. Annie acquired kitchen and tableware that James made of materials found in the colony—wood, iron, and, eventually, pewter. Annie also wove from flax yarn she had spun an extensive store of linen table and bed linens. In their fireplace, they continue to use candlewood, the smoky pine logs cut in half, but now have the forms to make their own candles for light.

Making shingles as it was done in colonial days. From George Francis Dow, *Every Day Life in the Massachusetts Bay Colony* (Boston: Society for the Preservation of New England Antiquities, 1935).

The Houses of the Gentry

Boston dwellings as early as 1637 and 1640 were described as elegant and spacious with large rooms. The usual fine houses of clapboard or wood and stucco were soon faced or rebuilt of imported brick or stone. These ever-expanding houses at first included two or three great rooms on the ground floor, two bedrooms on a second full floor (which overhung the first floor), and a garret above that. In the first fifty years, even fine houses were rarely painted inside or out, but paper was hung, rather than glued, on the inside walls. For those who could afford it, the paper was the painted kind imported from England. By the eighteenth century, many fine houses had four rooms, a hall, and a kitchen on the first floor, and three or four rooms on a second floor that were finished inside and out with precision and some sense of good design. A few houses had servant or slave quarters in the basement or under the rafters. Some New England cities, like Portsmouth, Rhode Island, boasted houses of three full stories. In the usual design, the shingled roofs were very tall and steep, sloping almost to the ground in back to cover the one-story sheds

The Parson Capen House, Topsfield, Massachusetts, 1683. From George Francis Dow, *Every Day Life in the Massachusetts Bay Colony* (Boston: Society for the Preservation of New England Antiquities, 1935).

and kitchens. But as early as 1636, the finer houses had mansard roofs with gables.

The houses of the governors and their friends were designed with a lively social life in mind. The centerpiece of these houses was a finely carved staircase. Unlike James Haselden, these men had the luxury of choosing ornamentation for their houses, though Puritan families were not inclined to extravagance. They did have very fine carved wood, brass hardware, leaded glass, and tapestries in the downstairs rooms, entryways, staircases, and front doors.

Furnishing in the Houses of the Elite. By contrast to the Haseldens' belongings, much of the furnishings in the households of the well-to-do were imported from the first. Instead of being confined to native woods like maple and oak, such households included mahogany. Instead of homespun sheets and tablecloths, these settlers imported the finest cotton and linen. Instead of using tableware made exclusively of pewter and wood, they also made use of silver.

Governor Bellingham's Hall. Nathaniel Hawthorne, who did exten-

This room from the 1683 Parson Capen House is an example of a typical colonial parlor. From George Francis Dow, *Every Day Life in the Massachusetts Bay Colony* (Boston: Society for the Preservation of New England Antiquities, 1935).

sive research in the Boston Athenaeum before writing *The Scarlet Letter* (1850), describes in that novel the 1640s "mansion," as he calls it, of Governor Richard Bellingham, which stood not far from the Boston Common on Beacon Hill. Contrast this with the first shelter and first log house of the ordinary citizen:

It had indeed a very cheery aspect; the walls being overspread with a kind of stucco, in which fragments of broken glass were plentifully intermixed; so that, when the sunshine fell aslant-wise over the front of the edifice, it glittered and sparkled as if diamonds had been flung against it by the double handful. The brilliancy might have befitted Aladdin's palace, rather than the mansion of a grave old Puritan ruler. . . .

They approached the door; which was of an arched form, and flanked on each side by a narrow tower or projection of the edifice, in both of which were lattice-windows, with wooden shutters to close over them at need. . . .

With many variations, suggested by the nature of his building materials, diversity of climate, and a different mode of social life, Governor Bellingham had planned his new habitation after the residences of gentlemen of fair estate in his native land. Here, then, was a wide and reasonable lofty hall, extending through

The provincial governor's house. From Annie Haven Thwing, *The Crooked & Narrow Streets of the Town of Boston 1630–1822* (Boston: Marshall Jones Company, 1920).

the whole depth of the house, and forming a medium of general communication, more or less directly, with all the other apartments. At one extremity, this spacious room was lighted by the windows of the two towers, which formed a small recess on either side of the portal. At the other end, though partly muffled by a curtain, it was more powerfully illuminated by one of those embowed hall-windows which we read of in old books, and which was provided with a deep and cushioned seat. Here, on the cushions, lay a folio tome, probably of the *Chronicles of England*, or other such substantial literature; even as, in our own days, we scatter gilded volumes on the centre-table, to be turned over by the casual guest. The furniture of the hall consisted of some ponderous chairs, the backs of which were elaborately carved with wreaths of oaken flowers; and likewise a table in the same taste; the whole being of the Elizabethan age, or perhaps earlier, and heirlooms, transferred hither from the Governor's paternal home. (71, 72)

By the eighteenth century, the colonial houses of many residents had three full floors, multiple fireplaces, an elegant entryway decorated with leaded glass, a mansard roof with as many as seven or eight gables, thirty or forty shuttered glass windows, and well-manicured grounds.

ATTIRE

The Stereotype

We know something of the clothing worn in colonial New England from a number of sources. The body of laws of the Massachusetts Bay Colony indicates something of the attitude toward apparel and its connection to class distinctions. There are also inventories of clothing provided by the colony to Salem men, inventories of possessions left in wills, communications sent to England ordering clothing, and portraits, chiefly of families of the gentry.

The appearance of Puritans in England was distinctive and often parodied. The excessively plain, drab dress seemed to match the gloomy, judgmental faces of the men who disapproved of play-acting, stained-glass windows, and the singing of hymns. It was as if Puritan disapproval of ornamentation and extravagance in the house of God spilled over into their attitude toward the clothing of human beings. But although Puritan doctrine did have an impact in restricting ornate fashions in colonial New England, the stereotype we have (going back to the early seventeenth century in England) of a people wearing only black, white, and gray is a false one.

Clothing and Economy

In the New World, frontier economics and the necessity to remain frugal to survive buttressed the Puritans' bias against extravagance in clothing. Four years after the founding of the Massachusetts Bay Colony, on September 3, 1634, the Puritan Court of Assistants found it expedient to publish a law against the buying of extravagant clothing. The law is very specific about the styles and materials that are prejudicial to the common good and therefore prohibited:

> The Court, taking into consideration the great, superfluous, and unnecessary expenses occasioned by reason of some new and immodest fashions, as also the ordinary wearing of silver, gold, and silk laces, girdles, hatbands, etc., hath therefore ordered that no person, either man or woman, shall hereafter make or buy any apparel, either woolen, silk, or linen, with any lace on it, gold, silk, or thread, under the penalty of forfeiture of such clothes.
>
> Also, that no person, either man or woman, shall make or buy any slashed clothes, other than one slash in each sleeve, and another in the back; also, all cutwork, embroidered or needle-work caps, bands . . . are forbidden hereafter to be made and worn, under aforesaid penalty, also gold or silver girdles, hatbands, belts, ruffs, beaver hats are prohibited to be bought or worn hereafter, under the aforesaid penalty. (Shurtleff, vol. 1: 126)

Note the plain style of this wealthy man, Edward Rawson. From George Francis Dow, *Every Day Life in the Massachusetts Bay Colony* (Boston: Society for the Preservation of New England Antiquities, 1935).

Five years later, on September 9, 1639, various watchdogs, probably the clergy, complained to the magistrates that some of the colonists seemed to have forgotten the restrictions on the use of lace, and flamboyant styles: "Whereas there is much complaint of the excessive wearing of lace, and other superfluities tending to little use or benefit, but to the nourishing of pride and exhausting of men's estates, and also of evil example to others." (Shurtleff, 274). So the court again reminded the citizens of Massachusetts Bay that lace, "immoderate great sleeves," "double ruffles," "immoderate great breeches," cuffs, and immodest short sleeves were strictly against the law. Now, curiously, they seemed to turn the matter of enforcement over to the churches and, more understandably, local law enforcement.

Class and Clothing

The laws of Massachusetts Bay and local communities indicate that rules concerning clothing also arose from religious dogma with reference to class. We have seen that social status affected work profoundly. People were expected to work only at a calling appropriate to the social class into which they were born. Similarly, the admonition to "remain in that calling to which one is called" was intended in a less drastic way to limit what people could wear. Puritan men and women were not to dress in a manner unsuitable for their social station.

In the early days of the New England colonies, this class consciousness with regard to clothing was strongly legislated by the Court of Assistants, with the backing of the clergy. A law published in 1651 gives us a hint of the fashions of the day and reveals the impact of class consciousness on dress, for it is especially directed to people of "mean condition," meaning lower-class citizens:

> . . . and also to declare our utter detestation and dislike, that men or women of mean condition, should take upon them the garb of gentlemen, by wearing gold or silver lace, or buttons, or points at their knees, or to walk in great boots; or women of the same rank to wear silk or . . . hoods, or scarfs, which though allowable to persons of greater estates, or more liberal education, yet we cannot but judge it intolerable in persons of such like condition. (*General Laws And Liberties*, 5)

Such fashions were forbidden specifically to those whose "visible estates . . . shall not exceed the . . . value of *two hundred pounds*" (5). To emphasize the class determination with regard to apparel, the magistrates instructed the officers of townships to be on the alert for any persons of low status who wore clothing forbidden them. However, such officers were to be aware of important exceptions to this law:

> Provided this Law shall not extend to the restraint of any Magistrate or publick Officer of this Jurisdiction, their Wives and Children, who are left to their discretion in wearing of Apparel, or any settled Military Officer, or Soldier in the time of Military service, or any other whose education and employment have been above the ordinary degree, or whose estate have been considerable, though now decayed. (*General Laws And Liberties*, 5)

We see that it was considered prideful and wasteful for any person whose goods were worth under £200 to wear lace and silk scarves, unless they once had a lot of money. And if people whose goods were worth under £200 wore such fashions, they set a bad example—but not if they were magistrates, or a member of a magistrate's family, or a military officer.

Since certain kinds of clothing were prohibited from use only by the lower classes, we might expect to find a wide variety of clothing, and we might expect that clothing was used as an indicator of success and status.

Materials Used in Clothing

Clothing in colonial New England was made of both native and imported materials. Women's clothing and men's shirts, jackets, and pants were made primarily of linen and wool, which after 1640 were usually home produced. Shoes could also be produced at home from leather. Women usually wore caps and shawls of linen or wool. As plentiful as furs were and as cold as the climate was, women did not appear to wear fur coats and hats as

Portrait of Major Thomas Savage showing the ceremonial costume of a man of privilege. From George Francis Dow, *Every Day Life in the Massachusetts Bay Colony* (Boston: Society for the Preservation of New England Antiquities, 1935).

men sometimes did. Men also wore work clothes of tanned leather, usually in the form of buckskin breeches and jackets.

Most of the forbidden materials used in the making of clothing were imported. This applied primarily to silk, fine cotton, and gold and silver buttons and buckles. But other materials, readily home produced, were repeatedly forbidden: beaver hats and lace.

Items of Apparel

Inventories indicate the items of clothes worn by men and women. One such source is a list of clothes provided to laboring men who were sent to Salem in June 1629. Included in the list are four pairs of shoes and stockings, garters, shirts, doublets (or short jackets), breeches, a leather-lined wool suit, a cape, and various belts, caps, and gloves. On an ordinary workday, a man would wear a fairly snug doublet, a long shirt, breeches that came below his knees, long stockings, sometimes canvas boothose over these, and leather boots. On Sunday he might change his cap for a felt hat and his boots for black shoes.

A woman would wear a three-piece gown made up of a skirt, bodice,

The simplicity and modesty of this dress is typical of eighteenth-century religious women such as Elizabeth Freake. Note that the attire of her daughter Mary varies little in style from adult clothing. From George Francis Dow, *Every Day Life in the Massachusetts Bay Colony* (Boston: Society for the Preservation of New England Antiquities, 1935).

and sleeves. Over this she wore an apron. Under the gown she wore an underskirt of linen or a petticoat or both, and a chemise. Her underwear was a shift. Often a woman wore almost five layers of clothing. She also wore a kerchief, kept her hair under a cap, and wore stockings, leather shoes, and overshoes.

New England women, unlike English women, did not wear billowing skirts, headdresses, or jewelry, including a wedding ring.

Research has shown that New England children, from the time they could walk, wore the same kinds of clothing that their parents did.

Apparel Color

Descriptions that survive in inventories and orders for clothing discredit the enduring stereotype of Puritan settlers dressed only in black, white, and gray. It is true that for church meetings and other ceremonial occasions, both men and women favored black to denote the seriousness of the affair, much as a person from the twenty-first century might wear black to a funeral. But the record shows that everyday dress, especially coats, caps, and gowns, were very colorful, usually in soft shades of green, yellow, red, russet, orange, purple, and blue, colored from native dyes.

Wigs

One of the most controversial matters of fashion and attire was the wearing of powdered wigs. Male citizens found the vogue of wig wearing to be very seductive, especially in the last decades of the seventeenth century and the eighteenth century. Devout members of the community, especially the clergy, were appalled at what they considered to be ungodly and unnatural foppery. One illustration comes from the diary of Samuel Sewall, a lay minister and Puritan judge who made notations of his visits to admonish men who had taken up wig wearing. On Friday, November 6, 1685, he makes note of such a visit and the bizarre justification of the wig wearer:

> Having occasion this day to go to Mr. Hayward the Publick Notary's House, I speak to him about his cutting off his Hair, and wearing a Perriwig of contrary colour: mention the words of our Savior, Can ye not make one Hair white or black: and Mrs. Alsop's sermon. He alleges, the Doctor advised him to do it. (I:82)

On June 10, 1701, Sewall called on another wig wearer, this time a young man who put up a determined argument:

> Having last night heard that Josiah Willard had cut off his hair (a very full head of hair) and put on a Wig, I went to him this morning. Told his Mother what I came about and she call'd him. I inquired of him what extremity had forced him to put off his own hair, and put on a Wig? He answered, none at all. But said that his Hair was straight, and that it parted behind. Seem'd to argue that men might as well shave their hair off their head, as off their face. . . . Told him that it was condemn'd by a Meeting of Ministers at Northampton in Mr. Stoddards house. (I:448–449)

Changing Fashions

In the last decades of the seventeenth century and throughout the eighteenth century, the influence exerted by the British presence in New England increased, particularly with regard to fashion, and especially among those who lived in the cities and had money. No longer were homespun and simplicity the rule of the day. For women the adoption of fashionable wear meant stiffer, more cumbersome, more restrictive clothes. They adopted hoop petticoats, for example, which caused their skirts to make a wide circle on the floor. They wore whale-bone stays in their undergarments to pinch in their waists. They adopted high-heeled shoes, elaborate bonnets, and velvet, brocade, and silk gowns trimmed with ribbons and lace and set off with jewelry.

Gentlemen adopted not only wigs, but took to wearing large silver buckles on their shoes, ruffled shirts, and heavy brocade dressing gowns that were so expensive and impressive that they wore them when they had their portraits painted.

Still, both the primitive conditions in the New World and the Puritan displeasure with extravagance left an indelible impression in the eighteenth century on American attire and Europe's vision of Americans. Benjamin Franklin, while he presided over Philadelphia culture, might indulge himself by wearing a wig or a ruffled shirt, but when he went to France to represent America and Americans, he left his fancy European clothes at home and appeared in drab homespun, with only his own hair and a coonskin cap on his American head.

BIBLIOGRAPHY

Adams, James Truslow. *Frontiers of American Culture*. New York: Scribner's Sons, 1944.

Andrews, Charles M. *Colonial Folkways*. New Haven, Conn.: Yale University Press, 1919.

Bridenbaugh, Carl. *The Colonial Craftsman*. New York: New York University Press, 1950.

Candee, Richard M. "Wooden Buildings." Ph.D. dissertation, University of Pennsylvania, 1976.

Crawford, Mary Caroline. *Social Life in Old New England*. Boston: Little, Brown, 1914.

Cummings, Albert L. *The Framed Houses of Massachusetts Bay*. Cambridge, Mass.: Belknap Press, 1979.

Demos, John. *A Little Commonwealth*. Oxford: Oxford University Press, 1970.

Dow, George Francis. *Domestic Life*. Topfield, Mass.: Perkins Press, 1925.

Earle, Alice Morse. *Colonial Days*. New York: Macmillan, 1898.

Eberlein, Harold. *The Architecture of Colonial America*. Boston: Little, Brown, 1915.

The General Laws And Liberties of the Massachusetts Colony: Revised & Reprinted. Cambridge, Mass.: Samuel Green, 1672.

Halsey, Richard. *The Homes of Our Ancestors*. Garden City, N.Y.: Doubleday, Page, 1925.

Hamlin, Tolbert F. *The American Spirit in Architecture*. New Haven, Conn.: Yale University Press, 1926.

Hawthorne, Nathaniel. *The Scarlet Letter*. New York: Dover, 1994.

Kimball, F. *Domestic Architecture*. New York: Charles Scribner's Sons, 1922.

Langdon, William C. *Everyday Things in American Life*. New York: Charles Scribner's Sons, 1937.

Lockwood, Luke V. *Colonial Furniture*. New York: Charles Scribner's Sons, 1926.

McClellan, Elisabeth. *Historic Dress in America*. New York: Benjamin Blom, 1969.

Millar, Donald. *Colonial Furniture*. New York: Architectural Book Co., 1916.

Plain and Fancy, a Survey of American Folk Art. New York: Hirschl & Adler, 1970.

Pratt, Dorothy, and Richard Pratt. *A Guide to Early American Homes*. New York: McGraw-Hill, 1956.

Sewall, Samuel. *The Diary of Samuel Sewall*. 2 vols. New York: Farrar, Straus and Giroux, 1973.

Shurtleff, Harold R. *The Log Cabin Myth*. Cambridge, Mass.: Harvard University Press, 1939.

Shurtleff, N. B., ed. *Records of the Governor and Company of the Massachusetts Bay*. 6 vols. Boston: W. White, 1853–1854.

Tran, Arthur, Jr. *The Story of Everyday Things*. New York: Harper and Brothers, 1941.

7

Food and Health

FOOD

Food played a critical role in the immediate survival of the New England colonists, the developing character of the area, and their economy, for food determined what they imported and exported. Food played a role, as well, in their relations with the native peoples and in the events shaping their final break with England.

Early Settlements

Plymouth Plantation. The people who came as part of the first major settlement in New England, at Plymouth Plantation in 1620, faced an unexpected and perilous situation upon arrival in the New World. They stepped ashore not in Virginia, to which they had set sail and upon which they had planned, but in Massachusetts, with its much more brutal climate. Furthermore, they arrived in November, disembarking at Plymouth in December, when natural vegetation had already disappeared beneath the frost and when it was too late to plant. They had brought with them on the *Mayflower* 20,000 biscuits (what we might call crackers), salted bacon, dried fish, cheese, turnips, and other root vegetables. However, they discovered upon landing that most of the supplies that they had not eaten in the course of the two-month voyage had spoiled. Some settlers remained aboard ship until March; others foraged for food to last until spring.

A problem more immediately pressing than food was the need for potable water. However, one of the first exploration parties that left the ship found sufficient springs and ponds for drinking water. According to their leader, William Bradford, these groups of explorers found something else that kept some of them alive during the winter: food that had been stored for winter use by the Indians. That the corn and beans they found were meant for others could scarcely have escaped their notice, for great varieties of each were carefully placed in baskets and buried in mounds. The settlers found these mounds in the early days of winter, dug up the food, and carried most of it back to the settlement at Plymouth and to the *Mayflower*. This blatant thievery was described by their pious leader as God's Providence in watching over them. While the beans and corn was instrumental in keeping them alive, they paid dearly for their actions in terms of their relations with the natives, for the incident did not escape the notice of the tribe from whom they stole.

The most natural source of food in such a situation might be expected to come from the sea. But what we now call the pilgrims were not yet skilled in the art of fishing and were unable to sustain the entire community with the amount of fish they caught. Clams and mussels seem to have been more accessible to them for immediate consumption. Nor were they able to discover how to preserve the fish. The colony was actually established with the notion that it would set up a fishing industry, but the colonists' ineptitude in both catching and salting fish created one disaster after another, until they abandoned the fishing trade for the fur trade.

Once spring was on the way and the *Mayflower* had returned to England, the Plymouth settlers got down to the business of planting crops, the main one of which was Indian corn. Bradford tells us in his *Of Plymouth Plantation* (1981), that one tribe of natives instructed them in the art of fertilizing their crop by planting a tiny fish with each seed and kernel. Despite the success with their first crop, the pilgrims continued to starve and to live a marginal existence for several years. There were periods in which the entire allotment of food for one person for one day at Plymouth Plantation was six kernels of corn. But while many settlers in the Plymouth area went back to England and many died, the community was saved by important infusions of people and supplies.

The Salem Community. The Salem community of forty people, the next major New England settlement, was somewhat better provisioned, but they also ran into unforeseen problems, which resulted in their having inadequate supplies of food in the early months of their stay. They brought with them on their voyage in September 1628 the following food: salted beef, biscuits, oatmeal, salted fish, butter, cheese, water, beer, brandy, wine, vinegar, and oil. They judged that they would need enough food and drink to last for three months until they could begin growing their own food and fresh provisions were brought from England. For this voyage, they planned on enough food for 135 people for ninety days. What they did not take into consideration was the unpre-

Squanto, a Native American, teaching members of Plymouth Colony how to plant corn. From Ralph Henry Gabriel, *Toilers of Land and Sea* (New Haven: Yale University Press, 1926).

dictability of the voyage, which lasted much longer than expected—sixty-eight days—so the provisions that were supposed to sustain them on shore were seriously depleted on the voyage over. As a result, the Salem settlement lost many of their number to starvation and disease relating to inadequate food.

In June the next year, they were joined by four hundred more settlers who came with a welcome infusion of supplies. They and the subsequent newcomers to New England were fortunate to have the advantage of Salem's experienced pastor, the Reverend Francis Higginson. He strongly urged every person setting out for the New World to have provisions to last each individual for a year. This included, per person, eight bushels of meal, two bushels of peas, two bushels of oatmeal, one gallon of water, one gallon of oil, two gallons of vinegar (needed to preserve food), plus cheese, butter, bacon, sugar, pepper, cloves, mace, cinnamon, nutmeg, and dried fruits.

The Winthrop Party at Boston. Despite all of John Winthrop's organizational skills, the people who settled in the Boston area were also plagued by food shortages. By the time their ships landed, most of the provisions had been consumed. Fortunately, however, they did not suffer acute starvation. One reason was the settlers' skill at catching and preserving fish. For the first year, fish, especially cod, was the mainstay of their diet, supplemented by clams, mussels, and lobsters. Some of the natives and the Salemites shared their stores of Indian corn with them in the early days. The Boston settlers were also willing to learn and experiment with food that grew in the wild, especially onions, berries, and fruits. Still, food was not plentiful, and while ships occasionally brought new provisions, they also brought more people to feed.

One of their more immediate needs after arriving in the Charlestown-Boston area was fresh, drinkable water. The Charles River, which emptied into the Atlantic Ocean, was a relatively short, saline body of water. They did discover a plentiful spring of fresh water, but it was on the shoreline and completely under seawater except at low tide. This need for fresh water, more than anything else, led them westward—to Cambridge (then called Newtown), Watertown, and other points.

To the meager diet of fish they added wild game. Cattle, swine, goats, and sheep were packed in large numbers for shipment to the colonies, but the majority of them died on board ship. It would be several years before these animals were established on New England farms.

Winthrop reported a good crop as early as the fall of 1631, though another chronicler, Edward Johnson, suggested that food continued to be scarce until 1633, when the settlers began reaping successful harvests of such New World staples as Indian corn, pumpkins, herbs, squash, beans, and fruits. Corn, pumpkin, and herbs were native staples, which were puzzling to the newcomers. But they were well suited to the climate and soil and very plentiful.

Food continued to be adequate for two more years, until 1635, when a scarcity was caused by so many people emigrating to the colony without bringing enough provisions with them.

The Old World Influence

The New England diet during colonial days was strongly influenced by the eating habits of England, a heavy cuisine without the variety of ingredients and seasoning that was present, say, in the areas settled by the French, Dutch, Germans, and Spanish. The mainstays of their diet in England had been certain cuts of meat, a few kinds of fish, bread and other dishes made of wheat and oats, root vegetables like turnips, beans, and a few fruits. The scarcity of all kinds of foods forced the settlers to experiment with different ingredients that were native to the New World or that could be grown and processed there.

Raw Materials

The colonists' situation on the Atlantic Coast led them to a far greater dependence on food from the sea than most of them had been accustomed to. When they first landed, eels were a popular food in that they were easily caught. Then cod became the mainstay. They gradually added herring, bass, sturgeon, alewives, shad (a despised fish), and mackerel to their diets, as well as mussels, clams, and lobsters. They found that fish were so plentiful that a log thrown in a stream would trap a dozen fish. A farmer or merchant or artisan could not take the time to catch fish every day, nor could a housewife shop every day, and fish do not keep. They knew from experience in England that for fish to be a staple in their diets, it had to be preserved. This was done with salt. Salt was imported, gathered from the sea and mined from salt beds.

There was an abundance of wild game in the New World, but the lower classes in England did not own guns, so many of the settlers found it difficult or impossible to hunt when they arrived. Gradually, however, they came to depend on hunted wild game, especially rabbit and venison, which was the main game eaten by the natives. They found that squirrels, bear, and raccoon meat were also edible. This food had to be preserved because there was no refrigeration. The game was stripped of its skin or fur, for which the settler had many uses; it was gutted and then soaked in brine for several weeks. Afterward, the settler would hang it in a house designed for smoking it; those who did not have a smokehouse could usually use a public smokehouse. In this way, any meat could be preserved and hung in the garret of the house for the winter. Wild birds, especially turkeys (some reportedly weighing forty pounds), pigeons, and geese graced their tables too.

Goats, used for meat, cheese, and milk, were the first animals imported to New England farms. Cows, also used for milk products and meat, came a bit later. By 1640, an average farm in colonial New England had as a food supply about ten cows and six pigs. At slaughtering time, this meat would be preserved, most of it in the same manner as wild game.

Milk that was not immediately consumed was made into butter and cheese. Properly stored in a cool place, both could last for months without spoiling. Cheese, which could be served without much preparation, quickly became a main part of the diet.

Indian corn continued to be a chief source of grain. It was eaten fresh in season and dried, some of it ground, for use as a cereal or bread throughout the year. Dried corn was parboiled for twelve hours and pounded in a mortar into a kind of mush. It was ground into meal and cooked and served with milk. Cornmeal was cooked with water and sweetened, producing what was called Indian pudding.

The ordinary settlers had to wait far too long to have the fine-textured wheat bread they cherished from in England. It took a long time for wheat to become established in the few areas of New England where it would grow well, and then colonists had to depend on the services of a miller to grind it to a fine texture. So bread was of necessity made of hardier grains more suitable to the New England climate and soil, like corn, rye, and oats. Barley, also grown in early New England, was chiefly used for making beer. Hay and oats were the fodder for cattle.

But if wheat was in short supply, many kinds of fruit were not. The settlers found a plenitude of wild berries and other fruits in the New World, and they easily grew other varieties from imported seeds. Apples, pears, cherries, plums, and quinces were in good supply and were added to the winter diet by drying. Nuts grew wild and were a valuable food source. Apple orchards were established fairly soon, and the main drink of the settlers came to be cider, a drink with low alcohol content, fermented with some form of sweetener. Vegetables and some fruits and meats were preserved with vinegar, which could also be made from apples. The settlers joined the Indians in adding native pumpkins and squash to their cookery. Pumpkin could also be dried and reconstituted for pies and stews in winter.

Some parts of Massachusetts had up to 170 growing days annually. The main vegetables grown were turnips, parsnips, beans, cabbage, and pumpkins. More prosperous families added onions, peas, carrots, spinach, asparagus, and beets to their tables. The potatoes first imported for planting did not grow well. Not until 1720, when some of the first Irish who emigrated to New England brought potatoes, were they grown successfully. Nor did the settlers eat tomatoes, though they were available, from fear that they were poisonous.

New Englanders had no shortage of sweeteners. Imported cane and beet sugars were available in large blocks called sugar loafs, which had to be cut. Sugar mainly graced the tables of those who had accumulated money. But the main sources were native. Settlers were instructed by the Indians in the art of tapping maple trees and already knew the value of honey.

Many seasonings, like wild sage and dill, were available in the wild for adventuresome cooks, who learned from the natives how to use these. In port towns, those who could afford to imported pepper, capers, cloves, cinnamon, ginger, olives, and currents from England and tea and spices from the West Indies.

The settlers came to know the value of drinking lots of fresh water, a habit they did not bring with them from England. Tea was made from raspberry and blackberry leaves, sage, and goldenrod. They also made beer and cider. Rum, which was aged with apples, was distilled in New England and was regularly dispensed to workers.

Food Preparation

Laurel Thatcher Ulrich in *Good Wives* provides a picture of the rigors of preparing meals in seventeenth-century New England. The women of the house made butter and cheese only in the spring (though butter was considered a luxury for most people in the seventeenth century). The making of cheese

A typical colonial kitchen. From George Francis Dow, *Every Day Life in the Massachusetts Bay Colony* (Boston: Society for the Preservation of New England Antiquities, 1935).

was a tiresome process of multiple pressings, rinsings, and turnings. Summer and fall were the seasons for harvesting vegetables and preserving them. Grains, notably dried corn, were taken to the miller for processing into meal and flour. The women also usually did the job of slaughtering and butchering pigs, placing the meat in salt for three or four weeks, and then smoking it. The biggest job in the fall was adding sugar to apples for the great quantities of cider—from ten to thirty barrels—required throughout the year. The concoction was left in the cellars to ferment along with any beer the householders had made from barley. Pumpkins and apples were dried in the fall and stored in the house. Throughout the year there were stores of food in containers all over the house, from basement to garret.

Bread-making was done on a fairly regular basis using the leavening left over from each process or skimmed from the tops of fermenting beverages, mixed with flour ground from grain taken to the miller.

Meals were cooked in a large walk-in fireplace. Often several fires were going in a single fireplace, for each dish had to have a different fire in order to cook it properly. The popularity of one-dish meals derives in part from the need for only one fire in the fireplace. Biscuits were cooked in a frying pan or placed directly on the hearth and covered by an upside-down pan buried under hot coals.

Typical Meals

Breakfast came at a busy time of day in the New England household. The women were usually occupied with milking and other chores, so it was not convenient to prepare a cooked breakfast. This meal therefore consisted of foods that could be eaten without much preparation. A large breakfast might include left-overs like meat from the previous day, bread, cheese, and milk or beer. The usual meager everyday breakfast was corn mush and milk.

Dinner came in early afternoon and was the most substantial meal of the day. The New England dinner was exclusively a one-pot dish: a leek soup, or an eel pie, or a stew of pork and apples, for example. More often it was made of spoon-sized pieces of boiled meat with a sauce of vegetables like beans or peas. (Only in upper-class households were meat and vegetables cooked separately.) New Englanders had a great love for sweets so the meal usually ended with a fruit pie.

Supper was usually cornmeal mush and the juice from the day's dinner.

The settlers ate from what were called trenchers—carved wooden, usually poplar, bowls. Poor families usually ate from the same trencher. They drank from tankards made of wooden staves. The only utensils were spoons and occasionally knives. Forks did not make their way to New England until the late seventeenth century. As conditions and economics improved, settlers began to possess tableware made of pewter, horn, or silver. China began to be available in the eighteenth century.

Food and Witchcraft

Food and witchcraft in Salem are linked at least tangentially. Many theories have been advanced for the odd behavior and hallucinations of the young girls who were the chief accusers of witches in Salem and screamed and fainted at the witchcraft trials. Then there were the odd visions of the rest of the community: men who woke up to find their elderly neighbors lying on top of them or saw them flying through the air. One theory is that the community had been poisoned with a batch of bad barley that had been used in soup and beer. The argument is that the bad barley acted as a hallucinogen.

Food and Revolution

Food figured in the colonists' worsening relations with the British. The Navigation Acts, which prohibited trade with any country except England, kept the settlers from exporting foodstuffs to European and West Indies markets. And the tariff on tea resulted in the rebellious dumping of tea into Boston Harbor in 1773. Both Navigation Acts and tariffs affecting food import and export were serious contributors to the American Revolution.

HEALTH

Of all the colonists throughout the New World, the New Englanders were undoubtedly the healthiest. Some writers have theorized that this was because they ate lots of apples and consumed fair amounts of cider. Others have attributed their better health to a colder climate, where malaria and typhoid (though they did exist) were less likely to be the constant plagues they became in more southerly, swamp-infested climates. In New England the life expectancy for men and women who lived to be twenty years old was about sixty-five, much higher than in other parts of the country. Medical care may have been better provided for in New England. A physician named Samuel Fuller came to Plymouth on the *Mayflower*, and the Massachusetts Bay Company arranged in 1629 for a physician named Abraham Pratt and a surgeon named Robert Morley to join the company in the Salem and Boston areas. The ministers who were attracted to the New World were highly educated and usually trained in both theology and medicine at Cambridge University.

The better health of New Englanders could scarcely be attributed to better hygiene, though. Sanitation, disinfection, proper drainage of sewage, toothbrushes, bathtubs, and indoor bathing were almost nonexistent in the seventeenth century.

Chief Illnesses

New Englanders did grow sick and die of diseases and other serious maladies, even though the lack of highly populated and congested cities meant that epidemics were not as bad as in Europe. The illnesses mentioned most often were scurvy, malaria, smallpox, and measles. One of the earliest maladies was scurvy, which plagued each of the major communities—Plymouth, Salem, and Boston—in the early days of settlement. Scurvy was a seriously debilitating illness brought on by inadequate diet. William Bradford writes that half of the original settlers at Plymouth died of scurvy (and other diseases) within two months of arrival. There are mentions of an outbreak of scurvy in the Boston area in 1632, after months of scarce food. John Winthrop, who knew something of medicine (his son worked as a trained physician), understood even at this time that scurvy could be prevented by limes and lemons, and he ordered a shipment of them brought to the colony.

New England also had outbreaks of malaria. One reported in 1629 and 1630 in Salem took the lives of many citizens and may have been one reason that prompted Winthrop to relocate near Boston, which he considered less unhealthy than Salem.

Sporadic outbreaks of smallpox took their toll on the Massachusetts population, notably in 1660, 1684, 1689, and 1702. The Reverend Cotton Mather, associated with the Salem witch trials, was also a learned scientist and physician and tried to introduce a resistant New England to the practice of inoculation. Epidemics of scarlet fever and measles also occurred, a particularly virulent one in 1688.

Healers

Traditionally there were four professionals who practiced three distinct branches of medicine: the trained physician; the surgeon, who was qualified to pull teeth, do bleedings, and lance infections; the apothecary, who prescribed various medicines; and the midwife. By the eighteenth century, the first three positions had become one, and students of medicine now received their training by reading medicine with an individual doctor rather than from the university.

There were two primary schools of thought: the Galen school and the Paracelcus. The former prescribed only vegetable substances, and the latter preferred mineral substances. The chief cures were bleeding, applications of poultices (herbs wrapped in cloth and applied to the skin), and medicines taken by mouth. Settlers medicated themselves with substances they ordered from the apothecary or herbs they gathered themselves, often on the advice of native peoples, or that they bought from itinerant medicine men.

Bizarre Cures and Diagnoses

The state of colonial medicine in the eighteenth century is illustrated by the cures prescribed by Dr. John Perkins, one of Boston's leading physicians. For scrofula (a form of tuberculosis that attacks the glands), he recommended sow bugs soaked in white wine. For palsy (involuntary shaking), he recommended bathing in a hot bath of urine and absinthe. For nervous weakness of the eyes, he recommended shaving the head. Dr. Perkins also noted the causes of death of some of his patients. Widow Alcock, he wrote, died of a hot bread supper.

Cotton Mather, acknowledged as one of the leading scientists of his day recommended a poultice made from olive oil, red lead, white lead, and castile soap. Cooked and rolled into balls, it would cure many things. If placed on the stomach, it would relieve weak stomach and colic. If placed on the area of the kidneys, it would cure kidney ailments. It would make scraped legs heal and was good for any ache, bruise, or corn. For a consumptive cough (which usually meant tuberculosis), Mather recommended boiling eight or ten crawfish, grinding them up, and mixing them with some chicken broth. Another cure for consumption that he recommended was drinking donkey's milk, and for very bad cases that might involve internal obstructions, he recommended "millipedes," though he left no record of how they were to be used. The following remedy for consumption, which finally sounds like little more than an untraditional version of chicken soup, becomes somewhat bizarre in the relaying of instructions:

> Take two young Cocks, hatched in the Spring, and kill them with Strangling, not shedding any of their Blood; pick 'em and gutt 'em. Don't wash 'em. While they are warm now bruise them to a Mash, breaking all their Bones. Putt them into

a clean earthen Pipkin; adding two Quarts of water, and one Pint of sweet rich Wine, wherein boil the Cocks to Rags. Then strain it hard thro' a clean Cloth; and into the strained Liquor putt one Pound and a half of stoned Raisins; two Drams of Saffron; one Ounce of Harts-horn; one Ounce of Ivory; one Handful of Maiden-hair; two Ounces of the Roots of Colts-foot sliced; and lett it be well-boiled. (Cotton Mather, quoted in Beall and Shryock, 210)

Sickness and Dogma

Puritan religious doctrine played an integral part in the psychological and physical state of New England settlers and their attitudes toward illness. All psychological ills were ordinarily attributed to possession by demons and witches. Modern physicians have speculated that a repressive and frightening theology that stressed individual and collective guilt, graphic descriptions of the horrors of hell, and a lively demonic supernatural probably contributed to psychological problems. A typical example can be found in Samuel Sewall's diary as he worried about his daughter's anxiety, fainting spells, and physical debilitation brought on by her fear of hell.

Illnesses, both individual and collective, were invariably attributed by the clergy to sin. At the funerals of children who had died of natural causes, ministers attributed the deaths to the sins of the parents. Ministers were also convinced that epidemics of disease, and especially the deaths of Puritan leaders, were proof of God's anger toward a sinful community, which had brought disaster on itself.

BIBLIOGRAPHY

Andrews, Charles M. *Colonial Folkways*. New Haven, Conn.: Yale University Press, 1919.

Beall, Otho T., and Richard H. Shryock. *Cotton Mather: First Significant Figure in American Medicine*. Baltimore: Johns Hopkins University Press, 1954.

Bradford, William. *Of Plymouth Plantation, 1620–1647*. New York: Modern Library, 1981.

Brown, Sanborn C. *Wines and Beers of Old New England*. Hanover, N.H.: University Press of New England, 1978.

Conroy, David W. *In Public Houses*. Chapel Hill: University of North Carolina Press, 1995.

Crawford, Mary Caroline. *Social Life in Old New England*. Boston: Little, Brown, 1914.

Dow, George Francis. *Domestic Life*. Topsfield, Mass.: Perkins Press, 1925.

———. *Everyday Life in Colonial New England*. Boston: Society for the Preservation of New England Antiquities, 1935.

Earle, Alice Morse. *Home Life in Colonial Days*. New York: Macmillan, 1898.

Fisher, Sydney G. *Men, Women, and Manners*. Philadelphia: Lippincott, 1897.

Jamieson, Frederick, ed. *Johnson's "Wonder Working Providence."* New York: Barnes and Noble, 1967.

Langdon, William C. *Everyday Things in American Life*. New York: Scribner's, 1937.

Phipps, Francis. *Colonial Kitchens*. New York: Hawthorn Books, 1972.
Rutman, Darrett B. *Winthrop's Boston*. Chapel Hill: University of North Carolina Press, 1965.
St. George, Robert Blair. *Material Life in America*. Boston: Northeast University Press, 1988.
Ulrich, Laurel Thatcher. *Good Wives*. New York: Vintage Books, 1991.
Webster, Charles. *The Great Instauration*. London: Duckworth, 1975.
Weeden, W. B. *Economic and Social History of New England*. Boston: Houghton Mifflin, 1890.
Winthrop, John. *The Journal of John Winthrop, 1630–1649*. Cambridge, Mass.: Belknap Press of Harvard University Press, 1996.

8

Marriage and Sex

We learn about marriage in colonial New England by looking at a variety of records: personal letters written by prospective partners and their parents, the personal letters of husbands and wives, diaries, wills, legal disputes, and laws. A look at courtship and marriage in colonial New England reveals that they were not different in most ways from traditional practices in England at the time, but they were markedly different from those of our own time, even from attitudes and traditions grounded in conservative Christianity. At the same time, any such examination dispels some commonly held stereotypes about seventeenth- and eighteenth-century New Englanders. To begin such an examination, speculate about the validity of the following statements. Do you think they are true or false with regard to colonial custom?

1. Courtship began when a young man asked a young woman on an outing.
2. The usual procedure was for a young man to ask a young woman's father for her hand in marriage.
3. The usual procedure was for the couple's parents to draw up a property settlement after the couple announced that they had fallen in love and wanted to get married.
4. Colonial New Englanders married early—in their late teens.
5. First marriages required parental permission.
6. An engagement was a property settlement; the wishes of the couple were never consulted.

7. One of the chief considerations in choosing a mate was his or her social class.
8. In some cases, parents encouraged the practice of allowing an engaged couple to sleep under the bed covers together.
9. The engagement was formalized with a diamond ring.
10. Marriage was considered a religious sacrament.
11. Marriage ceremonies had to be performed by a minister.
12. The church insisted on a prescribed ceremony with vows similar to today's wedding ceremony.
13. Divorce was not recognized or legal in colonial New England.
14. Husbands were legally allowed to strike their wives.
15. A woman lost ownership of her property to her husband when she married.
16. Colonial New Englanders did not have prenuptial agreements.
17. Love was not considered important in a New England marriage.
18. A couple were not considered married until they had had sex.

All of the above are false except for numbers 5, 7, 8, 15, and 18. Each is covered in the discussion that follows.

THE FIVE STEPS TO MARRIAGE

Edmund Morgan in *The Puritan Family*, identifies five steps in "the proper accomplishment of a marriage" (30): a contract, showing an intent to marry; a public announcement of the contract, called a publishing of the banns; the marriage ceremony; a celebration following the ceremony; and physical consummation of the marriage in sexual intercourse

Before the Contract

In an idealized story of traditional courtship in the 1940s or 1950s, John and Mary may have known each other all their lives. They probably saw each other at school every day, went to parties where they saw each, and may have begun dating several different people in high school. Twice they may have fallen in love and broken up with other partners, but by their senior year in high school, John and Mary were going steady—going out exclusively with each other. They would describe themselves as being very much in love. They would likely see a great deal of each other's families, and their parents would come to know each other. It would come as no surprise when, in their senior year in college, John makes an old-fashioned visit to Mary's father to go through the formality—and it is only that—of asking for Mary's hand in marriage. That very evening, John probably gives Mary an engagement ring. An announcement of the engagement in the local paper and an engagement party would likely precede the church wedding.

Courtship in colonial New England was very unlike the twentieth-century practice of dating. Young unmarried men and women did not pair off to socialize with one another just for the pleasure of each other's company. A young man called on a woman at her house—a first date, one might say—not so much to spend the time with her, but usually with the specific idea of subtly exploring the possibility of marriage.

Typically a man might well have arranged to pay a visit to the young woman's house only after talking the matter over with his father, perhaps for weeks. In many cases, his father himself may have suggested the visit after consultation with her parents. In an extreme case, the two fathers may have been talking about the details of the marriage for months before the two young people even had a first conversation with each other, usually when they were in their thirties.

In colonial New England, discussion of marriage was not broached by parents whose children were of different social classes. Just as it was imperative to remain in the station to which God had placed one, so it was equally imperative to marry someone of the same class. Occasionally men would marry "beneath them," as did the Reverend Michael Wigglesworth, a highly educated, socially prominent professor-clergyman who insisted on marrying his servant girl. He was able to do this because it was not his first marriage, and there seemed to be no family involved in the decision. But the community never condoned such unions. Since no one could marry without parental permission (and records tend to prove that parents did not give their permission for their children to marry beneath them), and since one could run away with one's forbidden beloved only to a lonely and dangerous wilderness, elopements of "star-crossed" sweethearts of different classes seem to have been rare.

The Contract

The reason behind what we would consider an unusual sequence of events in a courtship is the belief that the arrangement of a marriage began not as the natural culmination of love between a man and a woman but as a business negotiation between their families. This is not to say that the couple were not consulted; they were. And it was hoped and understood that love or affection would follow. There are records of young people who resisted the marriage proposed by their parents because they were already in love with someone else. However, the usual sequence of events found a reluctant bride or groom deciding at least to try to be fond of the mate chosen for him or her.

The courtship leading up to the contract consisted of business discussions over just what property the families of the bride and groom would contribute to the marriage. Many prenuptial negotiations took on the intensity of a modern corporate merger. For a bride of property, the negotiations were especially critical, for any property she owned when she married would, by law, automatically become her husband's. Each family brought property or money to the couple's union, and the object of each was to get the other family to make a larger contribution. The father of the groom often deeded a portion of his land to the couple and sometimes agreed to build a house for them on the land. In many cases, a man of the second generation was forced to marry late because his father refused to turn over a deed to the land that had been promised him.

In the case of second marriages, particularly when widows were involved, financial negotiations took place between the couple themselves. The widow, who in some communities had a legal right to at least one-third of her deceased husband's property, had much to lose in placing it in the hands of a new husband. Records indicate an unusual situation for widows: while in England women had no authority to sign contracts, widows in New England had the power to enter into contracts on their own. An example conveys the sense of courtship as an economic negotiation. After Samuel Sewall's wife died, he entered into marriage negotiations with the widow of one of Governor Winthrop's sons. Sewall would have benefited from the handsome estate she inherited from her husband, but when she insisted on his providing her with her own carriage, the negotiations fell apart, and the courtship ceased.

Once the marriage contract was drawn up, it was signed by all parties and was as legally binding as any other contract regarding property. If either of the parties decided he or she did not want to be married to the other and attempted to withdraw from the contract, the person could be, and was, sued for breach of contract. From the signing of the contract, the couple were considered married, though it was expected that they would refrain from sexual intercourse until after the wedding ceremony.

The signing of the contract, known as the *espousal*, was often the occasion for an espousal ceremony performed by a minister. The espousal ceremony was required by law in Connecticut.

Publication of the Banns

The publication of the banns, announcing that the marriage contract had been made, might today be similar to placing an engagement announcement in a local paper. For the colonial New Englander, the publication of the banns was an absolute requirement, without which the marriage could not take place. The publication could be made as an announcement on three consecutive meetings at the meetinghouse or it could be left for fourteen days on the meetinghouse door. One effect of this was to thwart clandestine marriages, which might allow one of the marriage partners to evade his or her marital responsibilities or perhaps even to attempt a bigamous marriage.

The courtship following the espousal was often a critical period when couples who knew little of each other expected to learn to be fond of one another. Although sex between espoused couples was not officially approved of, it was sometimes condoned.

The practice of bundling, particularly in rural households, increasingly came to be an issue at this juncture of the courtship. Bundling was the practice of allowing two unmarried people to lie beneath the bedcovers fully clothed, perhaps with a divider between them. This was usually in the house of the bride-to-be. It was understood that although they lay in the same bed, they were not to have full sexual union. The remoteness of the bride's house in a rural area often made it inconvenient for the groom to visit. And bundling loses something of its daring when one realizes that in most households for many years, there was very little privacy, adults often slept in the same room or in both a main room and a loft without a wall or door between them. Still, some theories have it that the increased toleration of bundling increased premarital pregnancies. Another theory is that parents of young people who were reluctant to marry one another often encouraged bundling to heat up the romance and to make them grow more affectionate toward each other.

Marriage Ceremony

When Protestantism pulled away from Catholicism and Puritanism pulled away from the Church of England, their adherents shed most of the sacraments recognized by Catholicism and the Church of England. For our purposes, a sacrament can be defined as a ceremony imbued with a mysterious, supernatural, holy character because God is presumed to be present and he bestows his grace as a result of the ceremony. The Catholic church recognized a number of such sacraments, the marriage ceremony included. However, the Puritans who dominated New England reduced the number of sacraments to two only: baptism and communion. Unlike the Catholic church and the Church of England, they did not regard marriage as a sacrament or holy ceremony. Because of this and in reaction to the practice of considering marriage a sacrament, the colonists legally prohibited ministers from performing marriage ceremonies. Instead they were performed by public officials—magistrates. Not until 1686, with the loss of the charter and the interference in colonial life by the British Crown, were ministers allowed to perform ceremonies. It was a breach of colonial tradition that the Puritans in the colony adjusted to without much ado. Puritan diarist Samuel Sewall, who refused to tolerate wig wearing and refused to attend his cousin's wedding to a too-close relative of his former wife, seemingly had no problem with attending weddings performed by ministers. Moreover, after Sewall's first wife died and he was remarrying, he asked his son, who was a minister, to perform his own second marriage ceremony.

In keeping with its secular nature, the wedding ceremony usually took place in the house of the bride rather than in church. It seemed to have none of the formal nature of repeated vows that are customary in ceremonies today. Instead the gathering was informal and often consisted of the spontaneous remarks about marriage and the couple made by the guests.

The Wedding Celebration

The wedding feast was understood to be an official stage in the sequence of events that bound two people in marriage, being roughly equivalent to today's wedding reception. It had the function of further binding the couple to the community. Unlike twentieth-century tradition, in which the expenses are met by the couple themselves or the bride's family, the wedding feast was paid for by the groom's family.

The privileged nature of the wedding feast is seen in colonial legislation. In November 1637, the Court of Assistants issued a decree forbidding the sale of cakes or buns, "provided that this order shall not extend to such cakes as shall be made for any burial, or marriage, or such like special occasion" (Shurtleff, vol. 1: 214). While the guests expected alcoholic drinks to be served at any wedding feast, presumably there was little or no toasting of the bride or groom, an officially despised practice because it was regarded as an impetus to heavy drinking and drunkenness. There was probably also no dancing since it was frowned on and even outlawed in "public houses," that is, inns and taverns.

Physical Consummation of the Marriage

Although we ascribe to the Puritans the prudery of the nineteenth century, they were open in their acceptance of sex as a joyful and necessary part of marriage, so the final, and indispensable, stage in the completion of the union between a married couple was sexual union. If such a union did not occur for any reason, the marriage was considered to have never taken place. The laws of the various New England settlements reveal that any "natural incapacities" or unwillingness to complete the sexual union were reasons for annulling a marriage. A man's impotence was the chief reason for annulling a marriage on these grounds.

ROLES OF HUSBAND AND WIFE

In married union, the male was generally expected to exercise authority and the wife to assume a submissive role. The final decisions with regard to finances and property were his. The hiring and disciplining of servants, for example, was his role. He decided about the purchase or sale of any land. He decided how property was to be distributed when his own children married, and he decided how property was to be distributed in his will.

On all these matters, the law and the culture gave him the final authority. Nevertheless, in many marriages, the husband made decisions only after consultation with his wife. Sometimes the wife was the better business person and would actually, if not publicly, control the finances. She also came to be expected by society to have an equal role in matters regarding the children and in transfer of property that her husband owned because it came to him as part of the marriage contract, or because she had a hand in his being able to acquire it after marriage. Wives also had the ability and the responsibility of standing in for their husbands when incapacity or absence required it. Many women were, practically if not legally, equal partners with their husbands as farmers, merchants, and artisans.

EXPECTATIONS IN MARRIAGE

The laws of New England clarify the conditions that the culture expected in a marriage. They have been summarized by historians John Demos, Laurel Thatcher Ulrich, and Edmund Morgan in various ways. A husband and wife could expect from their marriage a peaceful life (that is, no violent behavior or abusive language), sexual union and faithfulness, economic support (a husband owned property and supported the wife, and the wife had an obligation to help maintain and increase her husband's property by using it wisely and working hard), and a life lived together (that is, no decision on the part of either husband or wife to live in a separate house, whether in the same town or miles away.)

It was against the law and subject to punishment for either partner to strike the other. Nor could either partner subject the other to abusive language. Furthermore, neither was allowed to force the other to do anything contrary to God's laws.

LOVE AND MARRIAGE

Love between husband and wife was understood to have certain limitations. Love was not considered necessary before a marriage took place. Nor should love between husband and wife ever be greater than their love for God. Moreover, public displays of love and affection were not typical of New England couples. Nevertheless, it was thought that husbands and wives did learn to love each other after marrying, if they did not already do so. Although they were to love God more than anything else, husbands and wives were thought to love each other more than anything else in creation.

There were obviously marriages in which husband and wife did not seem to love each other warmly, but letters and diaries show that many New England couples loved each other passionately. Edmund Morgan points to the marriage of John and Margaret Winthrop as an example. His letters to her typically ended "so with the sweetest kisses, and pure embracings of my kindest affection I rest Thine" (Winthrop, 163). Her letters to him in his absence are equally ardent.

In her support of the idea that colonists were sometimes ardent in their love, Laurel Thatcher Ulrich quotes from the papers of a colonial sailor named Ashley Bowen who met his wife-to-be after having dreamed of her. He anticipates finding "fair opportunity to examine her real moles and marks with real sweet kisses of real substance of lips and breasts and all the qualifications a young woman could be endowed with to make a man happy" (quoted in Ulrich, 124).

One of the most graphic examples of the passion of the colonial marriage is that of the poet Anne Dudley Bradstreet to Simon Bradstreet, at one time governor of the Massachusetts Bay Colony. Anne's feelings are expressed in the several poems, replete with sexual connotations, which she wrote about her husband and marriage. She speaks of her children as "those fruits which through thy heat I bore" and her breast as "the welcome house of him my dearest guest," and she declares that "his warmth such frigid colds did cause to melt" (quoted in Ulrich, III). Anne went far toward heresy in loving her husband too much. In one of her poems, she compares him with the sun (a symbol of Jesus Christ and God) around which she orbits, suggesting that she not only loved him more than God but regarded him as equivalent to God. In the following poem, the word *magazine* means warehouse, *Capricorn* means winter and *Cancer* means summer:

A Letter to Her Husband, Absent upon Public Employment

My head, my heart, mine eyes, my life, nay more,
My joy, my magazine of earthly store,
If two be one, as surely thou and I,
How stayest thou there, whilst I at Ipswich lie?
So many steps, head from the heart to sever,
If but a neck, soon we be together;
I, like the earth this season, mourn in black,
My sun is gone so far in's zodiac,
Whom whilst I joy'd, nor storms, nor frosts I felt,
His warmth such frigid colds did cause to melt.
My chilled limbs now numbed lie forlorn;
Return, return sweet Sol from Capricorn;
In this dead time, alas, what can I more
Then view those fruits which through thy heat I bore?
Which sweet contentment yield me for a space,
True living pictures of their father's face.
O strange effect! now thou art southward gone,
I weary grow, the tedious day so long;
But when thou northward to me shalt return,
I wish my sun may never set, but burn
Within the Cancer of my glowing breast,
The welcome house of him my dearest guest.
Where ever, ever stay, and go not thence,
Til nature's sad decree shall call thee hence;

> Flesh of thy flesh, bone of thy bone,
> I here, thou there, yet both but one. (From Lauter, 273)

Ironically, something of the sexual passion and emotional affection to be found in colonial marriage is suggested in the religious metaphors used by the clergy. Traditionally, the connection between Christ and the human church was expressed as a marriage between the two. Colonial ministers continued this metaphor, picking up details and attitudes from the marriages they observed around them. These metaphors thus became mirrors of sex and marriage in the culture. Edmund Morgan quotes the Reverend Thomas Hooker, who reveals something of that ardor for an earthly partner in a sermon about Christ's love for the church:

> The man whose heart is endeared to the woman he loves, he dreams of her in the night, hath her in his eye and apprehension when he awakes, museth on her as he sits at table, walks with her when he travels and parlies with her in each place where he comes . . . and his heart trusts in her, which forceth all to confess, that the stream of his affection, like a mighty current, runs with full Tide and strength. (62)

DISCORD AND DIVORCE

Despite the success of many colonial marriages, some of them were unhappy and ended in annulment and divorce, both legal in colonial New England. Marriages were terminated legally when it was discovered that the couple's marriage was not legal in the first place or when one or the other partner failed to live up to the marriage contract. Some of the situations for which the court recognized annulment or divorce were the following:

- The physical inability to have sexual intercourse, the usual reason being male impotence. If the husband was impotent from the start of the union, the marriage was nullified. In New Haven this was a written law. Massachusetts records reveal the dissolution of several marriages on this account.
- Bigamy, when it was revealed that one or the other was still married to someone else.
- "Criminal uncleanness," which likely had to do with bestiality or homosexuality.
- Incest, when it was found that the person to whom one was married was related in any number of ways. Mosaic law, for example, forbid the union of a man with his dead brother's wife or his own deceased wife's sister.

- Fornication before marriage with the kin of one's mate. If, for instance, it was found out after the fact that one's wife had had intercourse with the husband's brother, then one had grounds for divorce.
- Malicious desertion.
- The presumed death of an absent mate. A man who left for a potentially dangerous mission—going into the wilderness to hunt, for example—and did not return within the year might be presumed to be dead. The presumption was that his wife was no longer married and was thus free to remarry.
- Adultery, desertion, or absence—the usual reasons for divorce. Absence might occur, for example when a wife moved back into the house of her parents and refused to come back home.
- Fraudulent contract, which usually had to do with a misrepresentation of financial resources at the time of the marriage contract or a failure to provide the financial support promised in the marriage contract.
- Cruelty.

Records show that divorces cut across class lines and that although Massachusetts had no divorce laws as such, between 1639 and 1692 it granted at least twenty-seven divorces, thirteen of them for desertion or adultery. The Plymouth Colony granted six divorces, five of them for adultery.

SEX OUTSIDE MARRIAGE

Although the joys of sex in marriage were anticipated and celebrated, there were as many arrests for sex outside marriage as for any other single crime. Five of the sixteen laws carrying the death penalty were sex crimes. The following are some of the charges with regard to sex outside marriage that were punished by the magistrates:

Fornication—sex between a couple who were not married. This included fornication between a couple before they were married. If the couple had sex before the signing of the marriage contract, the fine was substantial. If it were after the signing of a marriage contract, the fine was minimal. Some examples of punishment for fornication follow:

On October 3, 1632, Nicholas Frost was severely whipped, branded in the hand with a hot iron, fined, and banished for theft, drunkenness, and fornication.

In November 1632, Robert Huitt and Mary Ridge were whipped for fornication.

On October 6, 1634, John Lee was whipped for several crimes, including enticing the governor's maid to "go with him into the cornfield."

On October 6, 1635, two men were fined for "knowing [their] wife[s] carnally before marriage."

On March 7, 1636, William James was set at the bilboes (an iron bar and bolt with shackles) in Boston and in the stocks at Salem and fined for "knowing his wife before marriage."

Adultery—sex between a married woman and a single or married man. Sex between a married man and a single woman was not strictly regarded as adultery or punishable with death. Although adultery was punishable by death in the Massachusetts Bay Colony, this mandate was a controversial one among the Assistants, many of whom had fought against such a measure. Partly as a result (to avoid executing adulterers), the courts found most of those accused guilty of lesser crimes (attempted adultery, uncleanness, or lasciviousness) that did not carry an automatic death sentence. On September 7, 1641, Thomas Owen "for his adulterous practices" was to be imprisoned and sent to stand on the gallows with a rope around his neck for an hour before being returned to prison.

Bestiality and sodomy, punishable by death. One such example occurred on December 10, 1641, when William Hatchet was hanged for having intercourse with a cow.

Rape. Rape of an adult was punishable by death or other appropriate punishment. Rape of a child was automatically punished by death.

Crimes of uncleanness and enticement to uncleanness, which warranted admonishment or punishment by fines. John Kempe, for instance, found guilty of trying to entice three young girls to "uncleanness," was in 1639 whipped in two towns "very severely" and given as a slave to Leift Davenport.

CONCLUSION

The records of colonial New England show a brutality in punishing illicit sex and an insistent invasion into the private lives of their citizens, but they also dispel the stereotype of Puritans as cold, passionless prudes. As Edmund Morgan writes:

> In short, the Puritans were neither prudes nor ascetics. They knew how to laugh, and they knew how to love. But it is equally clear that they did not spend their best hours in either love or laughter. They had fixed their eyes on a heavenly goal, which directed and informed their lives. When earthly delights dimmed their vision, it was time to break off. Yet even this side of the goal there was room for joy. (64)

BIBLIOGRAPHY

Bailyn, Bernard. *Education in the Forming of American Society*. Chapel Hill: University of North Carolina, 1960.

Benson, Mary Summer. *Women in Eighteenth-Century America*. New York: Columbia University Press, 1935.

Calhoun. Arthur W. *A Social History of the American Family*. 1917–1918. New York: Barnes and Noble, 1960.

Cott, Nancy F. *The Bonds of Womanhood: "Woman's Sphere" in New England, 1780–1835*. New Haven, Conn.: Yale University Press, 1977.

———. "Divorce and the Changing Status of Women in Eighteenth-Century Massachusetts." *William and Mary Quarterly*, 3rd ser., 32, (1976): 586–614.

Demos, John. *A Little Commonwealth*. London: Oxford University Press, 1970.

Dolen, Dana. *The Art of Bundling*. New York: Farrar and Rinehart, 1938.

Dow, George F. *Everyday Life in the Massachusetts Bay Colony*. Boston: Society for the Preservation of New England Antiquities, 1935.

Dunn, Richard S. *Puritans and Yankees*. Princeton, N.J.: Princeton University Press, 1962.

Earle, Alice Morse. *Child Life in Colonial Days*. New York: Macmillan, 1899.

———. *Colonial Dames and Good Wives*. Boston: Houghton Mifflin, 1895.

———. *Home Life in Colonial Days*. New York: Macmillan, 1898.

Flaherty, David H. *Privacy in Colonial New England*. Charlottesville: University Press of Virginia, 1972.

Fox, Vivian C., and Martin H. Quitt, eds. *Loving, Parenting, and Dying*. New York: Psychohistory Press, 1980.

Greven, Philip J., Jr. *Four Generations*. Ithaca, N.Y.: Cornell University Press, 1970.

Koehler, Lyle. *A Search for Power*. Urbana: University of Illinois Press, 1980.

Konig, David Thomas. *Law and Society in Puritan Massachusetts*. Chapel Hill: University of North Carolina Press, 1970.

Lauter, Paul, ed. *The Heath Anthology of American Literature*. Lexington, Mass.: D. C. Heath, 1990.

Lockridge, Kenneth. *A New England Town*. New York: Norton, 1970.

Morgan, Edmund S. *The Puritan Family*. New York: Harper and Row, 1944.

Shurtleff, N. B., ed. *Records of the Governor and Company of the Massachusetts Bay*. 6 vols. Boston: W. White, 1853–1854.

Smith, Page. *Daughters of the Promised Land*. Boston: 1970.

Stiles, Henry Reed. *Bundling*. Albany, N.Y.: J. Munsell, 1869.

Ulrich, Laurel Thatcher. *Good Wives*. New York: Random House, 1980.

Winthrop, Robert C. *The Life and Letters of John Winthrop*. Boston: Little Brown, 1869.

9

Arts and Amusements

H. L. Mencken, a twentieth-century wit, once described Puritanism as the haunting fear that someone, somewhere, was having a good time. Despite Mencken's obvious exaggeration for the sake of humor, any examination of arts and entertainments in the colonial period reveals more than a grain of truth in his wisecrack. Others might humorously conjecture that any discourse on arts and amusements in colonial New England would be the shortest possible chapter in any book ever written. Although New Englanders certainly did have their own artistic genres and their own entertainments, it is also true that a discussion of arts and entertainments among these people does turn, more often than not, on the negative, especially in comparing this aspect of their lives with that of other cultures. Determining how New Englanders used their imaginations and their spare time inevitably involves what they outlawed or discouraged.

A brief look at England illustrates the point. England in the seventeenth century was a country of thriving arts. It had drama in the tradition of William Shakespeare. It had the poetry of John Donne and Andrew Marvell. Its great cathedrals in London, York, and Durham were showplaces of religious art. Its people amused themselves with many games, sports, and celebrations: bowling, horse racing, bear baiting, fox hunting, fairs, and religious festivals. In contrast, the religious dissenters who dominated New England held views of the imagination, art, and leisure that caused them to discourage most of the arts and amusements enjoyed by the English and Europeans. New Englanders outlawed all theater, regularly banned books, prohibited the use of music or art in their churches, and criminalized many sports, amusements, and celebrations.

Three dogmatic biases lay at the bottom of the New Englander's negative view of most arts and amusements:

- The suspicion of the imagination as an agent of the devil, leading to immorality and God defiance
- The perception of idleness as one of the chief sins of human beings, causing them to forget the necessity to work hard in their callings and to lapse into immorality
- Their fierce disapproval of the Roman Catholic church and its sacraments and rituals.

VIEWS OF THE IMAGINATION AND LEISURE

New Englanders' suspicion of many artistic genres was grounded in their view of the creative imagination, from which literature, painting, and music spring. Most New Englanders regarded the imagination as an agent of the devil who, through appeals to human imagination, leads people to commit all manner of sinful overt actions as well as sins of the mind and heart. Moreover, the imagination was regarded with suspicion because it was not checked and limited as were other human faculties. The visions prompted by the emotions were checked by the intellect, for instance, but through the imagination, which has no checks on it, a person could conjure up erroneous visions (of dragons and monsters, for example) and lead to the embrace of falsehoods. William Perkins, one of the most influential English writers in colonial New England, wrote that "the Imagination of mans heart is evil even from his youth" (456). The imagination was dangerous for another reason: through the use of the imagination, a person could pretend to create a world of his own (like a drama or a novel) and create his own people (like the characters in a play or novel). Such an artist committed the worst of all possible sins: the sin of pride or God defiance in attempting to be like God the Creator.

Art was also discouraged because it promoted idleness, regarded as one of the worst sins in colonial New England. Art not only led one into immorality; it diverted one's attention from work in one's God-given calling—work that was required to keep the frontier community from collapsing.

In 1726, Cotton Mather, in *Manuductio Ad Ministerium,* has this to say of literary and dramatic art of all kinds:

> How much do I wish that such Pestilences, and indeed all those worse than EGYPTIAN TOADS . . . might never crawl into your Chamber! The UNCLEAN

SPIRITS that COME LIKE FROGS OUT OF THE MOUTH OF THE DRAGON, AND OF THE BEAST; which GO FORTH unto the young People of THE EARTH, and expose them to be dealt withal as the Enemies of GOD. (43)

THE LITERARY ARTS AND DANCING

The effect of such attitudes on the acceptance of traditional arts and entertainments in New England is all too apparent, especially in the seventeenth century, before the British presence mitigated the wholesale prohibition of many pastimes. On the negative side, most performing arts, and especially theater, were banned absolutely from the New England colonies until 1793. Traveling actors were inevitably arrested and thrown out of town, not only in Boston and New Haven, but in Philadelphia and Albany as well, throughout the eighteenth century. The exception was found in private theatricals staged by and for British troops stationed in New England after the revocation of the charter.

Dancing, another performance art as well as a social entertainment, was also outlawed in public houses in 1646. Two dancing masters tried to introduce dancing to Boston in November 1685 and were promptly thwarted in their attempts, one of them fleeing Boston in July 1686. Both were subject to stiff fines, which would be canceled if they agreed to leave the colony. By 1714, Judge Sewall indicated that a dancing master named Edward Enstone, an organist for the Anglican King's Chapel, was allowed to advertise his dancing school in Boston. But he also recorded on November 29, 1716, that he (Sewall) and others managed to discourage the governor from broadcasting his approval of dancing by attending a ball given by Enstone.

As Cotton Mather's comments make clear, literary arts like poetry and fiction were also denounced by the all-powerful Puritan and Quaker clergy. Although printers operated in New England cities, especially Boston, the clergy and the magistrates kept a close eye on the materials published, halting material deemed irreverent, irreligious, or treasonous and denouncing anything that promoted frivolity, immorality, or idleness. One of the most popular works written in New England, "Day of Doom," by Michael Wigglesworth, was a long poem, and several New Englanders—Anne Bradstreet, Edward Taylor, and Phillis Wheatley—are now known for their exceptional poetry. However, these seemed to have been exceptions—their cases proof of the widespread discouragement of poetry in general. Wigglesworth's poem, for example, was tolerated and admired because it met the criterion for the little poetry that was sanctioned: it served a permitted religious purpose. Wigglesworth's poem, which was important enough to be memorized by New England school children, was a fire-and-brimstone dramatization of Puritan doctrine as each damned soul argues with the Judge about why he or she should be saved. The Judge's responses are expositions on such things as innate depravity, the Fall, predestination, and infant damnation.

The poems of Anne Bradstreet, daughter of lieutenant governor (and then governor) Thomas Dudley, and those of Edward Taylor, Harvard College–educated minister in Westfield, Massachusetts, were little known in their lifetimes. Both seemed to realize that not only was their chosen genre questionable, but that what they had to say as poets would be unpopular and misunderstood. Bradstreet refers to the antiliterary attitudes of her day in "The Author to Her Book," one of the few of her poems to see print, when she calls her work the "ill-form'd offspring of my feeble brain," and in "The Prologue" writes, "I am obnoxious to each carping tongue / Who says my hand a needle better fits." I made reference in Chapter 8 to the unfitting irreligious sentiments of her poems in which she compares her husband to Jesus Christ.

The disapproval of poetry is suggested in the fact that the great body of Edward Taylor's poetry was never published in his lifetime, nor was it his intention that his marvelous poetry ever see the light of day, even after he died. Unlike Bradstreet, Taylor's subject matter was almost wholly religious, but he certainly sensed that much of his sentiment, however religious, might be misunderstood by his contemporaries. His "Meditation Eight," for instance, seems to endorse the popish notion of transubstantiation—the belief that the wafer and wine of communion take the form of the flesh and blood of Christ.

With the diminishing absolute power of the clergy in the eighteenth century, came more open tolerance for poetry. Yet even here the enduring verse has a sermon or message to deliver. Phillis Wheatley, an African slave living in eighteenth-century Boston, used poetry as a medium for expressing herself on religious subjects and the deaths of famous men. And the Revolutionary Deist Philip Freneau used poetry for propaganda. Although Freneau did not take his religious beliefs from the early colonists, he did demonstrate that literature can be justified only if it is useful.

The one literary genre that flourished in colonial New England was the treatise or sermon. This was the form that inspired early publishers in New England. Printing houses formed to publish sermons, and sermons became the publishers' mainstays, addresses of particular eloquence often appearing within weeks of their first oral delivery in the meetinghouse.

Popular publications were practical works or those religious works of a character acceptable to Calvinist dogma. Joining "Day of Doom" on the colonial New England best-seller lists were the Bible, *The Bay Psalm Book*, the almanac, and the *New England Primer*.

GRAPHIC ARTS AND MUSIC

In Europe and England, the Roman Catholic and Anglican churches had been and continued to be great sponsors of graphic and musical arts. We think of the many medieval triptychs telling the story of Christ's birth, the Sistine Chapel in Rome, where the grand stories of the Bible were painted on the ceiling by Michelangelo, of classic statues of the Old Testament's Moses and David by the same artist. We encounter the richness of biblical narrative and symbol in the stained glass windows and elaborately carved altars of cathedrals throughout Europe and England.

But in church-powerful colonial New England, founded on religious doctrine, no such religious art was tolerated, much less generated. Largely as a reaction to the rich ornamentation of the Roman church, the dissenters who settled New England repudiated all symbolic and decorative art within their churches. They considered any statue or painting in the meetinghouse to be popish idolatry. As a consequence, we see virtually no biblical scenes traditionally depicted in colonial paintings.

The chief pictorial art produced in seventeenth-century New England was portraiture. Few figures of stature or wealth left this world without having had their portraits painted. Sometimes these were single figures, and sometimes they were family group portraits. Portraits were painted of each of the influential governors and businessmen in the Winthrop family; of famous clergymen like Richard, Increase, and Cotton Mather; of the jurist and diarist Samuel Sewall; and of many wives and children of men of means.

The meetinghouse was cleansed of traditional church music as well as art. No instrumental music of any kind was allowed, and the only vocalizing permitted was the intoning in sing-song manner from *The Bay Psalm Book,* which had none of the lyricism of the King James *Bible.*

THE USEFUL ARTS

Throughout the seventeenth century, most of the artistic impulse went into the decoration of ordinary household objects. This useful or practical art primarily involved the design of quilts, coverlets, and other linens. The artists of this genre were woman, and the artistic instrument was the needle rather than the paint brush. From this, Nathaniel Hawthorne, nineteenth-century author and son of prominent seventeenth-century Puritans, constructed his novel *The Scarlet Letter* about a seamstress who becomes a representative of the artist.

A second example of a useful art began to grace New England tombstones in the second half of the seventeenth century. From the mid-seventeenth century, tombstone carvers were among the most prolific

Examples of tombstone art. The winged death head represented the flight of the soul from the body. Note the crossed bones worked into both designs. Photos courtesy of the author.

artists of colonial New England. The central figure found on the seventeenth-century tombs was a winged skull, signifying the flight of the soul from the earth. The mat area, around the square containing the name and dates of the deceased, was decorated with carvings of leaves and flowers, sometimes cupid-like figures carrying open books or closed coffins, crossbones, and hourglasses symbolic of the passage of time. Religious themes like crosses were rare on tombstones. Gradually the death-heads were replaced by highly stylized circular heads (sometimes with heads topped with coifed or curly hair) that seemed to be intended to resemble a particular person and sometimes with a romanticized cherub. In the usual cases, wings continued to be attached to whatever head was drawn. Each community had its own stone carver whose individual touch is identifiable in the cemeteries that display his art.

The poet Edward Taylor enumerates the images found on tombstones in his "Meditation One Hundred and Twelve":

> With empty Eyeholes, Butter teeth, bones bare
> And spraggling arms, having an Hour Glass
> In one grim paw. Th' other a Spade doth hold,
> To shew deaths frighfull region under mould.
> (From Thomas H. Johnson, 178–179)

GAMES AND AMUSEMENTS

The games and sports that amused the populace in England—bowling, card playing, dice throwing, billiards, shuffleboard, angling, hunting, and horse racing—were familiar to seventeenth-century New Englanders. We find mention of them in official documents, diaries, and letters. That poetic chronicler of New England life, Edward Taylor, chose games to build his religious metaphors, suggesting that games were commonplace in colonial days. In his poem, "The Preface," for example, Taylor writes that after God had worked so hard—like a blacksmith, a mason, and a housewife—to create the earth, he amused himself by bowling the sun. Using the technique of the rhetorical question, the line is, "Who in this Bowling Alley bowld the Sun?" The game of tennis was being played in England in the sixteenth century, though in the early form of it, the ball was struck with the flat of the hand rather than a racket. Taylor also used this to make a metaphor about the soul of man needing to undergo great trial before reaching spiritual heights: "I, as Tenis Ball, struck hard upon the ground, Back-bounce with shine." In "Meditation Eighteen," Taylor refers to several games in developing metaphors for the depraved human heart, mind, and will. In the following stanza, *Phansy* is fancy; *a Green* is a grassy park; *Barley-breaks* is a game in which one couple attempts to block two other couples from getting past various lines; *pingle* is a small, enclosed playing area; and *Coursey-Park* is a game of chase played by a girl and a boy:

> Mine Heart's a Park or Chase of sins: Mine Head
> 'S a Bowling Alley: sins play Ninehold here
> Phansy's a Green: sin Barly-breaks in't led.
> Judgment's a pingle: Blindeman's Buff's plaid there.
> Sin playes at Coursey-Park within my Minde;
> My Will's a Walke in which it aires what's blinde.
> (From Thomas H. Johnson, 157)

In the eighteenth century, with the infusion of more urbane Englishmen, games of various kinds became commonplace. There are many announcements of horse races, including one in Cambridge in 1715. There are also mentions of hog racing and bear baiting. A bowling green was established in Boston in 1700 and billiards and nine pins were openly played in the eighteenth century. In 1720 merchants were selling decks of cards in Boston.

But the religious New Englanders of the seventeenth century frowned on these games because they tempted men and women away from their work, wasted time, and encouraged gambling and general immorality. For the most part, if people did their work, did not create disturbances, and did not gamble or dishonor the Sabbath, they were left alone to play most games in their own houses, but participation in games in public houses was made illegal in 1646:

> *Upon complaint of the disorders, about the use of the Games of Shuffle-board and Bowling, in and about Houses of Common-entertainment, whereby much precious time is spent unprofitably, and much waste of Wine and Beer occasioned;*
>
> It is Ordered by this Court and the Authority thereof, That no person shall henceforth use the said Games of Shuffleboard, or Bowling, or any other Play or Game, in or about any such House. (*General Laws And Liberties*, 57)

The ambiguity toward games is illustrated in the diary of Samuel Sewall. In May 1689, when Sewall was a young man, he made the rounds of a number of taverns, ending up playing ninepins at one of them. In August 1715, some twenty-six years later, he helped break up a game of ninepins on what was officially referred to as Mount-Whoredom near what is now Louisburg Square on Beacon Hill in Boston.

In 1670, the court, responding to what it saw as an increase in card playing, made the mere possession of cards or dice a crime, because it was assumed that the playing of cards necessarily involved gambling. In 1674, under laws relating to soldiering, concern was expressed over members of the militia who often gambled away their weapons and ammunition.

Horse racing was also made illegal near towns and major roadways in 1677 because it involved gambling and misspending time, "drawing of many persons from the duty of their particular Callings" (*General Laws And Liberties*, 347).

FESTIVE OCCASIONS AND CELEBRATIONS

In the choice of celebrations, the life of New Englanders differed markedly from that of the mother country. This difference arose ultimately from the New Englanders' repudiation of the Church of Rome and its traditions. In England, Christmas was a special season of celebration, as were Easter and other religious holidays. But in discarding all "popish" rituals and sacraments, New Englanders refused to recognize any holy days or to allow the observation of Christmas as a special holiday. Official feeling was so intense on this matter that the celebration of Christmas was outlawed. The rationale for levying a fine for the celebration of Christmas is made clear in the 1659 law:

> *For preventing disorders arising in several places within this jurisdiction by reason of some still observing such Festivals, as were Superstitiously kept in other countries, to the great dishonour of God, and offense of others;*
>
> It is therefore Ordered by this Court and the Authority thereof, that whosoever shall be found observing any such day as Christmas or the like, either by forbearing labour, feasting, or any other way upon any such account as aforesaid, every such person so offending, shall pay for every such offense five shillings as a fine to the County. (*General Laws And Liberties*, 58)

In 1681, with the colonies now firmly under the authority of the British king, the law making the celebration of Christmas a crime was repealed. However, year after year, Samuel Sewall faithfully observed with great satisfaction that up to 1728, business seemed to continue on December 25 as usual, with little evidence that Christmas was being celebrated. He himself scolded a man in 1699 for going to a French Huguenot church to celebrate Christmas. In 1708, in keeping with the Puritan disapproval of holy and saints' days, Sewall blotted out the following on the calendar given him by the royal governor: St. Valentine's Day; March 25, in honor of the Annunciation of the Blessed Virgin; Easter; September 29, which was Michaelmas or the Feast of Saint Michael; and Christmas. Sermons against the celebration of Christmas, like one of Cotton Mather's in November 1712, continued well into the eighteenth century. Mather especially deplored the "Mad mirth," drinking, feasting, and gaming involved in the celebration. Disapproval of the celebration of Christmas continued in New England until the Civil War.

Although New England continued to ignore the usual religious holidays, on many other days, by dictate or from custom, the colonial New

Englanders gathered together for music, games, performances, and special feasting and drinking. One such occasion was the local fair, held in many communities and first established by dictate as early as 1633, three years after the settlement of Boston. Days of thanksgiving and election days (when important officials were to take office) were official occasions for colorful and festive celebration. One such election day, described by Nathaniel Hawthorne in *The Scarlet Letter* (1850), was celebrated by taking the day off from work, perhaps displaying one's wares as a craftsman, staging sporting events such as wrestling and fencing matches, and having parades in which the local magistrates marched in their most colorful attire.

Public days for feasting, drinking, and general celebration were occasioned by funerals, weddings, and annual town meetings. More informal excuses for amusements and relaxation came after the hard work involved with building houses or farming. Thus, the people of the community had food and entertainment after house raisings, corn-husking bees, and apple bees. Women gathered together to work and socialize during quilting bees and spinning parties.

DRINKING

Drinking alcoholic beverages was an accepted part of the colonial New Englander's socializing and relaxation, whether at home or public houses. Both private houses and taverns were stocked with hard cider, rum, ale, wine, and other alcoholic drinks, which were freely imbibed not only by ordinary citizens, but by the clergy and religious magistrates as well. One of the Reverend Phillips's allotments in 1630, for example, included a hogshead of malt. Importers of liquor, brewers, distillers, and tavern keepers were licensed to ply their trades in New England. Men met in taverns to drink while they heard speeches or considered matters of public importance. The religiously educated jurist Samuel Sewall is a good example. Sewall often mentions having a bottle of wine with his meals at home, serving his guests expensive wines, and being served wines and liquors at the houses of his friends or in taverns. He mentions that state business involving other members of the court and the governor routinely took place in taverns like the Patten in Boston. On July, 15, 1712, Sewall and his wife took a ten-quart jug of madeira to a barn raising.

It is no surprise that with the heavy drinking in New England came problems of public drunkenness. Nevertheless, drunkenness was not tolerated, and there were more arrests for disturbances due to drunkenness than any other crimes. The punishments were occasionally limited to fines, but often involved being placed in the stocks and beaten "severely" or "sharply."

CHILDHOOD GAMES/CHILDHOOD DANGERS

We can confidently assume that the games of children throughout time have a certain universality. There are in most cultures the equivalents of dolls and balls and jump ropes and marbles with which children amuse themselves. Paintings of children show their abiding relationship to animal playmates. The same kind of rhymes, games, and songs that amused children for centuries are handed down in oral tradition. Pat-a-Cake and Ring Around the Rosey were played by young children in the sixteenth century. New England children had much the same amusements.

However, several situations specific to seventeenth-century New England culture gave the amusements of children a special character. First was the basic idea that all people are depraved from conception and are bettered by the religion and education of civilization. Children were viewed not primarily as innocent but as fundamentally bad. Perhaps for this reason, New England children were not encouraged to prolong the time of childhood games, but were as quickly as possible ushered into a somber and useful adulthood. For this and other reasons, most children were put to work at an early age on the farm and in the household. The urgency of bringing children to God also meant that an inordinate amount of time not spent in work was given to Bible study and religious education. These more serious activities shortened the play time of colonial children.

Much of the free play was also regarded as suspicious. As we have seen, Puritans regarded many games as heathenish, immoral, and a waste of time, and such games in the hands of religiously immature children might well be dangerous for them.

The typical New England view of nature also affected child's play. Untamed nature was looked on as heathenish, satanic, and spiritually dark and dangerous. A child who spent too much time playing in nature could come under the influence of Satan. In *The Scarlet Letter*, Nathaniel Hawthorne drew on his intimate knowledge of the culture of his ancestors to characterize the children of the day. While Pearl, the little renegade in the novel, plays by brooks, with flowers, and wild animals, the typical child played at grown-up games—"what passed for play," he writes:

> She saw the children of the settlement, on the grassy margin of the street, or at the domestic thresholds, disporting themselves in such grim fashion as the Puritanic nurture would permit; playing at going to church, perchance; or at scourging Quakers; or taking scalps in a sham-fight with the Indians; or scaring one another with freaks of imitative witchcraft. (64)

The peculiar New England views of the child, nature, and play are apparent in the early days of the Salem witchcraft episode. In Salem a group of young girls spent some of their leisure time playing and dancing in the forest. The girls had also played a game of dropping raw egg into cups of hot water to see if the shapes it made suggested something about their future husbands. To a twenty-first-century mind, this might appear unremarkable, but to Salem Puritans, it was an ominous sign and a deadly combination, as the girls well knew. When confronted, to cover up their frolic in the woods, they lied, attempting successfully to absolve themselves of responsibility by implicating a servant in witchcraft. Thus, the whole sequence of horrendous events that violently divided New England and terrorized a community, killing and imprisoning innocent people and absolutely ruining literally hundreds of lives, was put into motion by the games of children.

MERRYMAKERS AND PURITANS

There was for a brief time in colonial New England a noteworthy exception to the community discouragement of entertainments and levity. This was in the 1626 settlement of Mare Mount or, as the Puritans called it, Merry Mount, in Massachusetts, not far from the Plymouth settlement. Its leader was Thomas Morton, an upper-class Englishman and member of the Anglican church. This group was anathema to everything the Puritans represented, and although the Puritans had some legitimate complaints against the Merry Mounters (who, for example, sold liquor and guns to the natives), it was the Merry Mounters' amusements that made them such an anathema to the Puritans.

Morton describes their revels in his book, *New English Canaan* (1637). They erected what the Puritans called a paganish idol of the Prince of Darkness, a Maypole, and dedicated their revels to the god of love, in anticipating that one day they would attract women to the settlement. Around the Maypole they reveled in all the amusements that the Puritans hated: laughing boisterously, drinking to excess, dancing, enacting scenes from plays, singing love songs, playing drums, and shooting off guns just to make racket.

In 1628 the Puritans arrested Morton and sent him back to England. When he returned in 1630, they burned Merry Mount to the ground and banished him again.

The Puritan stereotype arose largely from their antagonism to traditional art and merriment, however innocent, so it is fitting to end this examination of colonial New England life with a quotation from Nathaniel Hawthorne's story about the Merry Mounters and the Puritans, New Englanders whose radically different approaches to truth and goodness are represented in their amusements. With the license of literary exaggeration and humor, Hawthorne compares the traditional English amusements of the Merry Mounters with those of the Puritans:

When they met in conclave, it was never to keep up the old English mirth, but to hear sermons three hours long, or to proclaim bounties on the heads of wolves and the scalps of Indians. Their festivals were fast-days, and their chief pastime the singing of psalms. Woe to the youth or maiden, who did but dream of a dance! The selectman nodded at the constable; and there sat the light-heeled reprobate in the stocks; or if he danced, it was round the whipping-post, which might be termed the Puritan May-Pole. (Hawthorne, 365)

BIBLIOGRAPHY

Andrews, Charles M. *Colonial Folkways*. New Haven, Conn.: Yale University Press, 1919.

Crawford, Mary. *Social Life in Old New England*. Boston: Little, Brown, 1914.

Dow, George F. *Everyday Life in the Massachusetts Bay Colony*. Boston: Society for the Preservation of New England Antiquities, 1935.

Dulles, F. R. *America Learns to Play*. New York: Appleton-Century, 1940.

Earle, Alice Morse. *Home Life in Colonial Days*. New York: Macmillan 1898.

The General Laws And Liberties of the Massachusetts Colony: Revised & Reprinted ("A Supplement of Law & Orders"). Cambridge Mass.: Samuel Green, 1672.

Hawthorne, Nathaniel. "The May-Pole of Merry Mount." In *Tales and Sketches*. New York: Library of America, 1972.

———. *The Scarlet Letter*. New York: Dover, 1994.

Johnson, Claudia Durst. *American Actress*. Chicago: Nelson-Hall, 1984.

Johnson, Thomas H., ed. *The Poetical Works of Edward Taylor*. Princeton, N.J.: Princeton University Press, 1966.

Krout, J. R. *Annals of American Sport*. New York: United States Publishers, 1929.

Mather, Cotton. *Manuductio Ad Ministerium*. 1726. New York: Columbia University Press, 1938.

Perkins, William. "A Treatise on Man's Imagination." In *The Works of William Perkins*. Nashville: Abington Press, 1970.

Weeden, W. B. *Economic and Social Life*. Boston: Houghton Mifflin, 1890.

Wright, Louis B. *The Cultural Life of the American Colonies*. New York: Harper and Row, 1957.

10

Native Americans

TRIBES AND THEIR ORGANIZATION

In 1620, the native peoples who had inhabited New England for thousands of years numbered about 75,000, far more than the European settlers in the 1620s and early 1630s. They were organized into numerous tribal societies, which were in turn divided into villages. Some of the more prominent New England tribes were the Pawtucket of Cape Ann; the Wampanoag of Cape Cod; the Massachusetts of the Boston area; the Pequot, Paugussetts, and Mohegan of Connecticut; the Narragansett of Rhode Island; the Algonquin of Holyoke, Massachusetts; the Pocumtuck of Deerfield, Massachusetts; the Mohawk on the western frontier of Massachusetts, New Hampshire, and Vermont; and the Penobscot and the Abenaki of Maine.

A leader called a great sachem presided over each of the tribes. The means of choosing the sachem and the extent of his power varied from tribe to tribe. In southern New England, the sachem was a hereditary post passed down through the female line. In northern New England, the post of chief sachem was awarded to the man who demonstrated the greatest ability to lead. In the southern area, the great sachem held absolute power; in the north, his was an advisory post. On rare occasions, the chief sachem was a woman.

A complex organization of legislators and advisers formed the next layer of tribal government. Within the council, which usually included women as well as men, the elderly had great respect and influence. Any decision resulted from careful deliberation by the advisory council and the great sachem of every possible angle of an issue, including the wishes of the entire tribe, and lengthy argument. Depending on the enormity or controversial nature of the matter at hand, consideration might go on for hours or days. Decisions and actions seldom went forward without a unanimous recommendation from the great sachem and the council.

The New England tribes had no body of laws. Instead they were guided by the council, tribal custom, and public opinion. Boundaries between tribes were marked by distinct natural features like lakes, streams, or mountains.

VILLAGE AND FAMILY

Within the tribe were numerous villages over which sub-sachems, sometimes called sagamores, presided. Within the village, the basic unit was the nuclear family made up of husband, wife, and children, who usually lived in a single abode. In some cases, several families would have their own living spaces within a large structure. The assumption is that these constituted extended families, somehow related to one another.

With few exceptions (as in the case of a few powerful chiefs), marriages among native peoples were monogamous. Women were free to bed or marry whom they pleased. Rape was unknown among natives, a phenomenon that amazed European female captives. Intermarriage within the greater family was strongly discouraged. And there is ample evidence, in tributes and the frequent refusal to remarry after a mate died, that the unions of the natives were often strong and affectionate. Divorce, however, was not forbidden or unknown. Usually the dissolution of an unsuccessful union was accommodated when the female left her husband and joined another village. Family planning was enabled with the use of plants consumed to prevent conception or cause abortion.

In most families, women did all the work except hunting and breaking up the fields for the first planting. Women cared for the domesticated animals; grew the crops; put up the houses and cleaned them; gathered wild berries, fruits, and medicines; ground the corn; and otherwise prepared the food. Most of the medical treatments were administered by the women.

The idea that native women were slaves, perpetuated by many Europeans, was universally refuted by white captives.

CONCEPT OF LAND AND OWNERSHIP

The native American concept of ownership is one of the most important ideas to grasp in studying the relationship between Indians and

Native Americans planting and reaping corn. From Ralph Henry Gabriel, *Toilers of Land and Sea* (New Haven: Yale University Press, 1926).

European settlers during the colonial period in New England. In contrast to the English businessmen who controlled New England and whose first consideration was the accumulation of great tracts of land, the natives had little idea of personal ownership of land. Within the tribal boundaries, they hunted, fished, and gathered food, medicines, trees and plants for housing, clay for pots, plants and herbs for medicines, and skins for clothing. But such land was held in common by the community for use; it was not the private property of any one person. The nearest that any individual came to private ownership of land was the family's house and perhaps the patch of land attached to the house used to raise a few vegetables. Even so, within the year, the members of the whole village abandoned their houses and plots to move on to another area within the tribal boundaries, so as not to exhaust resources. Ownership of land was communal and temporary rather than personal and capitalistic.

CONCEPTS OF NATURE

The natives' view of nature, which is also to say their religion, was largely the same throughout New England. They viewed nature as a whole, regarding no one part, including human beings themselves, as greater or more sacred than another. A tree was to be looked on as just as sacred, meaningful, and important as a human being. Some aspect of the Creator, some god, dwelled in birds, bears, wolves, in stones, and flowers. The natives viewed themselves as sharing the earth with other animals, whom they saw as brothers.

Their gods lived in many natural elements—for example, the sea, thunder, wind, and rain. Roger Williams counted thirty-seven such gods sacred to the people of the Narraganset. John Eliot, Puritan missionary to the Indians and translator of Scripture, said with regard to the natives that every creature was a word or sentence in the native's holy scripture called the earth.

For the plan of the creator to operate, some individuals in nature were consumed in order that others could survive. A deer, however holy, might be killed to provide food and clothing for a human being and his family. And this was justified. But the killing was never done without gratitude to the animal, it was never done wantonly, and it was never done to excess. The hunter took only what was needed for survival, just as the wolf or bear killed only what it needed for survival.

This was in marked contrast to the European settlers who peopled New England, whose very motive for settlement was largely to secure as much of the natural resources as possible for export. Within a few decades of the arrival of the English, species of trees and animals that had been in ample supply were thinned to the edge of extinction.

The native peoples of New England were not image worshippers. Their religious life was in evidence in public rites of thanksgiving, prayers for assistance, religious dances, and rites of burial.

DWELLINGS

Dwellings were erected wherever a village decided to plant itself temporarily, usually for about a year or until some situation dictated a move. If firewood in the area ran low, for example, the village might decide that it was time to move to a new setting. Several conditions were considered in locating a village: enough elevation for a good view, protection from the elements, defensibility, availability of firewood, proximity to water for fishing and transportation, a good spring for drinking water, and land for cultivation. The new, temporary village was fortified with logs as a defense against unfriendly tribes and wild animals.

Tribes in different parts of New England built slightly different structures, called wigwams, but all with complex and tight frames. Some of the southern New England tribes preferred square or oblong structures with vertical sides. If several families used a single structure, the dimensions were from sixty to eighty feet long and twenty feet wide. The more usual structures, common in the north, were round, with twenty- to thirty-foot circumferences and domed roofs.

Upon arriving at a home site, women, and in some tribes men, cut saplings for the complex frame of the wigwam. The actual building, which fell to the women alone, began when the large ends of about twenty-four saplings were buried to form a circle. The tops of the saplings were then bent together and tied with cord to form a domed ceiling, leaving a foot and a half smoke hole for the fireplace. The vertical saplings were then braced with four or five layers of horizontal saplings tied into the structure. The point was to create a dwelling solid enough to withstand winter winds.

The outside of the wigwam was covered with tree bark sewed with needles made of bone and thread made of the roots of evergreen trees. The aim was to create a tight edifice that would keep heat in, keep cold and moisture out, and withstand wind. The inside walls might be partially covered with bark and hides, which were frequently decorated. The result was a water proof shelter.

The builder provided one or more doorways, covered with a flap of heavy hides that could allow access to the wigwam without letting snow in. The flap could also be pulled back to allow smoke out of the wigwam. Several flapped windows or doors were provided to assist in ventilation.

Inside, the builder constructed several platforms, each used for a different activity. The family slept on one platform, worked on another, ate on another, and so on. These were covered with seal skins and deerskins and grass mats. Skins were also used as coverings for sleeping. The women stored their supplies in baskets and bags placed underneath the platforms. Such supplies might include bark or wood vessels, gourds, turtleshell or seashell utensils, stone knives, wood or stone mortars and pestles, bone needles, and preserved food. In the center was the fireplace. Sometimes, to keep the wigwam from becoming too smoky, the wigwam was heated not with the fireplace but with rocks that were fired outside the wigwam and brought inside.

DOMESTICATED ANIMALS

The native American often counted his wealth in dogs. These animals, likely descended from wolves, were used for hunting, sometimes for hauling, and sometimes for companionship, especially for the women.

One family had at the least six of these wolflike animals, and wealthier families had many more. Although they treated their dogs with respect, they did not seem to feed them well, often leaving them to find their own food, which was inadequate.

New England natives also kept hawks as pets, primarily to scare the smaller birds away from the inevitable corn patches planted outside each of the wigwams.

CLOTHING

The clothing of the New England natives was made of skins and furs. The men wore loose, armless shirts made of a single bear, deer, or moose hide, with the fur side inside. Smaller hides, usually raccoon, were attached to the shirt at the shoulder to hang over the upper arm. Trousers and moccasins were also constructed of hides.

Women wore dresses or skirts that came to their knees, cloaks, leggings, and moccasins, all made of skins. In southern New England, some of the women made cloth of plant fiber, which they used as summer clothing.

Native children went naked in summer until they reached their teens.

Special costumes were stored and donned for ceremonial dances. Mary Rowlandson, who lived with the Wampanoag for a time as a captive, describes the costumes worn by the dancers on one occasion:

> He was dressed in his Holland [that is, linen] shirt, with great laces sewed at the tail of it, he had his silver Buttons, his white stockings, his garters were hung round with Shillings, and he had girdles of wampom [shell beads] upon his head and shoulders. She had a Kersey [wool] coat, and covered with girdles of wampom from the loins upward: her arms from her elbows to her hands were covered with bracelets; there were handfuls of necklaces about her neck, and several sorts of jewels in her ears. She had fine red stockings and white shoes, her hair powdered and face painted red, that was always before black. (From Rauter, 335)

Men in different tribes had special traditions for dressing their hair. One 1724 account by a Jesuit priest, the Reverend Joseph Lafitau, includes a description of the Iroquois. On one side of the head, the hair was cut short; on the other it was grown to full length and tied into two or three top-knots.

FOOD

From a range of ingredients available to the native New Englanders, they had a varied cuisine. Corn was the mainstay, but during the colonial period they cultivated other vegetables: several kinds of beans, pumpkin,

Jerusalem artichokes, and an array of squashes. From the sea they harvested cod, shad, smelts, swordfish, herring, halibut, bluefish, salmon, oysters, lobsters, crabs, clams, and mussels. They hunted deer, moose, bear, raccoons, rabbits, snakes, turtles, turkeys, and a variety of other birds. The New England natives avoided eating carnivores. From the wild, they harvested wild rice and a variety of fruits and nuts: plums, blackberries, blueberries, cranberries, elderberries, gooseberries, red and black raspberries, strawberries, grapes, watermelon, beechnuts, chestnuts, and hickory nuts.

Foods like wild meats, fish, pumpkin, and corn could be preserved by drying and salting. These provisions, prepared in seasons of plenty, would be stored in baskets and bags and stored in the wigwam or buried underground for use in winter.

Vegetables were usually boiled in a big clay pot over a fire inside or outside the wigwam. Meats were boiled, broiled, or roasted over a fire. Breads and cakes, of which there was a large variety, were baked on the hearth or on fireproof green birch bark or clay containers suspended over open fires. Corn and wild rice were boiled.

From roots and leaves gathered by the women, seasonings and spices were contrived. Salt was not a long-standing element in their diets, but sugar, from the maple tree, was widely used.

The dishes that were original with the New England natives included baked and boiled beans, pumpkin, and squash, succotash, bean soup, corn chowder, hominy, and corn on the cob. They also introduced berry cake and breads, chiefly of corn: cornbread, corn fritters, and jonnycake. But they also had breads made of nuts, squash, and pumpkins.

Mary Rowlandson, taken captive by the Indians in 1676 during one of the prolonged conflicts, speaks of the natives eating horse meat and wheat pancakes fried in bear grease, which she pronounced delicious. She was also given a soup thickened with meal made from bark and cooked with peas and ground nuts.

TOBACCO

Every garden outside a wigwam also included tobacco. The plant and the smoke from the tobacco plant were considered sacred. It seems to have been used sparingly, largely in pipes during social gatherings, for ceremonial purposes, often to seal agreements.

HEALTH

Before the arrival of the Europeans, the natives were a healthy people. Their diets and their physical activities served to keep them strong. They suffered from few diseases, had good teeth, healthy childbearing, a low death rate, few deformities, and an effective natural medical system. They often lived to be sixty, many to eighty, and some to one hundred years old. The ailments with which they did have to contend included arthritis, rheumatism, neuralgia, chills, fever and pleurisy, infections from injuries and wounds, eye trouble (probably caused by smoke-filled wigwams), and ear complaints. However, until the Europeans arrived, the devastating diseases were unknown: smallpox, malaria, typhus, tuberculosis, bubonic plague, diphtheria, measles, and probably syphilis.

While the men, as witch doctors, tended to psychological and spiritual changes and ailments, women ministered to the body with natural medicines, salves, spas, and casts for broken bones. Scholars have identified 450 plant remedies the women administered for various ailments. They also had effective ways to treat frozen limbs, for example, and a process using bark and cement for setting broken bones.

Like the plains Indians, the New England natives also used the sweat bath, akin to a sauna, as a cleanser of body and soul. This structure, tall enough to stand in, was built of stones and straw near some body of water. A stone floor was heated thoroughly by a fire before throwing water on it to make steam. Sometimes a whole family would remain in the sweat bath, singing and chatting for about an hour, then exit to submerge themselves in the nearby pond or stream before applying oil to their bodies.

Another tradition was the powwow, intended as a psychological defense against various disorders. The Europeans found the powwow, which involved dancing, chanting, and magic, to be very threatening.

Unlike European women, the deaths of women in childbirth were minimal in the native population. Labor and childbirth were accomplished with little discomfort or interruption in work. Babies were nourished with breast milk or a concoction made of pulverized nuts.

With the arrival of the Europeans, the good health of the natives came to an end because the newcomers brought all their diseases with them. The natives, having no physiological defense against these intrusive germs and viruses, began dying at alarming rates.

AMUSEMENTS

In the tribal gatherings at seaside during the summer and fall, the native Americans typically amused themselves with a variety of games—foot races, recreational swimming, games of marksmanship, and ball games similar to lacrosse.

Native peoples in New England also enjoyed games of chance and had several games in which stones were cast like dice. Children had their own games and toys like balls and tops to be spun. In the calm at the end of any vigorous day, both adults and children enjoyed singing and story telling to amuse themselves.

A TYPICAL DAY

A typical winter day began with the family's need for fire, food, and water. All three might be provided by the older children of the family, one of whom fetched firewood, one water from the village spring, and a third who killed some small game like a rabbit or squirrels for the family breakfast.

The mother's day began as she made the all-important fire, fed the baby, who was placed in a cradle board hanging on the wall, and cooked the morning meal, usually the most important of the day. For this meal, she would begin by boiling water into which were placed the game she had skinned and dressed, and the nuts, dried squash, or pumpkin from her storage baskets and bags. The family ate the morning soup using clam shells as scoops. Portions of this soup were available throughout the day as they felt hungry.

The rest of the woman's work for the day involved securing the necessary corn from an underground storage area, where it had been placed in the summer and fall, and grinding it for mush or bread. With her store of dried blueberries and the cornmeal she had ground, she would make small cakes on the hearth in the center of the house. Having finished the day's food preparation, she might turn her hand to making rope for fishing nets.

The father and older sons might do some ice fishing or go through the complicated, arduous process of making wooden bowls. A block of wood was charred and scraped, charred and scraped, until the bowl reached the desired shape. The laborious process usually took more than one day. When it was finished, it was smoothed with sand and then polished with bear fat.

At the end of the day, several men and women of the village got together in one wigwam to visit, smoke, and entertain themselves with stories. Finally each family returned to its own wigwam, banked the fires, and turned in under skins for a night's sleep.

In fair weather, the natives participated in many more outdoor activities. The men and boys did more hunting and fishing from canoes, the girls gathered berries, and the women planted or hoed vegetables, collected herbs, fruits, and nuts, collected clay and molded it into pots, strengthening and decorating them with dried sea shells, then drying them, and later baking them.

INTERTRIBAL RELATIONSHIPS

Like their fellow human beings in Europe and Africa and other areas of the world, the native tribes of New England had both harmonious and discordant relationships with their neighbors. Many tribes were on friendly terms, trading, not for necessities, but for decorative elements like beads and shells, copper, and tobacco pipes. Different tribes gathered to trade, socialize, and plan cooperative efforts. For example, some tribes joined to form a united front to discourage hostile actions from unfriendly peoples.

Before the arrival of the Europeans, most New England tribes were not warlike peoples, and hostilities were minimal, but they were not free of territorial disputes and other conflicts. Certain tribes were more aggressive than others and were not above raids on their neighbors' provisions or attempts at appropriating the territory of other tribes. The Pequot and Abenaki tribes, for instance, took advantage of weakened tribes and stole their crops. Sometimes defensive stances were taken against other tribes, especially those with different languages, from fear. Smaller, unarmed natives naturally feared the Iroquois, for example, who were a large and strong tribe, with a different language, who had invaded New England and secured firearms from the Dutch. When armed conflicts did occur, the fighting and torture of captives was brutal. The victors in any sustained conflict slaughtered their male enemies and took the women and children of their enemies into their own tribes. Scalping by native peoples is not mentioned until 1670, after it had been introduced to Indian culture by the Europeans. Thereafter, natives friendly to Europeans were encouraged to bring the settlers scalps of slain enemies as proof of loyalty, for which they were then rewarded.

With the advent of the Europeans, native people, for most of whom war was not a way of life, found themselves in continual armed conflict as tribes were pitted against tribes and enraged by the settlers in the disruption caused by European settlement.

RELATIONSHIPS WITH THE EUROPEANS

Initial Contact

Native peoples like the Massachusetts tribes enthusiastically welcomed European settlers to their shores up to the third decade of the seventeenth century. Their motives were mixed. Many thought the armed Europeans would protect them from their more powerful native enemies. They also welcomed the trade with Europeans in skins and hides, receiving wampum in the form of shells and beads in exchange. Natives generously shared with the settlers their belongings, supplies, food, and the skills necessary for survival in the New World. What the settlers gave them in exchange was destined to destroy them: disease, firearms, whiskey, a brutal religion totally at odds with nature, and a demand for material goods that would rob them of their independence.

Within ten years of the arrival of Winthrop and his party, the natives' welcome of the settlers had worn out. The settlers had appeared on the scene with two objectives in mind with regard to the Indians: secure their land and convert them to Christianity. The natives soon saw trade as the settlers' means of exploitation. Sachems began to resent missionaries as interlopers interested only in preparing the way for land grabs. The English made their own laws on what for centuries had been native soil and held natives accountable to English rules. Moreover, any breach of English law resulted in a native's being subjected to a public humiliation unknown in his or her own culture. Two examples from *Records of the Governor and Company of the Massachusetts Bay* on July 30, 1640, give some idea of this humiliation: "Two Indian women were adjudged to be whipped for their insolent carriage and abusing Mrs. Weld," and "Hope, the Indian, was censured for her running away, and other misdemeanors, to be whipped here and at Marblehead" (Shurtleff, vol. 1: 297, 298).

Relations were scarcely improved by the Puritan attitude toward the natives. To the European mind, the natives were subfiends in the service of the devil whose domain included any untamed land in the New World.

Resentment naturally mounted. But it was the differing views of land and the English determination to acquire New World land that caused open warfare to erupt.

Conflict with Settlers

It is within the context of the native view that land was to be held in common that one must understand the business arrangements between European settlers and the natives. Often the natives had no understanding of what it meant to sell land to the settlers. And according to Roger Williams, a Puritan minister in sympathy with the Indians, Europeans used the natives' naiveté in this regard to acquire huge tracts of land without fully explaining the exclusive rights they intended securing and without fair and proper payment. At first, the natives blithely "sold" tribal lands in small and large tracts, believing that "ownership" would not exclude them from using the land. They realized only later that what the Europeans were doing was rapidly acquiring exclusive private use of virtually all the tribal lands in New England and subjecting natives on these lands to the laws of the Massachusetts Bay Colony.

One instance that reveals the conflict that arose because of the differing views of land ownership centered on the area of Dedham, Massachusetts, which European capitalists had acquired from the natives. The owners of the land actually lived hundreds of miles away—not on the land they owned in Dedham. Seeing no activity on the land, the natives believed they were free to hunt, trap, fish, build houses, and cultivate gardens there. This attitude was not far removed from that of the philosopher John Locke, who so strongly influenced the thinking of the fathers of the American Revolution. He wrote that one could own the land only with which one mixed one's labor and could actually use. But the colonists were amassing great estates on which they might eventually establish business enterprises, and they strongly objected to the presence of the natives on land that they now owned. Similar quarrels began to occur throughout the colonies, leading to armed hostilities.

There were many conflicts between settlers and natives throughout the colonial period. One of the first major conflicts occurred in 1637. Word reached Boston in July that an English trader named John Oldham had been killed by Pequot Indians. The New England colonies raised a militia and waged war against the Pequot for a solid year. On June 5, 1637, a militia destroyed a large Pequot village at Stonington, Connecticut, and a little over a month later a military force made up of soldiers from three New England colonies tracked down the survivors of the Stonington village at a place near New Haven and slaughtered all they could find. Other Pequot men and boys who were eventually captured were sold into slavery in the West Indies. The women and girls became slaves to white settlers in New England. With their numbers decimated, their main villages burned, their stored food and supplies stolen, the few survivors in this tribe left for the west. This was the end of the entire tribe's presence in New England.

Although for forty years after this incident, there was no open warfare between settlers and natives, relations between them were hardly cordial. Individuals from both camps were guilty of murders and thefts, and the English continued to gobble up land. Land disputes continued, the one at Dedham in 1668 and 1669 being one of the most prominent. There were also quarrels with the Narraganset in Rhode Island where Massachusetts Bay businessmen, under the Atherton Company, began commandeering immense amounts of Indian land. In this case, the European settlers of Rhode Island sided with the natives against the settlers of Massachusetts Bay and Connecticut. After the embittered Narragansett caused property damage near some Connecticut plantations, the New England Confederation demanded that the natives either pay a fine, which was too large for them to meet, or forfeit all their lands to the business corporation. Immediate disaster was averted when the king of England, Charles II, intervened at Rhode Island's request to side with the Narraganset and voided the claims of the Atherton Company. Still, the company tried to ignore the king's dictate and continued appropriating Narraganset land.

Throughout the 1660s and 1670s, the General Courts of the Massachusetts Bay or Plymouth Colony made a habit of hauling tribal sachems before them to quiz them on rumors of conspiracies or allegiances with tribes or nationals that the bay considered unfriendly. Once these hearings were over, the court would present the defendant with a bill for court costs, as it did the Wampanoag chief, King Philip, in 1667. The reason for the disintegration of relations and the buildup of hostilities was simple: the colonists planned on and were determined to secure key

Indian land as part of the expansion into the Connecticut Valley, and the Indians were determined that this would not happen.

King Philip had historically been friendly with the settlers, but suspicions mounted, rumors raged on, and the English demanded that various tribes surrender their weapons. When the English suspected that the natives had not surrendered their weapons, they prepared for war in 1671, finally forcing the natives to pay £100 worth of goods to the colony, to recognize English law, and to accede to any colonies' decisions regarding the disposal of Indian land.

For four years, King Philip and other sachems inwardly seethed over the humiliation. Finally in June 1675, after Plymouth Colony's execution of three of King Philip's men for the murder of an informant, the Indian chief began his raids on settlements in a year-long war in which many native tribes sided with the settlers. Some fifty towns along the frontier were burned. By 1676, the English had lost about 2,000 people, and the natives had lost about 4,000 in battle.

With the decisive defeat of King Philip's forces in 1676 (King Philip himself was killed, drawn and quartered, and his head brought to Boston for display) came the virtual end of the native tribes in New England. There was no longer a question of negotiating for land or paying the usual £25 for an estate. All Indian land was now up for confiscation as the settlers dictated the terms for takeovers and appropriated Indian land as the spoils of war. Prisoners of war were executed by the scores, most without trial and many of whom had been friendly to the settlers. Immediately, however, New England businessmen realized the cash value of the prisoners, so many more were sold into slavery and shipped to the West Indies, Spain, and the Mediterranean. Those deemed less dangerous became bound servants in the colonies to alleviate the perpetual labor shortage. Natives, who fifty years earlier had called the whole New England area their home, to be held in common with their brothers, were restricted to reservations. The more fortunate of them were allowed to be tenant farmers or to work as hired hands. In the 1620s, they had numbered around 75,000 people. Their people had lived in New England for thousands of years. By the 1680s, decimated by disease, alcohol, and wars with the settlers, their numbers had dropped to 20,000, only half the number of the new European settlers.

One further notorious clash between native Americans and settlers in the colonial period occurred on February 29, 1704, during a time when many tribes had sided with the French in the fight between French and English over the domination of northern New England. A company of 28 Frenchmen and 200 native Americans launched an attack on Deerfield, Massachusetts, a town of three hundred residents, twenty miles south of what is now Vermont. Forty-eight Deerfield residents were killed, and 111 were taken hostage.

BIBLIOGRAPHY

Axtell, James T. *The Invasion Within*. New York: Oxford University Press, 1985.

Bowden, Henry W. *American Indians and Christian Missions*. Chicago: University of Chicago Press, 1981.

Bragdon, Kathleen J. *Native People of Southern New England*. Norman: University of Oklahoma Press, 1996.

Carpenter, Delores Bird. *Early Encounters—Native Americans and Europeans in New England*. East Lansing: Michigan State University Press, 1994.

Jennings, Francis. *The Invasion of America*. Chapel Hill: University of North Carolina Press, 1975.

Lauber, Almon Wheeler. *Indian Slavery in Colonial Times*. New York: Columbia University Press, 1913.

Lauter, Paul, ed. *The Heath Anthology of American Literature*. Lexington, Mass.: D. C. Heath, 1990.

Leach, Douglas Edward. *Flintlock and Tomahawk*. New York. Macmillan, 1958.

Nash, Gary B. *Red, White, and Black: The Peoples of Early America*. Englewood Cliffs, N.J.: Prentice Hall, 1982.

Russell, Howard S. *Indian New England: Before the Mayflower*. Hanover, N.H.: University Press of New England, 1980.

Rutman, Darrett B. *Winthrop's Boston: Portrait of a Puritan Town, 1630–1649*. Chapel Hill: University of North Carolina Press, 1965.

Salisbury, Neal. "'I Loved the Place of My Dwelling.'" In *Inequality in Early America*, eds. Carla Gardina Pestana and Sharon V. Salinger, 111–133. Hanover, N.H.: University Press of New England, 1999.

Shurtleff, N.B., ed. *Records of the Governor and Company of the Massachusetts Bay*. 6 vols. Boston: W. White, 1853–1854.

11

Africans

Very few black people made their homes in New England during the colonial period. At the turn of the eighteenth century, there were probably no more than 1,000 living in all of New England and only 550 in Massachusetts. The vast majority of these 1,000 were slaves, first brought from the West Indies and later from Africa. The exact year in which slaves first lived in New England is a matter of debate. There is some speculation that a man named Samuel Maverick, who built a house in the Boston area in 1629, before the arrival of the Winthrop settlers, brought two or three slaves from the West Indies with him. The first recorded instance of the presence of slaves in New England, found in Governor John Winthrop's journal of December 12, 1638, makes mention of a Captain William Pierce, who took Pequot Indians as slaves after the settlers' decimation of their villages in Connecticut. Pierce, deciding that the Pequot were too dangerous to use as slaves in New England, transported them to the West Indies to sell in exchange for salt, cotton, tobacco, and black slaves. Other early references to slaves include a 1639 record of a slave's being killed by his master in Connecticut, references in 1644 to black workers in Connecticut, a 1645 account of a sea captain's being ordered to return to Africa a black man who had been stolen, and a 1652 attempt by Rhode Island to limit slavery to ten years.

The term *slave* was rarely used, however. Owners preferred the less onerous term *servant* or the euphemistic *perpetual servant*.

THE SLAVE TRADE IN COLONIAL NEW ENGLAND

New England was ill suited agriculturally and economically to the kind of work done by slaves that caused their proliferation in the South. Nevertheless, colonial New England played a highly significant and notorious role in the expansion of slavery in the New World. Although there were comparatively few working slaves in New England, New England outlawed slavery in the eighteenth century, and although many New England voices were raised in the nineteenth century against the institution of slavery, it was New England that introduced and expanded the trade in slaves during the colonial period.

The slave trade began with the Salem-based ship *Desire* in the 1640s. By 1644, New Englanders were bringing in slaves from both the West Indies and Africa. In 1644, three vessels departed New England for Africa to bring back gold dust and slaves, the latter of which were brought to the West Indies and traded for wine, salt, sugar, molasses, and tobacco. The public records show ship after ship departing from New England ports for Africa to secure African slaves, but chiefly to take them to the West Indies, where they were traded for goods. Boston was the chief port for the slave trade.

In the later eighteenth century, the old Dutch and English monopolies against which the New Englanders had to compete withdrew from the business, and New England was left as the chief slave trading area of the Western world, supplying growers of rice and cotton in the American South with slaves and providing South America with 4,800 African slaves a year.

An infamous triangle of trade developed. Slave traders took New World beans, corn, lumber, fish, and other goods to the West Indies in exchange for rum. From the West Indies, they sailed to Africa, where they exchanged the rum for slaves, returning to the West Indies with the slaves and picking up rum, sugar, and molasses to bring back to New England. The healthiest, strongest slaves were always sold in the West Indies to the sugar planters. The comparatively few slaves kept in New England were, on the whole, the weakest physically. An acute shortage of labor in the eighteenth century prompted the importation of even greater numbers of slaves. Traders bought slaves for £4 and £5 in Africa and sold them in the West Indies for from £30 to £80. By the time of the American Revolution, slave trading was a cornerstone of the New England economy.

Slaves were transported on New England ships between the decks in an area that was three feet, ten inches high. In the eighteenth century, this space was lowered to three feet, three inches high. Ten to thirteen inches of surface was allowed per slave. During the long voyage, no adult slave could stand up. The crowding was such that they had to lie spoon fashion for most voyages.

Slave traders in colonial New England were not despised, lower-class outsiders, ostracized by religious and polite society. On the contrary, they occupied the highest places in colonial New England society, where they assumed political, economic, and social positions of leadership. Four of the most prominent were judges, and several were colonial governors and lieutenant governors. John Hancock, famous signer of the Declaration of Independence, was a partner of James Rowe, a slave trader. Peter Fanueil, known as the wealthy founder of Fanueil Hall in Boston, was a slave trader. The founders of Brown University in Rhode Island made their fortunes as slave traders. Two slave traders, John Brown of Providence, Rhode Island, and James DeWolfe of Bristol, Rhode Island, were elected to Congress.

BLACK SLAVERY IN COLONIAL NEW ENGLAND

The Body of Liberties of 1641, a poorly written, ambiguous law, legalized slavery in New England:

> It is Ordered by this Court and the Authority thereof; That there shall never be any Bondslavery, Villenage or Captivity amongst us, unless it be lawful Captives taken in just Wars, as willingly sell themselves or are sold to us, and such shall have the liberties and Christian usage which the Law of God established in Israel concerning such persons doth morally require; Provided this exempts none from servitude, who shall be judged thereto by Authority. (*General Laws And Liberties*, 10)

Some scholars have interpreted this passage as proving that slavery was not legal in New England, but court records and newspaper advertisements prove that despite the ambiguity in the law, slavery was very much legal in Massachusetts, as it was in other New England communities. In 1670 the law was amended to clarify an ambiguity: it specified that the children of slaves were to continue in slavery.

Slavery was justified on the economic grounds that slave trading was good for the economy and that slave holding assisted the industry and farming of New England during labor shortages. In 1645 Emanuel Downing wrote to his brother-in-law, John Winthrop, that slavery was good for New England because, for the cost of maintaining one white servant, one could keep twenty black slaves. Slavery was also justified on religious grounds. Cotton Mather believed that slavery brought black Africans out of darkness into the godly company of the chosen people.

Pious New England clergymen were not above owning slaves. The Reverend Ezra Stiles, for example, sent a barrel of whiskey to Africa as payment for a slave. And in 1726, the Reverend Devotion's congregation gave him £20 toward the purchase of a slave. Among the 162 leading slave-holding families in colonial New England were the Reverend Nathaniel Chauncey, the Reverend Jonathan Todd, the Reverend Joseph Elliot, the Reverend Jonathan Edwards, the Reverend Jared Elliott, the Reverend Ezra Stiles, the Reverend William Worthington, the Reverend Edward Holyoke, the Reverend John Oxenbridge, the Reverend Joseph Greene, the Reverend Nathan Webb, the Reverend James McSparran, and the Reverend Samuel Hopkins.

At the same time, there were Puritans who disapproved of slavery. Governor John Winthrop held no black slaves in his household, and John Adams strongly disapproved of slavery. An important document on the question was Judge Samuel Sewall's "The Selling of Joseph," published in Boston by Bartholomew Green and John Allen on June 24, 1700. Sewall contradicts the biblical arguments in favor of slavery, ending by contending that blacks and whites have a common father in Adam and that blacks should be treated by whites as brothers, not as slaves. In "The Selling of Joseph," Sewall wrote:

> *Forasmuch* as Liberty *is in real value next unto Life: None ought to part with themselves, or deprive others of it, but upon most mature Consideration.*
>
> The Numerousness of Slaves at this day in the Province, and the Uneasiness of them under their Slavery, hath put many upon thinking whether the Foundation of it be firmly and well laid; so as to sustain the Vast Weight that is built upon it. It is most certain that all men, as they are the Sons of *Adam*, are Coheirs; and have equal Right unto Liberty, and all other outward Comforts of Life. *God hath given the Earth* [with all its Commodities] *unto the Sons of Adam, Psal 115.16. And hath made of One Blood, all nations of Men for to dwell on all the face of the Earth, and hath determined the Times before appointed, and the bounds of their habitation. That they should seek the Lord. . . .* So that originally and naturally, there is no such thing as Slavery. *Joseph* was no more a Slave to his Brethren, than they were to him: and they had no more Authority to *Sell* him, than they had to *Slay* him. . . . And seeing GOD hath said, *He that Stealeth a Man and Selleth him, or if he be found in his hand, he shall surely be put to Death.* Exod. 21.16. This Law being of Everlasting Equity, wherein Man Stealing is ranked amongst the most atrocious of Capital Crimes: What louder Cry can there be made of that Celebrated Warning. (1–3)

By 1715, the time of the first reliable census by race, there were 158,000 whites living in New England and 4,150 blacks. By 1776, the number of blacks had increased to 16,034. Most of the black slaves in New England were concentrated in the hands of very few families. Less than one-eighth of New England families owned slaves.

THE DAILY LIVES OF BLACK SLAVES

Although Africans were considered to be barbarians, slaves were fully integrated into the households of the masters for whom they worked, creating a situation that fell somewhere between slavery and indentured servanthood, their daily lives differing little from that of their masters in terms of the work they performed and their food, shelter, and clothing. They also had access to New England courts.

Work

Black slaves in New England met a general need across the labor market in colonial times. Whereas in the South, most slaves who worked outside the house were engaged in the farming of cotton, rice, and tobacco, slaves in New England did almost every kind of work that white workers did. Each slave performed whatever work his or her master performed, generally working alongside the master. If the master were a shoemaker, his slave was also a shoemaker. On farms, slaves had to have a greater degree of skill and versatility than they had in the South. For example, they worked a variety of crops, including vegetable gardens, forage crops, as well as flax and hemp. They took care of livestock, did farm repairs, and shoed horses. Rarely were there more than one or two slaves working on a single New England farm. The exception was Rhode Island, where the greater acreage per farm was worked by from five to forty slaves.

Travelers to New England in the second half of the seventeenth century reported that almost every household in Boston seemed to have a black servant, which inevitably meant a slave. Women assigned to the house cleaned, spun and wove, did laundry, cooked, nursed the sick, and helped care for children. Men worked in wealthier urban households as coachmen, attendants, butlers, and valets. When wealthy men went outside the village, slaves traveled on horseback before them to clear the path and warn of any untoward situations.

Slaves worked in every conceivable industry in New England: shipbuilding, lumbering, forging iron, blacksmithing, tanning, printing, carpentry, barrel making, innkeeping, and distilling. They also worked as artisans for tailors, barbers, bakers, sawyers, and anchor and rope makers. Usually the master and his one slave worked side by side. In urban areas especially, black slaves had the responsibility of manager—of warehouses, stores and shops, even ships. Slaves were very much in evidence in seagoing trades, where they worked at fishing, whaling, trading, and even privateering. Often black slaves were impressed, that is, forced on board ships as sailors, and many were encouraged to run away from slavery by going to sea. It has been estimated that in the eighteenth century, after New England had developed whaling as a major industry, half of many of the crews were black slaves.

A few slaves in New England also entered professions in colonial days, having been apprenticed to physicians and doctors, ministers, and lawyers.

Slaves did much menial labor in urban areas, working as helpers, porters, errand carriers, teamsters, and ditch diggers. Until the end of the seventeenth century they were conscripted into the military, being trained and forced to fight in wars with the Indians. At the end of the century, however, legislatures decided it was too dangerous to place arms in the hands of slaves and forbade them from serving in the peacetime militia.

Family Life

In some ways, the family life of the black slave in colonial New England was very different from what he or she would face in the South. In the South, marriage between slaves was not legalized or formalized, but New Englanders encouraged marriage between slaves. Couples got acquainted at church meetings, socials like house raisings, and holidays celebrated on the village common. Courtship was convenient for the couple who were both owned by the same master, for they could visit with each other whenever there was a lull in work. But with so few slaves being employed on a single farm, the likelihood of this happening was remote. If a couple living at different locations fell in love, the man had to obtain a pass to pay court to the woman at her master's house.

Unlike laws in the South, New Englanders believed in the sanctity of marriage for both white and black people, so slaves were encouraged to marry rather than being forbidden to marry. Before the wedding occurred, the masters of both man and woman had to agree to the union and also to arrive at a prenuptial agreement. How was the male slave to be given enough time off to work in support of a family, for instance? Would either of the masters agree to contribute to the support of the couple? To which of the masters would any children belong? Who would support the children? After these matters were settled, banns were published, a ceremony was performed—usually in the living room of one of the masters—followed by a wedding feast.

Any children of the couple legally belonged to the mother's master. However, unlike the situation in the South, where so many hands were required in farming large acreage, children were often considered to be burdensome to the master, who was only too eager to have someone else assume responsibility for them.

Black slaves frequently married Indian slaves, free Indians, or free blacks. In such cases, the fate of the children depended on the mother's situation. If she were the free person in the union, the children would be free. If she were the slave, her children would be slaves.

New Englanders were eager to support the institution of marriage in the beginning of a union, but that support was often dissipated when it threatened the convenience of the master. As in the South, slave families were often broken up when mother or father was sold to someone who lived far away. As in the South, the death of an owner often meant that his estate, including his slaves, were divided up or sold off indiscriminately. Newspaper advertisements reveal that mother and children were separated at the whim of the owner. In some cases, infants considered burdensome were given away, occasionally even before they were born. The Boston newspapers carried the ads—for example "A fine Negro child of a good healthy breed to be given away—inquire of the printer" (from the *Boston Weekly News Letter* of June 26, 1760), and "a fine healthy female child to be given away." (from the *Boston Gazette or Weekly Advertiser*, June 25, 1754).

The darkest sides of slavery in New England, as in the South, included the sexual abuse of slave women by their masters.

Other Aspects of Daily Life

Other aspects of the colonial New England slave's life, especially that relating to housing and food, varied little from that of the white master's family. Slaves were fed very well in New England. They not only ate the same food provided for the master's table, in most cases, they ate at the same table as the master, a custom so widespread as to cause comment on the part of travelers to New England who were unused to seeing servants eating with their masters.

The quarters of the slaves were also decent on the whole. In most instances, in both rural and urban areas, slaves lived in the houses with the master's family and their accommodations were little different in quality. Some slave families occupied the entire second floor of the house. In smaller houses, they could be found sleeping in the same room with their master and his family. Occasionally in Rhode Island and parts of Connecticut, where the acreage was larger and the slaves more numerous, they occupied separate cabins, as they did in the South.

The health of slaves was not as good as that of whites. They seemed to be especially subject to death from smallpox, measles, respiratory disorders, rheumatism, and mumps. Many were injured at their work, as was true of white workers, as well, but in New England records we do not find the evidence of disfiguring beatings and mutilation that were described in wanted posters for runaways in the South, though beatings were certainly administered to both black and white servants alike.

Sick slaves were attended by the same physician who treated the master's family, and the children of slaves were delivered by white midwives.

New Englanders did not forbid or limit the education of their slaves as southerners did. Rather, kind masters and concerned clergymen encouraged their slaves to become literate, well read, and well trained. For many slaves, who took on the same work performed by their masters, education and training were necessary for them to do their jobs. Moreover, they were often offered an elementary education in language and mathematics, sometimes followed by industrial training. One of the most striking examples is Phillis Wheatley, an African slave and one of the first poets of colonial New England, who was given a classical education by her owners.

The amusements of black slaves were largely the same as those enjoyed by whites: quilting bees, barn and house raisings, and fairs on the village common. In addition, black slaves loved meeting together to dance, play violin music, and share stories of Africa.

There was one institution of amusement that was peculiar to black people alone in colonial New England. This was a special election day, paralleling the Puritan election day, when a black governor was elected by free blacks and slaves. Masters generally gave their slaves and servants holidays at this time of year so they could fully participate in the celebration, and owners even contributed monetarily to the campaign of those vying for governor and to see that their own slaves were handsomely attired and had the use of horses and carriages for the event. Voting usually took place around ten o'clock on the morning of the election, after which votes were counted to determine the winner, who assumed a position of some importance as a leader and figurehead of the African community. The declaration of the winner was followed by an elaborate inauguration ceremony with extensive feasting and games.

There were several legal impediments and limitations on slaves' social lives. Because of the fear of a slave insurrection, slaves were eventually barred from participating in Artillery Day and Gun Powder Day, with their full array of guns and ammunition. Furthermore, the fear of conspiracy led the legislature to forbid slaves from visiting in the houses of free blacks.

Religion

Some members of the religious community, Cotton Mather among them, strongly believed that it was the duty of Christians to convert the slaves to Christianity, even though there was little evidence that conversion would cause the community to change its view of them as barbarians. Slaves were taught to accept their lowly position in life; it was not their masters who had enslaved them, they were told, but God himself. A few argued that Christianizing the slaves would make them more manageable and submissive because doctrine would teach them that obedience to a master was equivalent to obedience to the Christian God.

But other members of the community strongly objected to conversion of slaves on several grounds, all of them economic. Any slave converted to Christianity would be forced to attend church on the Sabbath, and his or her work would be lost to the master at such time. Furthermore, many whites believed that Christianity gave black slaves a false sense of equality, which made them less malleable and therefore less marketable. Some worried that allowing slaves to join the church might give them grounds to argue for suffrage. But the argument that bothered most religious New Englanders was this: the biblical warning that no Christian could hold another Christian in bondage. Thus, to convert a slave to Christianity and retain him or her as a slave was a violation of God's Word. To get around this impediment, apologists for slavery began arguing more heavily from a position based on race: they might be Christian, but they are still black and therefore sons of Ham and meant to be enslaved.

Phillis Wheatley, born in Africa in 1753 and brought to the New World as a slave in about 1760, was a member of the second church established in Boston. In one of her poems, "On Being Brought from Africa to America," written in 1773, she defies those in her community who argue that it is useless to convert black people because they are sons of Cain or Ham in the Bible and meant by God to be damned:

> 'Twas mercy brought me from my *Pagan* land,
> Taught my benighted soul to understand
> That there's a God, that there's a *Savior* too:
> Once I redemption neither sought nor knew.
> Some view our sable race with scornful eye,
> "Their colour is a diabolic die."
> Remember, *Christians, Negros*, black as *Cain*,
> May be refin'd, and join th' angelic train. (Fron Lauter, 718)

By 1776, at the end of the colonial period, most New England black slaves were not converted to Christianity.

FREE BLACKS

The first mention of free black people in New England occurred in 1646 when New Haven's governor, Theophilis Eaton, freed his two slaves and built them a house. But no accurate record of the actual numbers of free blacks exists. Subsequent to 1646, there were increasing numbers of free blacks in New England. Several situations added to this population. Some masters made agreements with prospective workers from the first to take them on as indentured servants, with given, limited terms, after which they would be free. In some cases, masters chose to free their slaves after a period of service, even without the initial agreement. And many masters freed their slaves in their wills. Until 1670, when the law was clarified, the courts found that children of slaves were free. Some slaves successfully petitioned the courts for their freedom, and some were able to purchase their own freedom.

Free blacks often found their economic situation to be harder than that of the slaves, for slaves were able to perform any work that their masters performed. But the freed black did not have the sponsorship of any white person and was competing for work with white laborers, who often attempted to bar blacks from certain trades. Most free blacks were limited to domestic service. Colonial records do show that some were able to establish their own businesses as basket makers, shoemakers, barbers, musicians, music teachers, cooks, bakers, grocers, and caterers. Rarely did they expand beyond a small subsistence-level business, however, because they were unable to get credit for expansion.

Despite their legal status, free blacks were considered the social inferiors of whites and basically lived with most of the same limitations and discrimination that burdened slaves.

LEGAL RESTRICTIONS PLACED ON FREED AND ENSLAVED BLACKS

The following restrictions on the social and economic life of black people were legally in place in one or more, but not all, New England communities:

- They were not allowed to leave their villages without a pass.
- They were not allowed to ride ferries.
- They were not allowed to be on the streets after 9 P.M.
- They were not allowed to buy merchandise for themselves, only through white men.
- They were not allowed to be on the streets during church.
- They could not hold social gatherings out of doors.
- They were forbidden from carrying sticks or canes unless they were physically disabled.
- They could not keep domestic livestock.
- Free blacks were not allowed to entertain black or mulatto slaves or natives in their houses.
- They could not own certain kinds of property.
- They could not own swine.
- They could not serve on juries.
- They were not considered full citizens.
- They were taxed but could not vote.
- They were excluded from the peacetime militia yet subject to the draft in time of war.
- They were socially ostracized and segregated in harborside ghettos.
- In New London, Connecticut, free blacks were forbidden to own any property at all and forbidden to reside in the community.
- Their children were forbidden from attending public schools.

THE END OF SLAVERY

The black people, both free and slave, in New England, were, as Lorenzo Johnson Greene writes in *The Negro in Colonial New England*, little more than chattel. But special conditions served to modify their situation by the time of the American Revolution. The topography, climate, and soil made slavery an impractical arrangement on small New England farms, very unlike the vast spreads of single, money crops on southern plantations where slavery flourished. Moreover, the fervor of New England Puritans and other religious dissidents placed troubling doubts and a decided distaste for slavery in the minds of the majority of the New England population, despite the unfettered exploitation of a comparatively few wealthy merchants and land holders. Because of this, the lot of the New England slave was never as hopeless or hard as it was in the South, and by 1790, slavery had been outlawed in all of New England.

BIBLIOGRAPHY

Fogel, Robert W. *Without Consent or Contract*. New York: Norton, 1989.

Franklin, John Hope. *From Slavery to Freedom*. New York: McGraw-Hill, 1994.

The General Laws And Liberties of the Massachusetts Colony: Revised Reprinted. Cambridge, Mass.: Samuel Green, 1672.

Genovese, Eugene. *Roll, Jordan, Roll: The World the Slaves Made*. New York: Pantheon Books, 1974.

Greene, Lorenzo Johnston. *The Negro in Colonial New England*. 1942. Rpt. New York: Atheneum, 1968.

Jernigan, Marcus W. *Laboring and Dependent Classes in Colonial America, 1607–1783*. Chicago: University of Chicago Press, 1931.

Jordan, Winthrop D. *White Man's Burden*. New York: Oxford University Press, 1974.

Lauter, Paul, ed. *The Heath Authology of American Literature*. Lexington, Mass.: D. C. Heath, 1990.

Leach, Douglas Edward. *Flintlock and Tomahawk*. New York: Macmillan, 1998.

Moore, George H. *Additional Note on Negro Slavery in Massachusetts*. New York: n.p., 1866.

Nash, Gary B. *Red, White, and Black: The Peoples of Early America*. Englewood Cliffs, N.J.: Prentice Hall, 1982.

Phillips, Ulrich B. *American Negro Slavery*. New York: D. Appleton and Co., 1918.

Sewall, Samuel. *The Diary of Samuel Sewall*. Boston: Massachusetts Historical Society, 1878.

Thornton, John. *Africa and Africans in the Making of the Atlantic World, 1400–1680*. Cambridge: Cambridge University Press, 1992.

Washburne, Emory. *Slavery as It Once Existed in Massachusetts*. Boston: John Wilson and Son Press, 1869.

12

Indentured Servants

Compared with other colonies in the New World, a small number of black and Indian slaves were held in New England until shortly after the Revolution, when slavery was outlawed. Another category of labor was more widely used: voluntary and involuntary Caucasian servants. There was one big, essential difference between Caucasian "slaves" as they were sometimes called and slaves of color. Unlike black and Indian slaves, white servants were not in servitude for life, nor were their children automatically slaves.

The primary voluntary servants in New England were designated not as slaves but as indentured servants, of whom there were fewer in New England than elsewhere in colonial America. Yet they constituted an important element in the social fabric of the region.

Both a religious attitude and an economic condition encouraged the importation of servants into New England. The religious attitude arose from the doctrine of calling, which specified that some people were called to be masters and some were called to be servants. Therefore, New Englanders, most of whom had enough money to hire help, had little hesitation in legally binding servants for up to twelve years and working them extremely hard.

An acute shortage of labor of all sorts encouraged the importation of servants. It was next to impossible for a couple to clear untamed land alone or to set up businesses without help. And for £5 or £6 apiece, a family could pay the passage of servants and own their labor for several years. For servants, this was a way to have their passage paid to the

New World and to be taken care of for a period of time before becoming independent laborers and, in many cases in the seventeenth century, business or land owners. Perhaps the situation was not ideal, but it might enable a man to reach a point of economic ownership and independence that would have been impossible in England, Scotland, or Ireland.

The term *servant* in colonial New England, describing men and women who were hired to do various kinds of work on farms, in houses, on ships, or for craftsmen, covered several kinds of servitude. The term described people who were hired by the day or for a few weeks or months to help at times, like planting and harvesting, requiring intense labor. It was also applied to apprentices—young people who worked under the direction of an adult to acquire specific training, as a printer or blacksmith, for instance. It described an independent class of servant who worked on shares, splitting the profits generated by their own labor with the owners of land or businesses.

There was yet another large category of servant: a person who voluntarily or involuntarily was legally bound to a master for a considerable period of time, from two to twelve years. These were called *indentured servants*, and there were several kinds. *Redemptioners* were a class of people who, in order to get to the New World, sold themselves to a ship's captain to pay for their passage. The captain, in turn, sold their labor to a settler. Usually upon reaching Boston, a settler and the ship's captain would sign a contract whereby the settler agreed to pay the £5 or £6 fare of the servant, furnish him or her with decent food and shelter though rarely pay, and at the end of a specified number of years provide the servant with termination pay. The usual termination pay was £10 or two suits of clothes or, less frequently, a plot of land. The servant bound himself to his master for from one to twelve years. In the early days of the settlement, the terms were low, from one to six years, but as the labor shortage became more acute with the growth of business, the terms lengthened, a few running to twelve years.

In the first three decades, there were other varieties of limited, bound labor. For example, English companies contracted with laborers who were sent to the New World to be bound to company employees to work for a term of years in businesses like the fur trade or fishing business. Sometimes a laborer was sent to the New World to make money for an absentee master living in England.

Sometimes settlers who could afford servants requested that friends in England or Ireland find and arrange to have servants sent to them in New England. On their trips back to England, settlers hired servants for themselves.

The business of providing servants for New England colonists became a lucrative one for some entrepreneurs. An employment service was run by sea captains, English businessmen, and Boston merchants. An advertisement for the sale of servants ran in the *Boston Gazette* in 1729:

> ***Plaids from Glasgow***
>
> Plaids of sundry Sorts both fine and ordinary, Choice Linens of several Sorts, Bed Ticking, Handkerchiefs, and Muslins, with some Young Men and Women's Time of Service, to be Sold at Mr. George Bethune's Warehouse in Merchants Row. Boston (November 24–December 1, 1729)

The typical arrangements in all cases were identical in nature to that made with the redemptioner. The servant's passage was paid, and he or she was promised upkeep for a period of years and about £10 at the end of the period.

Some of the arrangements were patently exploitative. For example, one man in Massachusetts in 1643 was bound to his master for ten years to pay his passage of £5; regular hired hands could earn £6 in one year.

The typical contract below, dated February 7, 1717, is with an employer-master, William Gibbs, who has arranged from Boston for Ebenezer Kingsby to be sent to Massachusetts from England:

> This Indenture made the Seventh day of February in the Year of our Lord God One thousand Seven hundred and seventeen Between Ebenezer Kingsby of the one Party and William Gibb of the other Party. Witnesseth That the said Ebenezer Kingsby doth hereby Covenant, Promise, and Grant to and with the said William Gibb his Exec.s adms. and assigns from the Day of the Date hereof until the first and Next arrival at Boston in New England and after for and During the Term of four Years to Serve in Such Service and Employment as the said William Gibbs or his assignes Shall there Employ him according to the Custom of the Country. In the Like Kind In Consideration whereof the said William Gibb do hereby Covenant and Grant to and with the said Ebenezer Kingsby to pay for his Passage and to find and allow Meat Drink apparel and Lodging with other Necessarys during the said term and at the End of the said Term to pay unto him the usual allowance according to the Custom of the Country. In the Like Kind In Witness where of the Partys above mentioned to these Indentures have interchangeably set their hands and Seals the Day and Year above written.

With the permission of the authorities, the indenture could be transferred to another master. At the time of the master's death, the indenture was either terminated or transferred to someone else. One employer, Thomas Baguley, was fined on April 29, 1641, for selling his servant's time, contrary to the wishes of the court.

INVOLUNTARY SERVITUDE

Another category of service was involuntary. Certain people were ordered by the courts to be bound over for a period of years to work for masters whom the magistrates deemed to be responsible family men. Many children—orphans, delinquents, or the offspring of disreputable parents—were bound as indentured servants to local masters. All men and women who remained unmarried were ordered to enter indentured service. Sometimes the courts ordered idle men and women to work as indentured servants for a specified employer. Working-class people who were judged to be immoral were placed in indentured positions, where a strong master could oversee their behavior. Finally, criminals and debtors often found themselves ordered into temporary "slavery" by the courts, which also specified the time of the service. A thief, for example, had to work until he had recompensed the person he had stolen from. The case of John Kempe shows the court's personal manner of dealing with a criminal: "John Kempe, for filthy, unclean attempts with three young girls, was censured to be whipped both here, at Roxberry, and at Salem, very severely, and was committed as a slave to Leift Davenport" (Shurtleff, vol. 1: 269).

On the same day, William Androws, who had been sentenced to slavery in the previous year for assaulting his employer, was freed from his slavery, bound over as a servant in the Endicott household, and made to pay the man he assaulted. And on June 2, 1640, Thomas Savory was whipped and sold for a slave until "he have made restitution" for thefts (Shurtleff, vol. 1: 297). A number of citizens of the Massachusetts Bay were judged to be so incorrigible that they were sold as slaves to masters outside the colony.

A debtor had to work until he had paid his creditor. Although there were occasional home-grown criminals or debtors serving limited time as "slaves," New England accepted extremely few convicts or debtors from Britain, as Georgia and other colonies did.

New England did accept numerous involuntary bound servants of another category, however. These were largely Scottish and Irish prisoners of war who had been supporters of Charles II and had been taken in the battles of Dunbar, Preston, and Worcester. A few figures indicate that the numbers were substantial. In 1651, 150 prisoners of war were sent to Boston on the ship *Unity*. Eighty prisoners were sent to work in the Saugus Iron Works. In 1652, over 200 were sent to Charlestown. It should be reemphasized that even these various categories of people, considered to be lower-class servants, were only bound for ten or twelve years at the most, not for life.

THE PASSAGE OVER

The voyage that voluntary and involuntary servants endured was often compared with that endured by African slaves. The usual number of passengers was supposed to be 300, but to make more money, ship captains would often cram as many as twice the recommended number onto fairly small boats. The amount of space allotted each adult was six feet by two feet between decks. There was no opportunity to change clothing, which had to be worn for the duration of the voyage, up to four or five months. Storms not only made the voyage longer, but forced the passengers to lie flat on the floor for days. The unventilated space was made more foul by the many diseased passengers. Those who died were often left to lie where they had died. The sick received no medical attention. Food and water were scarce and were sometimes rationed out at three ounces a day. One servant, Gottlieb Mittelberger, claimed in 1750, that their only food was rotten biscuits, full of dirt, red worms, and spider webs. Many passengers ate rats and mice.

As many as half the passengers died on these voyages. Children were especially vulnerable; chroniclers claimed that children from ages one to seven rarely lived to reach the New World. Eyewitnesses claimed to have seen as many as thirty-two corpses of children dumped overboard on such a voyage.

Upon arriving at a port city, little care was given to these passengers, especially to the old and sick, who would bring the least money as servants. Many were quarantined indefinitely to what were called "pest houses" to keep them from infecting the general population. In a number of cases, families would be separated when it served the best interests of the captains who were selling them and the employees who were buying them.

WORK

In the 1630s, servants arriving in New England on ships from the mother country made up about 21 percent of the passengers. The average family in New England had one or two servants, but the upkeep and business on large estates owned by the original members of the Massachusetts Bay Company, for example, like Governor Winthrop, required many more than the usual one or two servants. Winthrop brought four large families to New England as servants, eleven members of whom died within the first year. To assist him in his business, he occasionally "ordered" as many as seven servants at a time from England. William Pyncheon, an original member of the Massachusetts Bay Company who established the town of Springfield as his fur trading empire, employed half of the adult population of that town. For his agricultural interests alone, he employed between fifteen and forty men each season. In his house, he had thirty female servants. He had even greater numbers working for him in trading, canoeing, building, tanning, and other specialties. Contractors who had bought the time of servants would transport them to Springfield and sell them to Pyncheon.

The work most frequently assigned to indentured servants was farmwork and domestic house work. The jobs for men on the farm were varied and included threshing grain, tending livestock, planting crops, slaughtering, herding, tanning hides, husking corn, cutting wood, and felling trees. Farms located on the western frontier required the hardest work, as wild land had to be cleared of trees, stumps, and boulders before it could be broken up for planting. Women servants cooked, tended children, cleaned house, sewed, spun, wove, preserved foods, tended poultry, and milked.

Indentured servants worked in every conceivable job in village businesses. They were in special demand in the building of ships and houses, barbering, cabinetmaking, blacksmithing, and distilling.

Although servants and masters worked side by side, the hours demanded of servants were in excess of those worked by the owner and his family. Servants were instructed that they were on call twenty-four hours a day. They were to rise before the owner family and usually finished their labors at sundown. Owners expected a ten- or twelve-hour day and a six-day week of work from their servants. The community believed that long hours were for the good of both master and servant. Long hours put money into the pockets of the owners. They were also good for servants, for "idleness was the devil's workshop," and hard work kept them from getting into trouble.

MISBEHAVIOR AND DISCIPLINE

The servant was taught that every action in life was to be for the betterment of the owner. His master was an agent of the Lord, one whose God-given calling allowed him to give orders and punishment without question. The servant was to obey even a harsh master without objection. The misdemeanors for which servants were most often punished fell into the categories of running away, getting drunk, sexual looseness, impudence, idleness, and theft. Between 1620 and 1750, there were 700 recorded instances of runaways in the Massachusetts Bay Colony. This was considered one of the most heinous of crimes because the master lost the passage he had paid for the servant, the work for years bargained for, the clothes and supplies that the servant usually stole to aid in the escape, and the expense of tracing down the servant and getting him or her back. In order to limit the success of runaways, the authorities passed laws forbidding servants to go aboard ships in the harbor or to ride ferries, the first of which could facilitate escape by sea and the last escape by land.

The Massachusetts Court of Assistants made the following ruling in 1634:

> [I]f any boy (that hath been whipt for running from his master) be taken in any other plantation, not having a note from his master to testify his business there, it shall be lawful for the Constable of the said plantation to whip him and send him home. (Shurtleff, vol. 1: 140)

The punishment for running away always involved whippings. On March 4, 1633, the court ordered two men whipped for running away from their masters. Christopher Darling, who had stolen food when he left, was to be whipped "severely."

Beatings were also administered to servants who sneaked out of the master's house at night to have some time to amuse themselves, for it was taught that the totality of a servant's time—twenty-four hours a day—belonged to the master. A servant was due time to rest, but not to amuse himself away from the master's property. A notation for July 29, 1641, reveals the following:

> James Laurence, for going out of his masters house in the middle of the night unseasonably against his express order, was censured to be sharply whipped, and also for keeping company with a lewd woman. (Shurtleff, vol. 1: 334)

At the same meeting of the court, two other servants were sentenced to be whipped: William Pilsberry for "defiling his master's house" and Dorothy Pilsberry for her "uncleanness and defiling her master's house" (334).

Employers constantly complained about servants' stealing from them, especially when the family was absent from the house. Pilfering was a particular problem on Sundays when the family were in church. It was generally assumed that any commodity that was sold or traded had been stolen from an employer. To discourage stealing, laws were passed by the Court of Assistants forbidding servants from giving, selling, or trading any commodities without express permission of their masters

NECESSITIES, EDUCATION, AND AMUSEMENTS

The shelter, food, and clothing that most masters provided for their servants were little different from those enjoyed by other members of the household. They ate the same food at the same table and slept in the same house, sometimes in the same room, with the master and his family. They were provided with decent clothes and the same medical care in case of illness. The courts considered seriously servants' complaints about insufficient care, on occasion ordering employers to dress a servant better or see to his or her health.

Employers also had the obligation to provide their servants with education. Servants were to be taught basic reading and arithmetic and to receive continuous religious education. Work and study were intended to consume every waking hour. Any master who failed to educate his servants had them taken from him.

The amusements of servants were drastically curtailed. Their absence from the farm, business, or house at any time was frowned upon. The indentured servant's time belonged to the master, not to himself. Employers believed that when servants were not actually working, they should be resting up for the next day's labors. Tired or hung-over workers frequently did not get up to begin work on time and performed poorly at their labors. Servants who partied without or within their master's property reflected badly on and shamed the family, and masters often complained of sexual misconduct on the part of servants. To discourage drinking and gambling, the two favorite leisure-time activities of servants, local courts passed laws forbidding tavern keepers and sailors aboard ship from entertaining servants.

LEGAL POWER BUT PRACTICAL LIMITATIONS

Although the master legally owned the time and labor of his indentured servants, circumstances limited his power over them. One reason was the keen labor shortage throughout the colonies. If an owner of a farm or business kicked his unruly servant out—perhaps selling him to another person—acquiring another servant was an arduous, expensive, time-consuming, and risky business. Thus, many masters quietly tolerated laziness, incompetence, and insolence rather than exchange a known problem for an unknown one.

A master was also well aware that a wily servant whom he had made angry could retaliate. Sometimes a vengeful servant could be very dangerous. A house servant named Mehitabel Brabrook, for example, put a huge toad into a kettle of the family's milk after being scolded. Later, she set the master's house on fire.

In extremely rare cases, the skills and responsibilities of indentured servants were so highly valued that they were exceptionally well recompensed. The manager of the ironworks at Lynn, Massachusetts, was such a man. Although this manager was bound, the owner of the ironworks paid him handsomely in order to keep him happy and productive, making the servant one of the richest men in Lynn.

In the tight labor market, it behooved owners to treat their servants well for another reason: at the end of the indentureship, a good servant often agreed to work as a free hired hand for his former owner.

A SERVANT'S PROTECTIONS

Despite the belief that masters were the agents of God and should be obeyed no matter how harshly they acted, they were not free to misuse their servants. The community made it clear that no servant could be asked to do something evil. Frequent sexual abuse on the part of the master fell into this category. The records indicate that the testimony of female servants was generally believed by the magistrates, and offenders were strictly dealt with. For example, a maidservant in John Harris's house complained that Harris and his son, John, had tried to rape her. Her testimony was deemed truthful, and the two men were found guilty. They were whipped twenty stripes each and imprisoned. In another case, a young woman finally complained that her master's brother had made indecent advances toward her repeatedly. She had delayed asking her master for protection, she told the court, because she well knew that she would not be believed because of her low station in life. She feared that she would suffer for revealing her story. When she finally did approach her master with the story, her fears proved to have had substance, for the whole household turned against her. She was forced to go to the authorities, who did believe her and removed her from her situation.

Nor were masters free to administer brutal beatings or to maim or in any way cruelly punish a servant. The physical evidence of cruel punishment was clear enough to the courts. In 1640, the General Court of Massachusetts found that Samuel Gifford had been misused by his master. The servant was taken from his master and assigned to another man for three years, at six pounds per year. Other masters, guilty of cruel beatings, were themselves severely whipped. In the case of serious maiming, the servant would be set free and the master ordered to pay him for his suffering.

Although running away from a master was ordinarily considered a grievous crime, a servant who was misused had the legal right to escape a master's cruelty by seeking sanctuary in a good neighbor's house, to be cared for until the authorities resolved the dispute.

CONCLUSION

The life of indentured servants was hard. For the time they were bound, they were without any personal freedom. Yet life as a servant in New England was not as hard as life in England, because the New England authorities saw that servants had the necessities of life and even an education.

Nor can the situations of indentured servants be equated with those of black and Indian slaves. True slaves could be held indefinitely and passed on as slaves to the owner's heirs. Moreover, the progeny of slaves were also slaves. Indentureship for the poor, criminals, debtors, and even prisoners of war was a way for a new beginning in the New World. Although life in service could be hard and even unjust, servants could often look forward to economic independence and well-being, through eventual land and business ownership, that they could never dream of in England.

BIBLIOGRAPHY

Demos, John. *A Little Commonwealth: Family Life in Plymouth Colony*. New York: Oxford University Press, 1970.

Galenson, David W. *White Servitude in Colonial America*. Cambridge, Mass.: Harvard University Press, 1981.

Handlin, Oscar. *The Uprooted: The Epic Story of the Great Migration That Made the American People*. Boston: Little, Brown, 1952.

Innes, Stephen. *Labor in a New Land*. Princeton, N.J.: Princeton University Press, 1983.

Jernigan, Marcus Wilson. *Laboring and Dependent Classes in Colonial America*. Chicago: University of Chicago Press, 1931.

Konig, David T. *Law and Society in Puritan Massachusetts*. Chapel Hill: University of North Carolina Press, 1977.

Morgan, Edmund S. *American Slavery, American Freedom*. New York: Norton, 1975.

———. *The Puritan Family*. New York: Harper and Row, 1966.

Morris, Richard B. *Goverment and Labor in Early America*. New York: Octagon Books, 1965.

Nash, Gary. *Race, Class, and Politics*. Urbana: University of Illinois Press, 1986.

Pestana, Carla Gardina, and Sharon V. Salinger, eds. *Inequality in Early America*. Hanover, N.H.: University Press of New England, 1999.

Shurtleff, N. B., ed. *Records of the Governor and Company of the Massachusetts Bay*. 6 vols. Boston: W. Whiter, 1853–1854.

Smith, Abbot Emerson. *Colonists in Bondage: White Servitude and Convict Labor in American 1607–1776*. Chapel Hill: University of North Carolina Press, 1947.

Towner, Lawrence William. *A Good Master Well Served: Masters and Servants in Colonial Massachusetts, 1620–1750*. New York: Garland, 1998.

Wechsler, Louis K. *The Common People of Colonial America*. New York: Vantage Press, 1978.

13

Education

The main business of most settlers in New England was day-to-day survival in an untamed frontier. But the leaders of the Massachusetts Bay Colony, in particular, had the wealth to become established fairly early and to turn their attention to matters other than the basic needs of food and shelter. One of their concerns, made more urgent because of religious doctrine as well as the ever-pressing need for labor, was the education of youth. Pragmatic economics dictated that the community's children should be trained as quickly as possible to become the blacksmiths, weavers, carpenters, and other workers that were so desperately needed in the New World. The religious doctrine that taught that idleness was evil inspired the founding Puritans to train their young to be productive. Work was good for the soul. It was also imperative for every citizen to know Protestant religious principles and to be able to read Scripture, for the devil was a very real threat to take over the lives of those ignorant of religion and the Bible.

Just what the motives of the colonials were is a matter of debate. Some have argued that the chief purpose of education in the minds of the colonial founders was to reinforce the religious creed. Others argue that the purpose of education was primarily to secure a caste system. Others more friendly to the Puritans contend that indoctrination has been unfairly overemphasized and that their chief educational aim was to prepare their people for citizenship.

There were several tiers of education:

- Religious education of children, apprentices, and servants
- Religious education of Indians
- The home teaching of basic reading, writing, and arithmetic to young children, apprentices, and servants
- The home training of apprentices and children in vocational skills
- Dame schools for the teaching of basic reading, writing, and arithmetic
- Elementary schools
- Secondary schools (called grammar or Latin schools)
- Vocational schools
- Schools for girls
- On-the-job training in a profession or trade for married women
- Universities
- Divinity schools

RELIGIOUS TRAINING

The Reformed Protestant's view of human nature, the character with which a child was born, necessitated an early form of religious education. Because of Adam's Fall, everyone was born depraved and evil at heart. Satan could have his way with every child who was not buttressed with elements of civilization: religious, church society, moral instruction, biblical knowledge, and religious catechism. Ignorance breeds heresy, the Puritan contended, so it behooved the New England colonists to see to the souls of their children, which is to say to the religious instruction of their children, as soon as possible. Education saved not only the child but the godly community that the children would eventually comprise.

The tendency in the seventeenth century was to place the responsibility for religious instruction in the family first and only secondarily with the clergy. Families were encouraged to begin the religious training of infants as soon as possible. Every moment was an opportunity to teach a religious precept.

Legislation in 1642 specified that masters were to catechize their servants and apprentices in the grounds and principles of religion at least once a week. It also gave students the expectation that they would be examined on their religious studies. Mention is made of their being able to read the "Capital Laws," that is, the Ten Commandments. The wording of one part of that 1642 law follows:

> Forasmuch as the good Education of Children is of Singular behoove and benefit to any Common-wealth, and whereas many Parents and Masters are too indulgent and negligent of their duty in the kind:
>
> It is ordered, that the Select men of every Town in the several Precincts and

quarters, where they dwell shall have a vigilant eye over their brethren and neighbors, to see, First that none of them shall suffer so much Barbarism in any of their families, as not to endeavor to teach, by themselves or others, their Children and Apprentices, of much learning, as may enable them perfectly to read the English tongue, and knowledge of the Capital Laws: upon penalty of *twenty shillings* for each neglect therein.

Also that all Masters of families, do once a week (at the least) catechize their children and servants in the Grounds and Principles of Religion, and if any be unable to do so much; that then at the least they procure such children and apprentices, so learn some short Orthodox Catechism, without book, that they may be able to answer unto the questions, that shall be propounded to them out of such Catechism, by their parents or masters, or any of the Select men when they shall call them to a trial, of what they have learned in that kind. (*General Laws And Liberties*, 26)

The law of 1647, known as the "Old Deluder Satan Law" reinforced the need for education, primarily on religious grounds. The preamble makes clear that Satan's main object was to keep people from being able to read the truth of Scripture for themselves, an unflattering allusion to the Anglican and Roman Catholic practices of having only priests read and interpret Scripture for lay believers. The Puritans and other Reformed Protestants believed that Satan, working through what they believed were heretical clergy, was able to delude the masses of ignorant people. Furthermore, if the settlers did not attend to the religious education of their children, God might well punish the whole community:

It being one chief project of Satan to keep men from the knowledge of the Scripture, as in former times, keeping them in unknown Tongues, so in these latter times, by persuading from the use of Tongues, that so at least the true sense and meaning of the original might be clouded and corrupted with false glosses of Deceivers; to the end that Learning may not be buried in the Graves of our fore Fathers, in Church and Commonwealth, the Lord, afflicting our endeavors. (General Laws And Liberties, 136)

Religious education continued in the household with regular meetings during the week and with a meeting on Sunday afternoon, when the earlier sermon in the meetinghouse would be discussed.

Although, until the end of the seventeenth century, the emphasis continued to be on religious education generated within the family, some ministers assumed the burden of religious instruction from the very early days of the Massachusetts Bay Colony. The Reverend John Cotton, for example, a member of the early settlement, for twenty years conducted religious schools for young people on Sunday afternoons, when he repeatedly reviewed religious writings. Even in the late 1640s, other ministers in some communities held meetings for religious study on weekday evenings—often two or three evenings a week. And sometimes the heads of households objected that religious education was taking up too much time from their workers—their older children and servants—who had chores to do at home.

By the end of the seventeenth century and throughout the eighteenth century, religious instruction was conducted primarily by schoolmasters or by ministers at special meetings in their houses, the meetinghouses, or the houses of the students. These church groups, often as large as 200 students, included a wide range of ages, from about seven to thirty-one. Girls and boys were instructed separately on different days of the week, and while boys received instruction until they were well into their thirties, girls were dismissed at age sixteen.

A large part of any religious education, as the old Deluder Satan Law implied, was learning to read the English language in order to read Scripture. The other half of religious education was what was called *catechism*, or a body of religious beliefs that the students first memorized and the teacher then explained. The religious content of the catechism was fairly uniform. There were many books of catechism, sometimes written and published by the minister of the local community. But by far the most widely used were John Cotton's *Spiritual Milk for Boston Babes* and the *Westminster Assembly's Shorter Catechism*, which were later appended to the primary textbook, the *New England Primer*. These presented a series of questions and answers on fundamental religious principles. Following are a few of the questions and answers from the *Westminster Catechism*:

Quest. What is the chief End of Men?

Answ. Man's chief End is to Glorify God, and to Enjoy Him forever.

Q. What Rule hath God given to direct us how we may glorify and enjoy Him?

A. The Word of God which is contained in the Scriptures of the Old and New Testament, is the only Rule to direct us how we may glorify and enjoy him.

Q. What do the Scriptures principally teach?

A. The Scriptures principally teach, what Man is to believe concerning God, and what duty God requireth of Man. (Ford, Appendix)

Young students, around seven or eight years old, were assigned to memorize the catechism. It was generally understood that young children would scarcely be able to understand what they were memorizing. Still, they would be asked the stock questions with regard to the catechism and would be expected to provide the stock answers from memory.

The next step was helping students reach an understanding of the catechism. At first, the teacher's questions were fairly simple and could be answered yes or no: "What? Is there then a God, who made all things? Did you make yourself? Who then made you?"

Older children were required to engage in discussion based on the catechism, to cite scriptural proofs and explain them, and to connect theory with practice.

The religious folk of New England were usually suspicious of poetry unless it was free of any lyrical cadences and could be used for proper religious purposes. Such is a poem, written in 1683, assigned to be memorized for the edification of young children:

> I in the Burying Place may see
> Graves shorter there than I;
> From Death's Arrest no Age is free,
> Young Children too may die;
> My God, may such an awful Sight,
> Awakening be to me!
> Oh! that by early Grace I might
> For Death prepared be. (From Lauter, 309)

One of the texts found to be most useful was a gory, morbid poem by minister and Harvard professor Michael Wigglesworth, entitled "Day of Doom." Young children throughout New England were assigned to set to memory this poem about the last day on earth, when people ran about in panic, tearing the flesh off their bodies in horror and foolishly trying to kill themselves. The most pedagogically useful verses show various individuals coming before the throne of the Judge to argue why they should not be damned. The Judge's retorts comprise lessons in the Puritan doctrines of election, depravity, and damnation. For example, when infants who had died before they were born are damned, they argue that they had never done anything bad because they had never lived. But the Judge damns them anyway, telling them that sin and damnation are like an inheritance. If you *had* lived, he told them, you would not have turned down the good that you would have inherited from Adam, so you have to take it all, the bad with the good, and the bad part of the inheritance is damnation. The damned infants respond that it is not fair for God to save Adam, who by his actions caused everyone to be damned, yet send infants who never lived to hell. But the Judge tells him that God is so great that he is free to do whatever he wants to do, and he wants to save his first creation, Adam, and does not want to save the infants. When a group of "Civil, Honest Men" protest to the Judge that they have always done good deeds and never committed any sin, he tells them that even though they have not committed any bad actions, they had evil in their hearts: they wanted to commit sins, and that is what damns them. Each group that protests its own damnation allows the Reverend Wigglesworth to explain a sticking point of Puritan doctrine that seemed too unjust to be believable. The poem ends with monsters dragging the damned down to an eternal fire of damnation, while the saved people in their white robes look on smuggly. The poem was constructed in a rhyming, singsong cadence that made it easy to memorize.

RELIGIOUS EDUCATION OF NATIVES

New England settlers believed that it was in the best interests of both natives and settlers to give natives religious instruction. It was assumed that the settlers would be better off if they could erase cultural differences in their surroundings and that natives who could be made to share their religion would be less likely to attack. They believed that converting the natives to Christianity would turn them from godless barbarianism. It is unlikely that Calvinist doctrine would allow for the eternal salvation of any native, even one who became Christian, but at least such a native convert would know the truth, as the Puritans perceived it, and God would probably see that he had an easier life on this earth.

To this end, missionaries, John Eliot most prominent among them, spent most of their lives among the Indians. Eliot even created useful texts for his students. In 1653 he published *Catechism in the Indian Language*, the first book printed in a native language. And in 1661, he published a translation of the Bible into the Algonquian language.

The irony, as James Axtell points out in *The School upon the Hill*, is that the Indians taught the English settlers far more than the English taught the Indians. The natives had their own religion, their own culture, and their own values and despite the efforts of the Reverend Eliot and others, they resisted negating their own beliefs in order to assume English beliefs. Conversely, natives had the kind of knowledge that the English had to have to survive. The information they conveyed so generously transformed every aspect of everyday life in New England: their habits of planting, eating, hunting and fishing, construction, clothing, and traveling. Furthermore, the natives often made converts of settlers, many of them captives, to their own way of life. Recent statistics indicate that as many as 70 percent of Indian captives between 1689 and 1713 may have chosen to remain with the Indians.

LITERACY AND VOCATIONAL HOME EDUCATION

Doctrine taught that boys were to give their most serious attention to the matter of identifying the calling for which God intended them. Practically speaking, only a small percentage of boys had such a luxury. Most of them were expected to learn the trade of their father and, from a tender age, to help on the family farm or in the family business. However, some fathers were able to contract with tradesmen and artisans to place their seven- or eight-year-old children as apprentices so that they could learn a trade. The boys were trained by working side by side with a skilled craftsman. Girls learned to spin, weave, and sew. Usually the agreement also obligated the master to teach his apprentice to read as well, and sometimes to read, write, and figure.

Young sons and daughters were often taught at home by their parents or by school dames, women with young children who conducted classes in reading, writing, and figuring for their own children and those of others. Later in the seventeenth century, dame schools were conducted in rented rooms or meetinghouses to students as young as two or three years old.

ELEMENTARY SCHOOLS

Even before legislation required communities to set up schools, New Englanders in some areas had already done so. For example, Boston had a school in 1635, Newport in 1640, Hartford in 1642, and Windsor, Connecticut, in 1644. The Old Deluder Satan Law of 1647 specified that communities were to see to the education of their children. Every town of fifty householders was instructed to pay someone to teach reading and writing. Children could still receive this elementary education at home, but a school had to be provided for those who were not receiving a basic education from their parents or masters. Some communities paid for these first schools by assessing parents, some by a form of taxation, and some by a combination of revenue sources.

The first structures in which this public instruction took place were rented rooms, barns, shops, or meetinghouses, but soon buildings went up for the expressed purpose of schooling. They were generally small, crude, dark, cheerless, drafty buildings, about twenty by eighteen feet wide with ceilings six or seven feet high. Within this structure were a central room, a foyer, and a loft. There were from two to three windows eighteen inches square. On the walls from floor to windows were rough boards; from windows to ceiling was lime plaster.

On three sides, desks made of rough planks were attached to the walls. In front of the desks were unfinished planks set on pegs—the students' backless seats. They were usually gummy with resin and full of splinters. At the end of the room, opposite the foyer, was a fireplace, meant to supply both light and heat, and the schoolmaster's desk. In winter, the small building was kept closed up, and a fire blazed in the fireplace, creating a dark, smoky chamber. The fire also consumed most of the oxygen in the room, causing the students to nod off. Their extremities freezing cold in the drafty school, the students often raised their hands to request permission to approach nearer the fireplace briefly to thaw out their fingers. One schoolmaster in Roxbury complained to the town fathers that the cold wind blew in the broken window glass in his school, that the floor was ripped up to feed the fire, and that the seats were burned and out of kilter.

Some of the parents paid their children's tuition with wood for the fireplace, but inevitably the local school would run out of wood in winter and would be closed until more could be procured. If a parent could not pay with money or wood, his child would be suspended.

The teaching of reading was the primary aim of the elementary school. Writing was considered a distinct skill to be developed after reading had been mastered. The text, which was formally published as *The New England Primer*, began with letters of the alphabet, moved to simple two-letter combinations, then to words of one syllable, then two, then three, four, and five syllables. The first sentences, designed to reinforce the child's grasp of the alphabet, often taught a biblical or a moral truth. The "A" sentence was: "In Adam's Fall We sinned all." The "F" sentence was: "The Idle Fool was Whipt at School." "P" was "Peter denies His Lord and cries." Other texts included a hornbook (a sheet of paper protected by a layer of transparent animal horn) for the teaching of the alphabet and the Lord's Prayer, a speller, and a catechism.

GRAMMAR SCHOOLS

The Old Deluder Satan Law of 1647 also made provision for grammar schools in towns of 100 families. As the law stipulates, grammar schools were originally intended for students who planned to go to college. To enter, a student, around seven or eight years old, had to be able to read a passage from the Bible or from the psalter. These programs, which lasted seven years, were variously called grammar schools, writing schools, Latin schools, and secondary schools. Here is where more serious teaching of writing began, and Latin grammar, arithmetic, and the classics were taught through rote memorizations. The books to be studied included the Bible and Dr. Watts's *Hymns for Children*.

The grammar school structure was not different from the old elementary school. Schoolmasters were notoriously poor; they were usually nineteen- or twenty-year-old ministerial Harvard graduates who taught for a year before moving to a church assigned to them. The numbers of young men in these schools was never large, in part because only the wealthy could send their sons to a grammar school and then on to Harvard. The most famous of these schools was the Boston Latin School, founded in 1636, which was publicly supported, but never had more than 100 students during the seventeenth century.

For most of the seventeenth century, girls were taught reading, writing, and arithmetic only. They were not at first allowed to enter the grammar schools. In the mid-eighteenth century some of the grammar schools were opened to both girls and boys who were taught not the traditional Latin curriculum, but only the three R's.

MEN'S VOCATIONAL SCHOOLS, WOMEN'S PRIVATE SCHOOLS, AND ON-THE-JOB TRAINING

The apprenticeship system never flourished in New England, yet there was a pressing need for skilled labor of all sorts. To train young men for New England industry, vocational schools taught them such subjects as navigation, seafaring, surveying, shipbuilding, mathematics, accounting, and business.

Young women from comfortably situated families went to schools that taught the "female arts," as they were called: piano, voice, French, sometimes dancing, needlework, and painting.

Women were not welcomed into trade or professional schools, but they received on-the-job training when they worked beside their husbands. As wives of physicians, lawyers, printers, and artisans, they became experts in their husband's vocation. Although the community would not allow them to be institutionally trained, they accepted professional and trade skills in the wife of a tradesman, who often took over her husband's business when he died or became incapacitated.

COLLEGES AND UNIVERSITIES

Higher education came to New England in 1636 when the Court of Assistants allocated £400 for an institution based on the model of Cambridge University in England, where most college-educated New Englanders had received their training. Despite some Protestant arguments that the Bible was sufficient learning for any Christian and despite the Puritans' general antagonism to classical learning, New England's conviction that a godly man should be highly educated prevailed, and in 1637 the plan was implemented for a college on a one-acre lot in Cambridge. A board of overseers was appointed and one professor hired. In 1638 it opened to its first freshman class. In September of that year, a businessman named John Harvard died, leaving his 400-volume library and a little under £800 to the new establishment. As a result of John Harvard's bequest, the institution was named for him. Other colleges opened in New England before the American Revolution—Yale in 1701, Brown in 1764, and Dartmouth in 1769, for instance—but for most of the colonial period, Harvard set the standard and dominated the field.

Its early president, Nathaniel Eaton, who stole money from the college, deprived his boarding students of food and decent lodging, and beat them and his own assistants brutally, was promptly dismissed. Under the leadership of President Henry Dunster, a solid curriculum was developed and adequate faculty hired; in 1652 a four-year bachelor's degree was established in the English tradition. The curriculum consisted of grammar, logic, rhetoric, arithmetic, geometry, astronomy, metaphysics, ethics, natural science, Greek, Hebrew, and ancient history. It was not intended to be practical in any way, but to provide a knowledge of God through his word and works. Latin, which students had mastered in grammar school, was the language of instruction. Most textbook materials were also in Latin.

The first Harvard students ranged from ten to thirty years old, though most were around fifteen. As in the elementary and grammar schools, discipline at Harvard College was severe. Students under eighteen who misbehaved were whipped or had their ears boxed. Older students were fined or publicly admonished.

The Harvard students were fortunate enough to have a young, learned clergyman, the Reverend Michael Wigglesworth, for a teacher. Like the model Puritan guide of the young, Wigglesworth was concerned not just with his students' mental development; he was obsessed with the condition of their souls. In June 1653, his student John Haines had left the campus to go to Salem for three days without permission, which put Wigglesworth in agony. When Haines came back and did not bother to explain his behavior, Wigglesworth collared him for a lecture:

> I told him not only of his evil carriages in this business. . . . I told him that danger of backsliding from former attainments how Satan enters in with no spirits worse than himself and the latter end of that may become worse than his beginnings. . . . I asked him further if himself did not see that to be true that I had spoken to him that his heart was gone after pleasure and off from those good ways he had sometimes walked in. . . . I told him also of the dangers of pleasure and how they had like to have been my ruin. (27)

Wigglesworth was disappointed later that his lecture to his student had not had the effect he intended because he saw Haines "at play I think among the students" that very evening after his lecture. The next day he found that Haines was with "ill company playing music, though I had so solemnly warn'd him but yesterday of letting his spirit go after pleasures. And again I see light and vain carriage in him [he was smiling and laughing] just at night on this last day at even." This last was a particularly damning observation since the sabbath began on Saturday night, and Haines's "light and vain carriage" was a desecration of the Sabbath.

Something of the demeanor and mind-set expected of the students is suggested in Samuel Sewall's account of one of his fellow students at Harvard in 1674, Thomas Sargeant, who was examined by several trustees of Harvard and found guilty of speaking blasphemously of the Holy Ghost:

> [H]e should be therefore publickly whipped before all the Scholars. 2. That he should be suspended as to taking his degree of Bachelor. . . . 3. Sit alone by himself in the Hall uncovered at meals, during the pleasure of the President and Fellows, and be in all things obedient, doing what exercise was appointed him by the President, or else be finally expelled from the college. He kneeled down and the instrument Goodman Hely attended to the President's word as to the performance of his part in the work. Prayer was had before and after by the President. (5)

The first substantial building at Harvard was "Old College," consisting of a dining hall on the ground floor to accommodate fifty people and a dormitory above that included a library, sleeping quarters, and small individual studies.

Although there appeared to be the occasional scholarship for the poor, deserving student and although some students paid their way with farm produce, most students were from families with money and position. Going to Harvard was extremely expensive, costing as much as the entire income for two full years of an average laborer. One-half of 1 percent of the men of New England went to college. Fewer than 500 students graduated from college in the entire seventeenth century in New England.

For 144 years, Harvard practiced a blatant form of caste ranking that was perhaps in keeping with the Puritans' seventeenth-century doctrine of the elect, and a policy that was taken up by other institutions of higher education in New England. Students were ranked in two ways: by social standing of the student's family and by the student's perceived value to the community when he graduated. On the student's first day on campus, the steward of the college ranked all freshman by the "Supposed Dignity of the Families." Ranking had an impact on every aspect of everyday college life: the order of recitation in class and before the faculty, when he could serve himself in the eating hall, where he could sit in the eating hall, where he could sit in chapel and march in academic processions, and where his name would appear in the student catalogue.

The top 10 percent in the ranking were sons of magistrates, and the next 20 percent were the sons of college graduates in order of degree date. The lower 70 percent were then ranked according to their potential usefulness to society. In 1723, finding the ranking according to merit too cumbersome, the college dropped it and ranked only by "the Degrees of their ancestors." Finally, with perhaps some revolutionary theories of democratization in the air, Yale College ended its rankings in 1767 and Harvard in 1772. One student's father, the Reverend John Cotton of Plymouth, revealing the general snobbery of the times, was enraged at

Yale when that institution dispensed with rankings. In this Plymouth minister's mind, the removal of rankings even smacked of heresy:

> I believe it will be a general Discouragement to Gentlemen at a Distance and particularly in our Province to Send their Sons amongst you (whatever Esteem they May have of your Society upon other accounts) if they must in this Sort be degraded and no Distinction be made between them and the lowest Sort. Upon the Whole, I would query, whether the new method does not Savor too much of *the doctrine of Levellism*, which has not much Credit in the present Age. (Quoted in Axtell, 223)

GRADUATE THEOLOGY

Graduate study was available at Harvard in theology. The course of study included books on Protestant theology and the Bible, studied in Hebrew and Greek. Much of the study included copious note taking on written and oral sermons, on which students could expect to be examined. These graduates moved on to school teaching for at least one year before being assigned to a congregation. The minister-physician-poet Edward Taylor took that route. Other brilliant students, like Cotton Mather, became leaders in New England. Some, like Michael Wigglesworth, became both ministers and professors of divinity at Harvard. A few graduates of the school of theology, having attended school to enlarge their minds rather than to train for a profession, entered business after graduate school. Judge Samuel Sewall falls into this category.

In 1726 Cotton Mather published *Manuductio Ad Ministerium*, one of the most important practical books of advice for divinity students.

CONCLUSION

Historians have disagreed vehemently over the aims and characteristics of education in colonial New England. The system was fraught with class distinctions that kept virtually all but well-to-do males from grammar schools and colleges. On one hand, a broad curriculum of humanities and natural sciences was introduced at the grammar school and college levels. On the other hand, everything seemed to be doctrinally motivated and shaped. None of the scientists and social and political philosophers of the day were included in the curriculum. As historian James Truslow Adams concluded, there was education, but the end result might have been more narrowing than broadening. Nevertheless, that colonial New England introduced—even insisted on—education and literacy for all children, irrespective of social standing and means, is of immense importance.

BIBLIOGRAPHY

Adams, James Truslow. *The Founding of New England*. Boston: Atlantic Monthly Press, 1921.

Axtell, James. *The School upon the Hill*. New Haven, Conn.: Yale University Press, 1974.

Bailyn, Bernard. *Education in the Formation of American Society*. New York: Norton, 1960.

Brayley, Arthur Wellington. *Schools and Schoolboys of Old Boston*. Boston: L. P. Hager, 1894.

Bridenbaugh, Carl. *Cities in the Wilderness*. New York: Ronald Press, 1955.

Cremin, Lawrence. *American Education: The Colonial Experience*. New York: Harper and Row, 1970.

Ford, Paul Leicester, ed. *The New England Primer*. New York: Dood, Mead, 1897.

The General Laws and Liberties of the Massachusetts Colony: Revised Reprinted. Cambridge, Mass.: Samuel Green, 1672.

Holmes, Pauline. *A Tercentenary History of the Boston Public Latin School, 1635–1935*. Cambridge, Mass.: Harvard University Press, 1935.

Johnson, Clifton. *Old-Time Schools and School-Books*. New York: Macmillan, 1904.

Lauter, Paul, ed. *The Heath Anthology of American Literature*. Lexington, Mass.: D. C. Heath, 1990.

Martin, George H. *The Evolution of the Massachusetts Public School System*. New York: D. Appleton, 1923.

Morrison, Samuel Eliot. *The Founding of Harvard College*. Cambridge, Mass.: Harvard University Press, 1935.

———. *The Intellectual Life of Colonial New England*. New York: New York University Press, 1956.

Rutman, Darrett B. *Winthrop's Boston*. Chapel Hill: University of North Carolina Press, 1965.

Sewall, Samuel. *The Diary of Samuel Sewall*. 2 vols. New York: Farrar, Straus and Giroux, 1973.

Seybolt, Robert F. *The Public Schools of Colonial Boston*. Cambridge, Mass., Harvard University Press, 1935.

Small, Walter. *Early New England Schools*. Boston: Gunn and Co., 1914.

Wigglesworth, Michael. *The Diary of Michael Wigglesworth*, ed. Edmund S. Morgan. New York: Harper Torchbooks, 1946.

14

Fear and Persecution in Daily Life

The history of colonial New England, so irrevocably stamped with notorious cases of brutal persecution, cannot be discussed without reference to the New England authorities' attempts to abrogate the freedom of speech and freedom of religious expression, especially in the cases of Anne Hutchinson and members of the Quaker sect. Nor can one adequately discuss the daily life of the period without reference to the persecution of hundreds of ordinary citizens accused of witchcraft in the colonial period. One might argue that these infamous cases directly involved the daily lives of only a small percentage of New England's total population, but the truth is that these events impinged on the daily life of every citizen in New England. The attitudes that led to these various events, the horror of the events as they unfolded, and the lessons that the events left in the minds of individuals brought a constant fear to their lives long after the events were over. Those ever-pressing lessons perpetually warned that anything one said, any association one had, any enemy one made, could lead to being branded as a criminal, subject to prison or public corporeal punishment or worse.

To explore the topic of fear and persecution in the lives of colonial New Englanders brings us back continually to the idea of the abrogation of basic freedoms, which would eventually be granted in the Bill of Rights, ratified in 1791 after the American Revolution. Freedom of religion, of expression, and of the press had no place in the colonial New England governments, minds, and daily lives, especially with regard to matters touching individual conscience. Colonial legislators and governors would not pretend that any resident had the freedom to speak his or her mind, or to publish any opinion he or she wished, or to hold just any religious belief. In all of New England, only Rhode Island allowed freedom of conscience.

LEGALIZING INTOLERANCE

Religious intolerance was legislatively sanctioned in 1646. The following legislative opinion speaks to the major heresies that the Puritans perceived within Christianity and would not tolerate. Notice that this includes the Baptists, who were also immigrating to the New World to escape persecution (and then were arrested, beaten, and exiled by the Puritans.) The passage also gives to the authorities Godlike powers that must not be challenged:

> It is therefore Ordered and Declared by the Court; That if any Christian within this jurisdiction, shall go about to subvert and destroy the Christian Faith and Religion, by broaching and maintaining any damnable Heresies: As denying the immortality of the Soul, or resurrection of the Body, or any sin to be repented of in the regenerate, or any evil done by the outward man to be accounted sin, or denying that Christ gave himself a Ransome for our sins, or shall affirm that we are not justified by his death and righteousness, but by the perfections of our own works, or shall deny the Morality of the fourth Commandment, or shall openly condemn or oppose the Baptizing of Infants, or shall purposely depart the Congregation at the administration of that Ordinance, or shall deny the Ordinance of Magistracy, or their lawful Authority . . . or shall endeavor to seduce others to any of the Errors or Heresies above mentioned; every such person . . . after due means of conviction, shall be sentenced to Banishment. . . . And every person that shall publish and maintain any heterodox or erroneous doctrine, shall be liable to be questioned and censured by the county court where he lives, according to the merit of the offence. (*General Laws And Liberties*, 59, 61)

The law goes on to indicate that any person who denies that any book of the Bible, which are named specifically, is the infallible word of God will also be punished. The punishment was severe for anyone caught saying the wrong thing, on land or on sea:

> [The person] shall be committed to the prison at Boston, without bale . . . , there to be safely kept till the next County Court, where upon sufficient testimony brought against the said delinquent, he shall be adjudged for his offense after legal conviction, to pay such a fine as the Court which shall have cognizance of the crime shall judge meet, not exceeding the sum of fifty pounds, or shall be openly and severely whipped by the executioner, whether constable or any other appointed, not exceeding forty strokes, unless he shall publicly recant before his sentence (which if he do) he shall not pay above the fine of ten pounds to the

treasurer for the use of the Common-wealth, or be whipped in case he pay not the fine.

And it is further ordered and enacted, that if the said offender after his recantation, sentence or execution, shall the second time publish, and obstinately, and pertinaciously maintain the said wicked opinion, he shall be banished or put to death as the court shall judge. (*General Laws And Liberties*, 59, 60)

The heresy law dictated the burning of books (most frequently banned were those recommending the Quaker religion) and the arrest of anyone who was found with a banned book in his or her possession. Anyone who discovered that a neighbor had a banned book and turned that person in received half of the fine:

It is ordered, that all and every of the Inhabitants of this Jurisdiction, that have any of the Books in their custody, that go under the names of John Reeves, and Lodowick Muggleton . . . which are full of blasphemies, and shall not bring or send in all such books in their custody to the next magistrate, shall forfeit the sum of ten pounds for every such book found in his hand, the one half to the informer, the other half to the country.

And as many of the said books, as are, or shall be in custody, shall be burnt in the market place at Boston, on the next lecture day, by the common executioner. (*General Laws And Liberties*, 60)

On March 4, 1634, Israel Stoughton, a resident of Cambridge (what was then called Newtown) decided that his own book, which had been disapproved by the magistrates, was going to get him in trouble, so he asked the legislators to burn it.

INDIVIDUAL CASES OF INSUBORDINATION

A number of private citizens, whose names are not recorded in the history books, felt the strong arm of government come down when they dared express a view that was not in keeping with Puritan doctrine or was critical of those in power. Long before the Court of Assistants provided the Massachusetts Bay community with a body of written laws, citizens were arrested and punished for criticizing their leaders. On May 3, 1631, for example, Thomas Walford was fined "for his contempt of authoritie." In June, Phillip Ratliffe did not get off so easily. For "uttering malicious and scandalous speeches against the government and the church of Salem," Ratliffe was to be whipped, fined, have his ears cut off and banished from the colony. In September, Henry Lyn was whipped and banished for writing letters back to England that were critical of the colonial government. In 1632, a Mr. Batchelor was warned to cease his "contempt of authority," among other things. In March 1632, Thomas Dexter was set in the stocks, disenfranchised, and fined "for speaking reproachful and seditious words against the government here established, and finding fault to diverse acts of the Court, saying this captious government will bring all to naught, adding that the best of them was but an attorney." (Although Governor Winthrop was a lawyer, Puritans had no love for lawyers and considered Dexter's comment the supreme insult.) Ensigne Jennison was fined for "upbrading the court with injustice, uttering these words: 'I pray God deliver me from this court.' " On the same day, John Lee was sentenced to be whipped and fined for "speaking reproachfully of the Governor, saying he was but a lawyer's clerk, and what understanding had he more than himself; also taxing the Court for making laws to pick men's purses," as well as other crimes. William Knop was called before the court in 1637 for publicly criticizing the governor, this time, Governor Henry Vane. On September 4, 1638, Katherine Finch was whipped and imprisoned for "speaking against the church, magistrates and elders." And John Underhill was banished in the same month for "verbally abusing the court."

THE CASE OF ANNE HUTCHINSON

Anne Hutchinson's lengthy ordeal was a singular case of insubordination (here essentially the criticism of authorities in the expression of religious belief) that split and traumatized the community. Hutchinson, born in 1591 in England, was a highly educated, very religious young woman who came under the influence of a young Puritan minister named John Cotton. When Cotton moved to Boston in 1633 to become the second pastor of the community's church, Anne and her husband and children followed him. Her activism began immediately as she became a self-appointed angel of mercy, calling on the aged, the ailing, and the sick at heart. Soon, however, she found that she was called on to explain the morning's sermons to a little group of women, much as the heads of households were expected to do after services to help their uneducated children and servants to understand religious doctrine and Scripture. As innocent and even praiseworthy as this action might sound, it was fraught with danger. Although a mother was expected to provide constant religious instruction for her children and even, when called on, for her neighbors' children, Hutchinson and any other woman laid herself open to attack when she gave instruction to adults, for this was solely a male prerogative.

Then several things began to happen that blew these simple Sunday school lessons into full-scale hostilities. Hutchinson's religious sessions became enormously popular, attracting not a few women but scores of people who clamored for her lessons. It became obvious very quickly that Hutchinson was much more popular as a religious teacher than any of the powerful ministers working in the Massachusetts Bay. Clerical jealousy of Hutchinson was a major cause behind her persecution by authorities. Another change that escalated the unhappiness of the authorities with Hutchinson was that men as well as women began eagerly attending her meetings. She began holding separate sessions for men, and the authorities accused her of holding sessions in which both men and women were present. On the basis of these integrated religious meetings, clergymen began to accuse her of encouraging sexual misbehavior. And, finally, though she denied it, clergymen accused her of criticizing all of them personally, except for John Cotton. This, in itself, was enough to accuse her of treason. The ministers were the chief authorities in New England, and to criticize a legislator or a minister was to denounce and undermine one's "country."

One of Hutchinson's consistent observations during her lessons was that God-fearing people needed to place more faith in God's gifts and grace and less on their own works or deeds. Whether her presentation of this idea was in serious conflict with the doctrines preached by the Puritan community is difficult to determine objectively. That she had been taught by the second minister, John Cotton, and never judged that her beliefs were different from his would suggest that she was scarcely unorthodox. Nevertheless, New England ministers decided that she was preaching the heresy of *antinomianism*, or the belief that human beings are saved by grace alone and that we know God primarily through our own heart, not primarily through our intellect.

The clergy of New England, especially John Wilson, the first pastor of the Boston church, became enraged. They saw themselves in a power struggle with this woman who now attracted an army of ardent followers. They declared that she had defied authority and was preaching antinomianism, which, carried to its natural conclusion, would mean that ministers were unnecessary as explicators and guides. To get rid of Hutchinson was not a simple matter because she was a strong-willed, intelligent woman, with important connections. When she was ordered to cease her meetings, she refused.

As a consequence, many of her male supporters were openly chastised and deported. In the middle of the controversy, Henry Vane, who supported her, had a bitter argument with former governor Winthrop during a series of meetings in May 1637 to consider the situation. Eventually Vane lost the governorship to John Winthrop. This was bad news for Hutchinson, for Winthrop was a close ally of the Reverend John Wilson, whose hatred of her became all the more virulent when he discovered that Hutchinson's sympathizers planned to replace him with Anne's brother-in-law, the Reverend John Wheelwright. The following passage, from John Winthrop's assessment on October 21, 1636, of the ministers involved, shows just how perilous the election of Winthrop was for her:

> One Mrs. Hutchinson, a member of the church of Boston, a woman of a read wit and bold spirit, brought over with her two dangerous errors. . . . There joined with her in these opinions a brother of hers, one Mr. Wheelwright, a silenced minister sometimes in England. . . .
>
> Mr. Wilson made a very sad speech of the conditions of our churches, and the inevitable danger of separation, if these differences and alienations among brethren were not speedily remedied; and laid the blame upon these new opinions risen up amongst us, which all the magistrates, except the governor [Vane] and two others, did confirm, and all the minister but two. (Winthrop, 195–205)

Vane was so furious that he immediately returned to England, giving his house and land to the Reverend John Cotton, Hutchinson's mentor.

In August 1627, the ruling clerics announced that after studying the matter, they had decided that Anne and all of her supporters were no longer permitted to speak on religious matters or to hold any further meetings or in any way criticize any clergyman. At this point, John Cotton, the man of God whom she had followed so faithfully and had been her religious teacher, deserted her and declared himself to be in total agreement with the other ministers in New England.

After intense political struggles, on November 2, 1637, Anne was brought to trial before a civil court on charges of treason. The two-day trial was held in Newtown (what is now Cambridge) because it was feared that she had too many supporters in Boston. She was found guilty and sentenced to be banished. For four months afterward, she was held in Roxbury, under house arrest, in the home of one of her bitterest enemies. Although she was in poor health, she was constantly subjected to inquisitions by New England clergymen, seeking to find specific proof of her heresy. Her supporters claimed that her questioners berated the sick and weakened woman so mercilessly that she often said things that she did not mean. In August, a tumor was expelled from Hutchinson's uterus, leading her enemies to spread the news that Anne had given birth to a monster, fathered by the devil.

On March 15, 1638, Hutchinson was brought back to Boston for a second, church trial. The Reverend Cotton attempted at first to save her, but when the other ministers began to attack him, claiming that Anne said she only believed the same thing that the Reverend Cotton believed, he changed his tune. The following passage is from his testimony at the end of the trial, when he distances himself from her and calls her a liar:

> Mr. Cotton . . . though she have confessed that she sees many of the Things which she held to be Errors and that it proceded from the Root Pride of Spirit, yet I see this pride of heart is not healed but is working still, and therefore to keep secret some unsound opinions. God hath let her fall into a manifest lie, yea to make a lie and therefore as we received her in amongst us I think we are bound upon this ground to remove her from us and not to retain her any longer, seeing

she doth prevaricate in her words, as that her judgment is one thing and her expression is another. (From Adams, 385, 386)

In a church packed with clerical outsiders, Anne was examined, found guilty of heresy, and ordered to be banished. Her husband, William, had for months been scouting about for a haven outside the Bay Colony and had decided on the settlement at Rhode Island, which, thanks to the leadership of Roger Williams, tolerated people of all religious beliefs. Anne immediately left the Massachusetts Bay Colony for Rhode Island and later left Rhode Island for New York when persistent rumors reached her that the Massachusetts Bay Company was attempting to gain control of Rhode Island, in which case she would face a new trial and perhaps a death sentence.

The persecution of Anne Hutchinson was not a tightly contained government and church vendetta against a sole woman. On the contrary, it reached into the daily lives of almost every resident of Massachusetts Bay, certainly into the lives of every resident of Boston, Salem, Cambridge, and other nearby settlements. There was scarcely a resident of Boston who would not have been involved in some way because of Anne's immense popularity. Scores of people had attended her meetings, and their lives were traumatically disrupted when these meetings were halted, especially those who saw her as their religious mentor. (To judge her popularity, remember that the authorities were so afraid of her influence over the people that they transferred her civil trial outside Boston, placed her under house arrest so far outside Boston that she would be out of touch with her followers, and then packed the church trial with clergy from other areas of Massachusetts Bay.) Her popularity is attested to by John Winthrop himself in the following journal entry for October 21, 1636:

> The speech of Mr. Wilson was taken very ill by Mr. Cotton and others of the same church.... It was strange to see, how the common people were led, by example to condemn him [Rev. Wilson, Anne's enemy] in that, which (it was very probable) divers of them did not understand ... and that such as had known him so long, and what good he had done for that church, should fall upon him with such bitterness for justifying himself in a good cause. (Winthrop, 204–205)

Many of those who had attended her meetings were certainly afraid for their own lives when she was brought to trial. Furthermore, her family was large and very influential. Many citizens of Boston would have had daily business and personal dealings with her husband and grown sons. Moreover, her supporters included figures well known throughout the colony, Henry Vane, governor of Massachusetts Bay, among them.

All this suggests just how her ordeal must have dominated private discussion and occupied the thoughts of many in the colony.

The long Hutchinson trials had a measurable, lasting impact on the community. The direct result was even more government and church intrusion in the lives of citizens. The case prompted the government to become even more repressive and to act promptly and brutally to silence Quakers and Baptists. It made many citizens even more afraid, more eager to keep out of trouble with the government, more concerned with pleasing authority, as they were conditioned to do anyway. One sees the evidence of this at the departure of former governor Vane for England, and even as the church trial was underway, when the Reverend John Cotton, whose very teachings Anne had adopted and had gotten her in trouble in the first place, deserted her at the trial to protect himself. This fear is seen when, after having been found guilty and sentenced to immediate banishment from New England, Anne exited the church, obviously physically ill and faltering. Of all her many friends and supporters, many of whom had called on Anne for comfort and assistance, only one woman, Mary Dyer, rushed to her side to help her down the steps.

QUAKERS

In 1656 the Puritan fathers perceived another serious threat among them: the Quakers, founded by a former Puritan, George Fox. Much of the New England's antiheresy legislation was directed specifically against Quakers. And there was no question about Quakerism's being antithetical to Puritanism. Quaker philosophy taught that all persons had God/Christ within them and that if they were guided by this inner light, they would be saved from hell. This contradicted the Puritan belief in depravity and in a special group of the elect who alone are saved by God. The New England elite was equally offended and also frightened by the Quaker belief that ministers were unnecessary in reaching one's inner light and in knowing God. In the Quaker meetinghouse, there was no minister; each person, man *and* woman, was equally welcomed to speak as the spirit moved him or her. Any faith that dispensed with ministers was a threat to the power structure of New England.

Quakers were immediately banned from most areas in New England: the Massachusetts Bay, Plymouth, New Haven, and Hartford. Books about Quakerism were confiscated and burned. Ship captains were forbidden to bring Quakers into these colonies, and citizens who welcomed Quakers into their homes or openly sympathized with them were subject to fine or imprisonment.

Laws against Quakers were unusually harsh. The first time a Quaker appeared within these New England colonies, he or she was thrown out and told not to return. The second time, the law stated that the Quaker would be "directed to a Constable of the Town . . . be stripped naked from the middle upwards, and tied to a Carts tail, and whipped through the Town," before being thrown out of the borders of the colony. Upon a third appearance, the Quaker would be "Branded with the Letter R on their left shoulder, and be severely whipped, and sent away in manner as before." Any further appearance would result in the Quaker's being put to death. Throughout New England, Quakers were imprisoned, beaten almost to the point of death, and branded; they had their ears cut off or their tongue bored with red-hot irons.

In 1659, in an appeal to the king of England, a Quaker named George Bishop described some of the behavior of the Puritan officials in Salem toward Quakers. As a rhetorical device, Bishop pretends that he is addressing the Puritan officials directly, first about the beating of Edward Wharton and then of Ann Coleman:

> So he [Edward Wharton] was tied to a pair of cartwheels with a great rope about his middle, and a number of people to draw them about, where the executioner cruelly whipped him as in the warrant; and having loosed him, told him, "That he must prepare to receive the like at the next town," which was about fourteen miles from thence, through the woods; which being a long way for a man to travel on foot, whose back was so torn already, to serve their pleasure. . . .
>
> Not long after Edward Wharton's executions as afresaid, Joseph Nicholson, John Liddal, Jane Millard, and Ann Coleman were, by the said Hathorn's warrant, apprehended, and so cruelly whipped through Salem, Boston, and Dedham, that one of them, viz., Ann Coleman, was near death, being well-nigh murdered. She was a little woman, and her back, as hath been said, was crooked, and your executioner had her fast in a cart at Dedham, Bellingham, your deputy, having seen Hathorn's warrant, bidding them "Go on," and saying "The warrant was firm"; and so encouraging the matter, he so unmercifully laid her on with the rest, that, with the knots of the whip, he split the nipple of her breast, which so tortured her, that it had almost cost her life. (Bishop, 279)

But Quakers were persistent. In September 1659, Mary Dyer, once the faithful follower of Anne Hutchinson and now a convert to Quakerism, was arrested with two other Quakers, both men, and thrown out of town. All three returned to Boston a month later, on October 18, 1659, when they were arrested and condemned to death. Mary's family managed to get her a reprieve, based on her official membership in the Reverend John Wilson's Boston church, but her two companions were executed and thrown into an unmarked pit on Boston Common. In May 1660, Mary returned, was arrested, and sentenced to be hanged. This time there was no reprieve, and her former minister, the Reverend Wilson, came to curse her on the scaffold.

This was not just a case of a small group of outsiders invading Puritan territory. Although Quaker missionaries did arrive directly from England

and other provinces, there were converts to Quakerism living in New England, and there was strong pro-Quaker sentiment among the common people. Some Quakers, Mary Dyer included, were New Englanders who had supported Anne Hutchinson. That the persecution of Quakers touched the daily lives of many New Englanders is shown by the strong measures the Puritan authorities felt they had to take to keep citizens from harboring Quakers, bringing them food in prison, or even publicly expressing sympathy for them. Firsthand accounts reveal that armed soldiers had to surround the Quaker prisoners to keep the citizenry from interfering with their executions on Boston Common. The horror of the executions prompted the intervention of the English king to halt further killings of Quakers, and it undoubtedly intensified the terror in the community that was already conditioned to yield to authority without question.

WITCHCRAFT

The execution of accused witches throughout New England, ending with the wholesale arrests in Salem in 1692, was the worst instance of rule by terror that the colonists faced. The ordeal began in January 1692 when several young girls in the Reverend Samuel Parris's Salem household, in response to being scolded for dancing in the forest and playing games to predict the future, began accusing members of the community of bewitching them. Among the many arrested were Sarah Goode and her four-year-old daughter, Dorcas. Community leaders began to encourage citizens to turn in their neighbors as witches. Often the only way to avoid being arrested oneself was to accuse someone else first. Once accused, the only way to escape execution was to "confess." Hysteria and arrests began to mount. Throughout the spring, people were arrested and held in prison without benefit of trial. Soon the Salem jail was overflowing, and those accused of witchcraft were packed into the Boston jail.

When the trials began, all rules of evidence and other safeguards for the accused were totally ignored. The most notorious abuse of the legal system was the acceptance of *spectral evidence*. This meant that even though a roomful of people might say that a woman was sitting with them all evening, her "specter," or spirit, could have left her body and be out torturing her accuser at the same time. Here is one report of the trial of Martha Corey by a staunch believer in the witch threat, Deodat Lawson. He begins by talking about the effect the accused witch had on the young girls who had originated the witch hysteria to save themselves from punishment for dancing:

Painting by T. H. Matteson depicting the witchcraft trial of the Reverend George Jacobs. COURTESY PEABODY ESSEX MUSEUM.

> [T]hese are most of them at Corey's examination, and did vehemently accuse her in the Assembly of afflicting them, by Biting, Pinching, Strangling, etc. And that they did in their Fit see her Likeness coming to them, and bringing a Book to them, she said, she had no Book; they affirmed, she had a Yellow-Bird, that used to suck betwixt her Fingers, and being asked about it, if she had any Familiar Spirit, that attended her, she said, She had no Familiarity with any such thing. She was a Gospel Woman. (Lawson, 155)

By October, twenty people had been executed for witchcraft. Hundreds had been held in prison; some had died there. Dozens had to flee the area to save themselves; hundreds more who lived had had their land and possessions confiscated; and untold numbers had seen families, friends, and communities irrevocably broken apart.

Finally on October 3, 1692, Governor Phips, who had been lobbied by Increase Mather, forbade any further arrests. This marked the end of the executions, but it took a year to try and release the rest of the prisoners.

The intensity of the fear of witchcraft was a part of the daily lives of New Englanders long before the Salem hysteria. People who stood out in any way, especially those who were somewhat rebellious, the physically disabled, and the mentally ill, had good reason to fear arrest on charges of witchcraft. And for ten months in 1692, all citizens of New

Grave of George Jacobs, who was hanged in Salem for witchcraft. The families of most condemned witches never recovered the remains of their relatives, who were dumped into shallow graves without ceremony. Photo courtesy of the author.

England had good reason to live in terror of being accused of witchcraft by someone they had offended, someone with whom they had argued, someone who wanted their land, or someone who could in any way profit or receive satisfaction from their being jailed, humiliated, or even executed.

Despite a hard core of ministers and legislators who were convinced that the devil was abroad in Massachusetts and that God would punish them until they purged the colony of every suspected witch, and despite the success of these fanatics in manipulating many people, the general populace in 1692 did not share in the hysterical belief that witches lurked in every household in New England. As dangerous as it was to defy the magistrates, a few ordinary citizens put their lives on the line—unsuccessfully, it turned out—to save Rebecca Nurse, a woman known to be an angel of mercy. Thirty-five citizens put their names to the following petition:

Portrait engraving of Cotton Mather by C. E. Wagstaff and J. Andrews based on a painting by E. Pelham. The Reverend Cotton Mather encouraged the witchcraft trials. COURTESY PEABODY ESSEX MUSEUM.

> We whose names are hereunto subscribed, being desired by Goodman Nurse to declare that we know concerning his wife's conversation for time past,—we can testify, to all whom it may concern, that we have known her for many years; and, according to our observation, her life and conversation were according to her profession, and we never had any cause or grounds to suspect her of any such thing as she is now accused of. (Quoted in Upham, vol. 2: 272)

As in other matters, however, people were too terrified, too used to following the orders of their superiors, to mount a rebellion. They also immediately perceived that to criticize the witch accusers and the authorities was to bring accusations on themselves or members of their families. Many influential businessmen and ministers were convinced from the beginning that a grave injustice was being done. Many, like the Reverend Increase Mather, worked behind the scenes to influence powerful Englishmen to stop the reign of terror. Many others, like the Reverend Samuel Willard, had an underground railroad to help the accused escape. When a popular minister, the Reverend George Burroughs, was arrested and scheduled for execution, an uprising seemed sure to occur. A tentative groundswell of protest threatened to halt the execution. But the Reverend Cotton Mather, a firm believer in the dangers of witchcraft, galloped up to Salem from Boston at the last minute and confronted the grumbling crowd. After the people backed down, the execution went on.

THE EIGHTEENTH CENTURY

Beneath the surface of colonial New England life ran an underground stream of terror. For some, this was a fear that God would punish them individually or collectively, should they allow the slightest heresy or aberration to continue in their midst. For others, perhaps most, there was the constant terror that some idea would escape the lips of someone close to them, some association with a dangerous personage would become known, or some irritated and greedy neighbor or relative would come forward—something that they could not prevent would bring a terrifying knock on the door. And nothing they could say or do would prevent personal disaster.

The eighteenth century brought gradual changes. Instances of intolerance and repression, especially the witch trials, for which most participants had expressed remorse, had inevitably contributed to a backlash against the narrowness of Puritanism.

BIBLIOGRAPHY

Adams, Charles Francis. *The Antinomian Controversy*. New York: DaCapo Press, 1976.

Battis, Emery. *Saints and Sectaries: Anne Hutchinson and the Antinomian Controversy in the Massachusetts Bay Colony*. Chapel Hill: University of North Carolina Press, 1962.

Bishop, George. *New England Judged by the Spirit of the Lord*. London: T. Sowle, 1703.

Boyer, Paul, and Stephen Nissenbaum, eds. *Salem-Village Witchcraft: A Documentary Record of Local Conflict*. Boston: Northeastern University Press, 1993.

Bremer, Francis J., ed. *Anne Hutchinson, Troubler of the Puritan Zion*. Huntington, N.Y.: R. E. Krieger, 1981.

Cameron, Jean. *Anne Hutchinson, Guilty or Not?* New York: Peter Lang, 1994.

Dalglish, Doris N. *People Called Quakers*. Freeport, Me.: Books for Libraries Press, 1969.

Demos, John Putnam. *Entertaining Satan*. New York: Oxford University Press, 1982.

Dove at the Window: Last Letters of Four Quaker Martyrs. Lincoln, Mass.: Penmaen Press, 1973.

The General Laws And Liberties of the Massachusetts Colony: Revised & Reprinted. Cambridge, Mass.: Samuel Green, 1672.

Gragg, Larry Dale. *The Salem Witch Crisis*. Westport, Conn. Praeger, 1992.

Hall, David. D., ed. *The Antinomian Controversy*. Middletown, Conn.: Wesleyan University Press, 1968.

Hill, Frances. *A Delusion of Satan*. New York: Doubleday, 1995.

Ingle, H. Larry. *First Among Friends*. New York: Oxford University Press, 1994.

Karlsen, Carol F. *The Devil in the Shape of a Woman*. New York: Norton, 1987.

Lawson, Deodat. "A Brief and True Narrative." In *Narrative of the Witchcraft Cases*, ed. George Lincoln Burr. New York: Charles Scribner's Sons, 1914.

Plimpton, Ruth Talbot. *Mary Dyer*. Boston: Branden, 1994.

Report on the Trial of Mrs. Anne Hutchinson, communicated by Franklin Bowditch Dexter to the Massachusetts Historical Society. October 11, 1888.

Upham, Charles W. *Salem Witchcraft*. 2 vols. Boston: Wiggin and Lunt, 1867.

Williams, Selma R. *Divine Rebel: The Life of Anne Marbury Hutchinson*. New York: Holt, Rinehart and Winston, 1981.

Winthrop, John. *History of New England*. Boston: Little Brown, 1853.

Conclusion

By the middle of the eighteenth century, the daily lives of New Englanders had profoundly changed from the early days when the Puritan church shaped every aspect of colonial life. These changes evolved from several developments.

A WIDER WORLD MOVES TO NEW ENGLAND

As we have seen, the attire of New Englanders (regarding ornamentation, wigs, and wedding rings, for instance), their amusements, and school study were modified by the weakening of the church, which had limited those aspects of their lives.

Daily life was also changed by improving economic situations. As commerce grew in areas such as shipbuilding, fisheries, fur and metal deportation, more people could find and pay for imported fabric, clothes, china, and silver. Many could afford commodious, comfortable, well-designed houses.

The taming of the New England frontier and establishment of European civilization meant that the majority of residents were not spending most of their time beating back the wilderness and just struggling to survive from day to day. There were more well-established roads and better means of transportation. Civilization brought a sufficient abundance of services and commodities, earlier available only to the rich, that people of modest means had had to spend many hours and much labor to provide for themselves. The services of tailors, furniture makers, stonemasons, and apothecaries, for example, could be used by the person of average means. On the intellectual front, there were printers of books and newspapers and better-educated school teachers.

In the larger towns, and especially the port towns, everyday lives were changed by the models of dress, ornamentation, and manners that the upper-class English brought with them to the New World. The plain style in clothes, for instance, gave way to ruffles, slit sleeves, and lace.

THE DECLINE OF THE PURITAN CHURCH

It was, however, ideas as much as circumstances that changed the ways colonials lived in New England in the eighteenth century. And the greatest change was attributable to the gradual decline of the most powerful force in their lives, the church. The demise of the Puritan church, as it was in 1630, was precipitated by a variety of factors, which include the following:

- The backlash against the Puritan-inspired witchcraft hysteria
- The cruelty and oppressiveness in dealing with the Quakers
- The absolute intolerance of other Protestant religions
- The introduction into New England of a nondissenting, British presence after the loss of the charter
- A backlash against seventy years of unrelieved church intrusion into both government and private life
- The difficulty in dealing with the Calvinistic idea of what appeared to be divine injustice
- The Puritan theologians' loss of balance between intellect and emotion
- The inability to keep spiritual concerns and material worldly success in proper perspective
- The infusion of new science and rationalism into the culture
- The halfway covenant

The Backlash

In all three major cases of Puritan religious persecution, the common people were entirely out of sympathy with the many powerful Puritan lay and church leaders, like John Wilson and, later, Cotton Mather, who were largely responsible for the turn of events. Not only the English Crown, but even their leaders' theological counterparts in England, were utterly appalled at colonial policies. During the witchcraft trials, many New Englanders felt that they had been duped, used, and rendered helpless by the mounting hysteria. Others were soon remorseful about their part in the horror. The classic case is diarist Samuel Sewall, a judge in the Salem cases who in 1697 arose in church meeting and walked to the pews reserved for the poor, where he stood penitently while the minister read his apology.

Some of the backlash was obviously disgust and horror at what had befallen decent people—their friends and neighbors—over matters of personal conscience. But part of the backlash came from less admirable motives. Earlier, they had been told by their leaders that God was punishing them with disease, fires, droughts, British intrusion, and Indian raids because they were not sufficiently vigilant in wiping out religious heresy and witchcraft. But God's punishment went on and on, and many people, Sewall included, drew their own conclusions from what they saw around them: that God was punishing them not because of their tolerance of evil but because of the part they had played in persecutions.

The Royal Intrusion

The English presence after the loss of the original charter gradually weakened the power that the Puritan church and clergy had once exerted in government. Various English kings over the years had tried without success to challenge some of the capital crimes (like the death penalty for older children who struck their parents), had ordered, with limited success, the cessation of Quaker persecution, and had intervened in the Salem trials to halt executions. Except in the Salem case, the Puritan leaders had once had the power to defy the king of England himself and avoid yielding to royal demands. They had been able to scoff at the opinion of their English Puritan colleagues in these matters. But the continual controversies began to erode their base of power, and they found that they had fewer and fewer influential friends and supporters outside the colony.

When British greed grew sufficiently great and their impatience sufficiently thin, they moved in, assuming more and more authority as the seventeenth century wore on. Royal governors gained more control, and the Crown insisted on more reforms at the same time that it inflicted taxes and troops on the colonies. The reforms included increasingly firm steps to break the monopoly of the Puritan church. The weakening of the church's influence in government and legislation was felt long before any weakening in the Puritans' social and cultural influence was seen outside direct legislation.

The decisive steps taken by the English, from the time of the loss of the charter to the Revolution, loosened Puritan control of government. Laws forbidding emigration to New England of members of "heretical sects," that is, those unsympathetic to Puritanism, were no longer in force. This meant the infusion of many people who diluted the Puritan mainstream. Furthermore, church attendance was no longer a legal obligation, and church membership was no longer a requisite for the suffrage, opening the franchise and government participation to many more independent-minded citizens who would not be manipulated by the Puritan clergy. Antiheresy laws were expunged, leaving the clergy with no legal weapons with which to fight their enemies.

After intense objection from the Puritan authorities, the English also insisted that members of other Protestant faiths be allowed to worship

King's Chapel, the first Anglican church in Boston. The cemetery, which is older than the church, is where John Winthrop is buried. Photo courtesy of the author.

openly in all New England. The Anglicans came with the royal representatives, and the Puritans were forced to share with them the Second Meeting House in Boston before the English built King's Chapel for themselves. The Baptists (who had been whipped earlier for daring to enter Massachusetts Bay) and even the hated and persecuted Quakers were allowed, through the intervention of the British, to become established within the community. Although anti-Catholic sentiment was very slow in dying in New England, there is little evidence in the eighteenth century of discord between ordinary Puritans and members of Protestant sects that their leaders had once persecuted.

All of these measures certainly weakened the Puritan oligarchy. At the same time, the reforms had to take great psychological pressure from ordinary citizens in their daily lives and cause them to be determined never to return to the old ways. By the early years of the eighteenth century, the nightmare of being mutilated or executed for holding a "wrong" religious belief or of expressing the wrong religious idea was largely over.

Although clergymen continued to have an indirect influence as lobbyists and mediators, they lost their direct stranglehold on the legislature. The cultural (as distinct from the legislative) influence of the church certainly diminished in many respects as Puritans lost the majority in leadership.

Doctrinal Problems

The demise of the Puritan church cannot be entirely laid at the door of British enemies and the other religious sects allowed in by the British. The clergy knew that their congregations had serious doctrinal problems with Calvinism. While Puritans taught that God was merciful, doctrine countered with a

God whose actions were capricious, vengeful, and unfair. Obviously, ordinary churchgoers never embraced the Puritan brand of Calvinism with the same fervor that their leaders did. Ordinary Puritans were specifically troubled by the idea that infants went to hell, even deserved to go to hell, and by the idea that good deeds had a negligible effect on one's salvation. The Puritan clergymen were aware of this and concentrated great effort, as Michael Wigglesworth did in "Day of Doom," to explain these particular matters about which their followers had excruciating reservations. As controversy erupted within the Congregational churches in the eighteenth century, these two troubling points arose again and again.

Division among Puritan Theologians

With the use of antiheretical laws, especially those against the antinomians, the Puritans had managed to maintain a delicate balance between head and heart, intellect and emotions. As the eighteenth century wore on, the church split in two along these lines. The side that began stressing the place of the emotions in religious experience grew into the Great Awakening. It was meant to be a revitalization of Puritanism but instead invigorated other Protestant churches, like the Baptists and emerging Methodists. The place of the intellect in religious experience came to be stressed by other Congregational clergymen, transforming that sect entirely and leading to the founding in New England of the Unitarian church.

The New Secularism

The New England Puritans had taken up the doctrine of secular calling with commitment and enthusiasm, adopting it with more crusade-like fervor than any other Protestant sect had done. It was a doctrine that seemed especially made for their situation in the bitterly cold, uncivilized world of New England. In the doctrine, the Lord's inspiring intent for a high community and individual purpose in this hard frontier life was joined with the requirement to work hard (the only way to survive in the New World as individuals and communities) and to be successful. The doctrine also laid the seeds of this pious people's doctrinal destruction, for their higher, more important message was that reality lay in the spirit, in the soul, in the divine presence. The religious calling to please God always, they taught, superseded things of this world, even the secular calling or work in this world. But the proper ratio between the spirit and the world could not be maintained with such a heavy (and perhaps necessary for survival) emphasis on work in this world. Despite the clergy's lip-service to things of the spirit, their actions usually rewarded success in this world. This attitude and the congregation's gradual exposure to other ideas of the time, like natural philosophy and Deism, which stressed observable fact in the visible world, cut away the very spiritual bedrock of Puritanism. Without it, it had no religious identity.

Benjamin Franklin represented a secular turn in social thinking in the eighteenth century. From Benjamin Franklin, *The Life of Benjamin Franklin* (Philadelphia: J. B. Lippincott & Co., 1874).

Natural Philosophy and Rationalism

The Puritans in the seventeenth century knew full well that the new philosophies and sciences would be dangerous for their church. For decades they had assiduously kept these ideas from their communities as best they could, not even allowing them into the Harvard curriculum. Newtonian physics, for example, which appeared in 1687 and was introduced to America in 1708, was not seriously considered in New England until Cotton Mather explained it in 1721, over thirty years after its appearance. In 1714 Mather was also the first learned man of influence in New England to support the Copernican theory of the universe—some 178 years after Copernicus offered his theory that the earth moved around the sun rather than vice versa.

The impact that the new ideas in philosophy and science were making in America in the eighteenth century is illustrated by the history of a young Bostonian named Benjamin Franklin. His ancestors had been religious dissenters whose leaders in America for seventy years censored and burned books that challenged Puritan belief. But at twelve years old in 1718, Franklin was able to read without fear Xenophon's *The Memo-*

rable Things of Socrates and books by such freethinkers as John Locke, the earl of Shaftesbury, and the Deist Anthony Collins. In his teens Franklin came strongly under the influence of Deism and, as he writes in his autobiography, "a real Doubter in many Points of our Religious Doctrine," arguing different points of religion with his friends and colleagues without hesitation. During his teenage years in Boston, his personal articles of faith (which he published in 1728 in Philadelphia and were made more widely known in his *Autobiography*) had already begun evolving. Franklin's views religious views were antithetical to Puritanism. He did not believe that the Bible was the revealed word of God; he was early on convinced that works were much more important than faith, writing in the *Autobiography* that "the most acceptable Service to God was the doing Good to man," and he did not belong to or attend church services, declaring himself to be left unedified by sermons—this, despite his claim to have no animosity toward the church.

Franklin's notions were shared by many of the intellectual men who founded the new country: Thomas Jefferson, who described himself as a Christian Deist, and Thomas Paine, who explained his Deist philosophy in *The Age of Reason*, primarily by attacking organized religion and its clerical spokesmen.

Although it is true that the masses of New Englanders, still Calvinistic in their beliefs, were in vehement disagreement with these philosophical radicals, the new ideas had a share in weakening the Old World Puritan view and had a profound impact on American life, especially in the formation of the rights and liberties of the nation.

THE INFLUENCE OF COLONIAL NEW ENGLAND

New England Puritanism exerted lasting cultural influence in the new country—not just in New England—long after the Puritan church itself was no more. As late as the twentieth century, the Puritan past reinforced a variety of other national influences, some negative, some positive, that shaped American society. We see its influence in a nation that is overwhelmingly Protestant. We see it in our sense of national mission, our discomfort with idleness, our national work ethic, our drive for material success. We see it in an occasional suspicion of art and entertainment, in our commitment to free education for all, in our fondness for simplicity and the plain style.

In a very real sense, however, much of what we value as a nation seemed to emerge as a reaction against New England Puritanism. One might argue that our fundamental rights and liberties came into being as part of the backlash against decades of Puritan oppression. In 1791, the first U.S. Congress, perhaps looking back with dismay on New England life in the seventeenth century, guaranteed in the First Amendment

A depiction of Boston Harbor in 1723 illustrating how the area changed since the early settlement. From George Francis Dow, *Every Day Life in the Massachusetts Bay Colony* (Boston: Society for the Preservation of New England Antiquities, 1935).

to the Bill of Rights, as a cornerstone of American life, freedom of religion, freedom of speech, freedom of the press, and freedom of assembly. Amendments Five through Eight, in reference to fair treatment for anyone accused of a crime, seem to be fashioned by citizens who held in national memory the details of the Salem witch trials ninety-nine years earlier, when every legal right imaginable had been disregarded. It is at least interesting to imagine that Roger Williams, Thomas Hooker, Anne Hutchinson, and Mary Dyer were looking over the shoulders of the founding fathers as they set about the task of framing the U.S. Constitution.

Index

About the Author

CLAUDIA DURST JOHNSON is Professor Emeritus at the University of Alabama, where she served as chair of the English Department for twelve years. She is the series editor of the Greenwood Press "Literature in Context" series, for which she has authored numerous works, including *Understanding* The Scarlet Letter (1995), *Understanding* The Crucible (1998) and *Understanding* The Call of the Wild (2000).